FOR ORGANS, PIANOS & ELECTRONIC KEYBOARDS

215

THE BEST CHRISTMAS SONGS EVER

ISBN 0-7935-0894-0

D1228057

Hal Leonard Publishing Corporation

7777 West Bluemound Road P.O. Box 13819 Milwaukee, WI 53213

CONTENTS

THE BEST CHRISTMAS SONGS EVER

All I Want For Christmas Is My Two Front Teeth

Registration 1
Rhythm: Swing or Rock

Words and Music by
Don Gardner

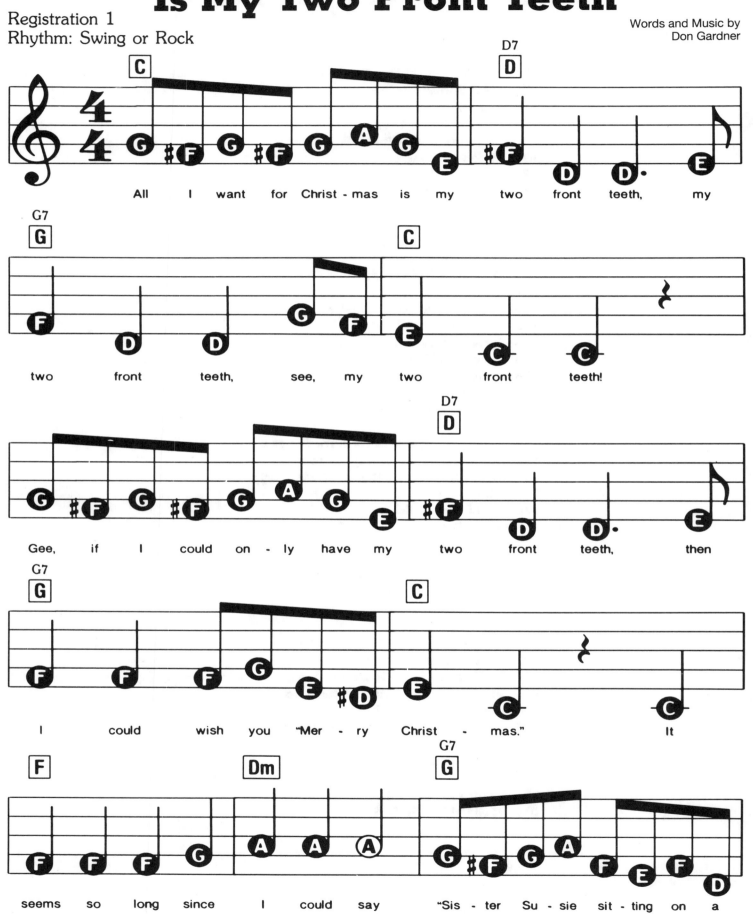

Angels From The Realms Of Glory

Registration 6
Rhythm: None

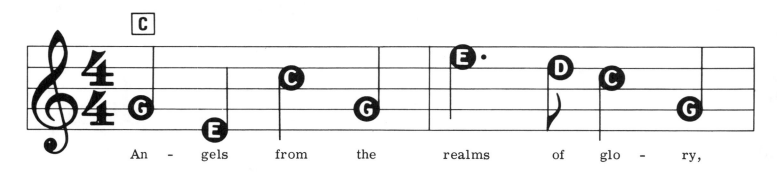

An - gels from the realms of glo - ry,

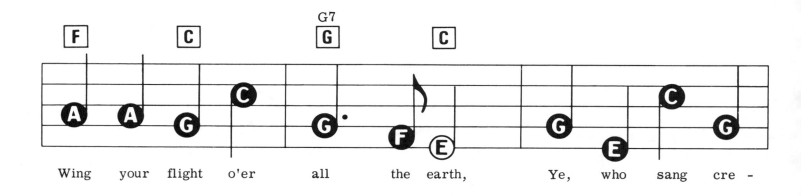

Wing your flight o'er all the earth, Ye, who sang cre -

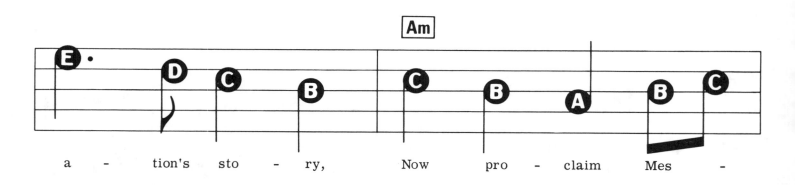

a - tion's sto - ry, Now pro - claim Mes -

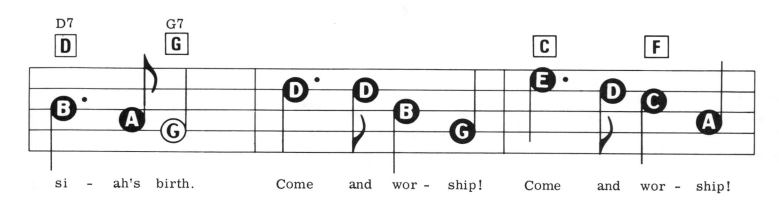

si - ah's birth. Come and wor - ship! Come and wor - ship!

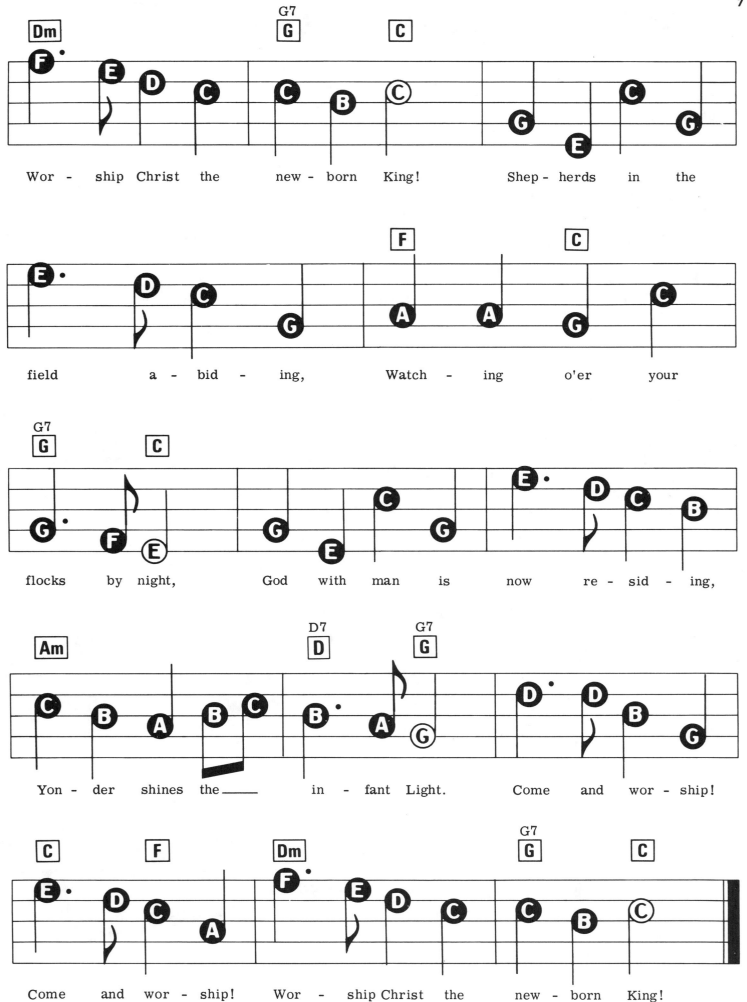

Angels We Have Heard On High

Registration 3
Rhythm: None

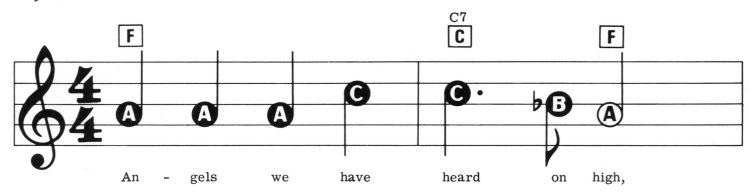

An - gels   we   have   heard   on   high,

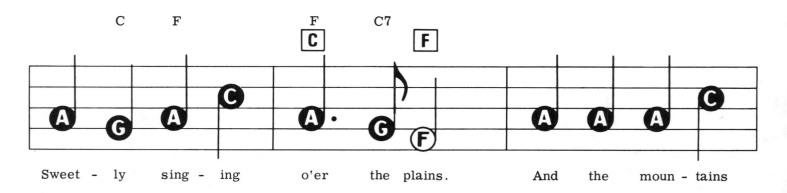

Sweet - ly   sing - ing   o'er   the   plains.   And   the   moun - tains

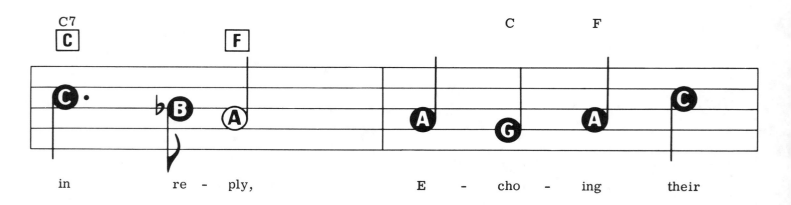

in   re - ply,   E - cho - ing   their

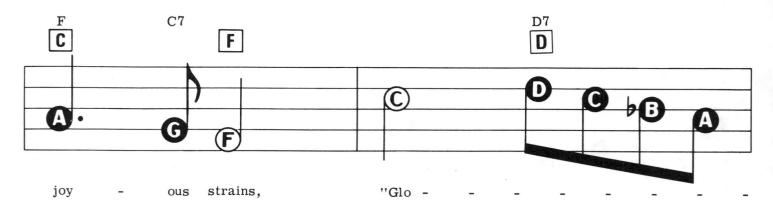

joy - ous   strains,   "Glo - - - - - - - - - - -

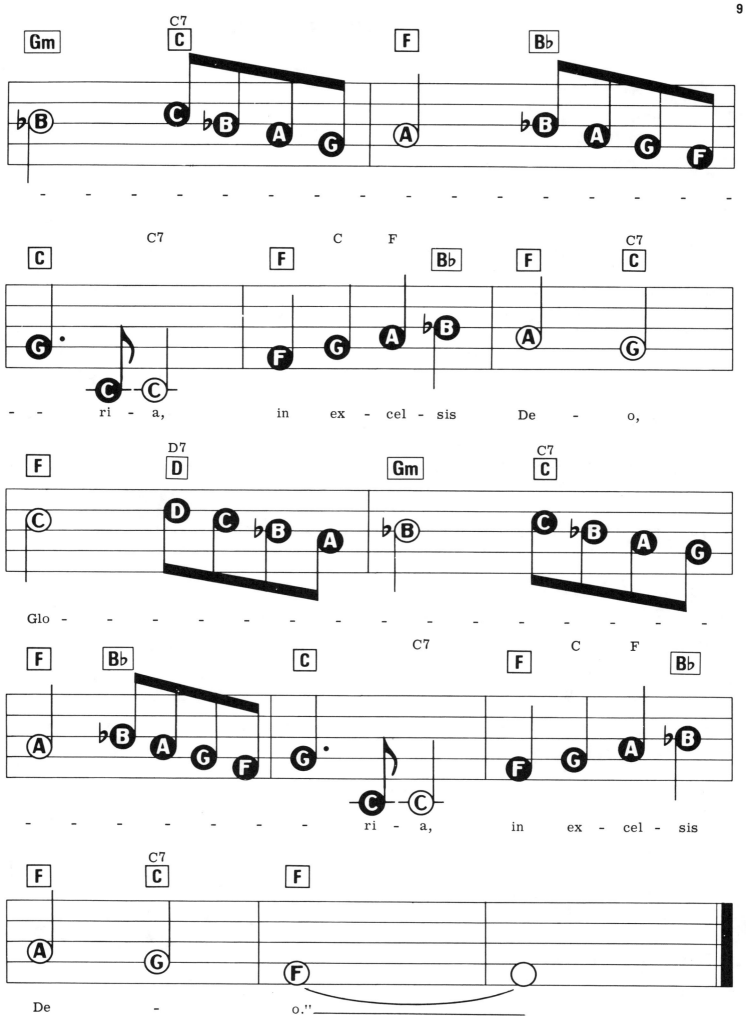

Auld Lang Syne

Registration 2
Rhythm: None

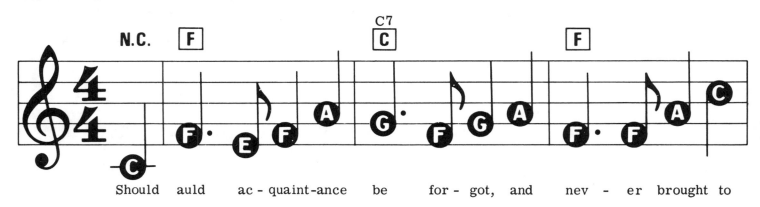

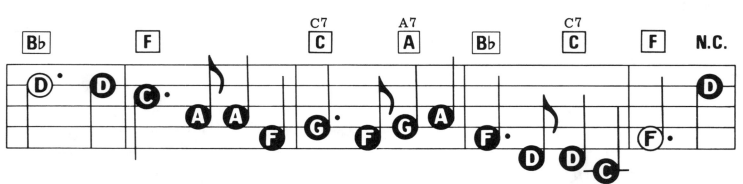

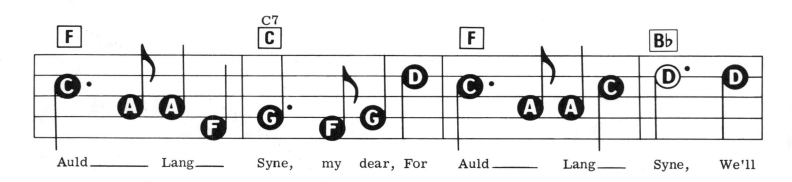

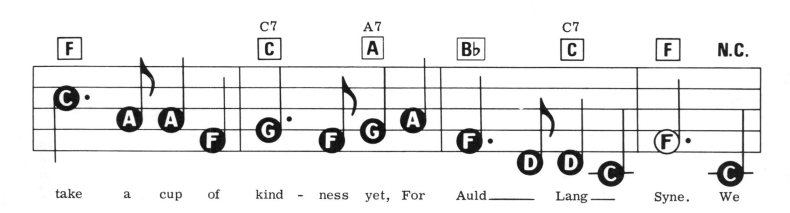

11

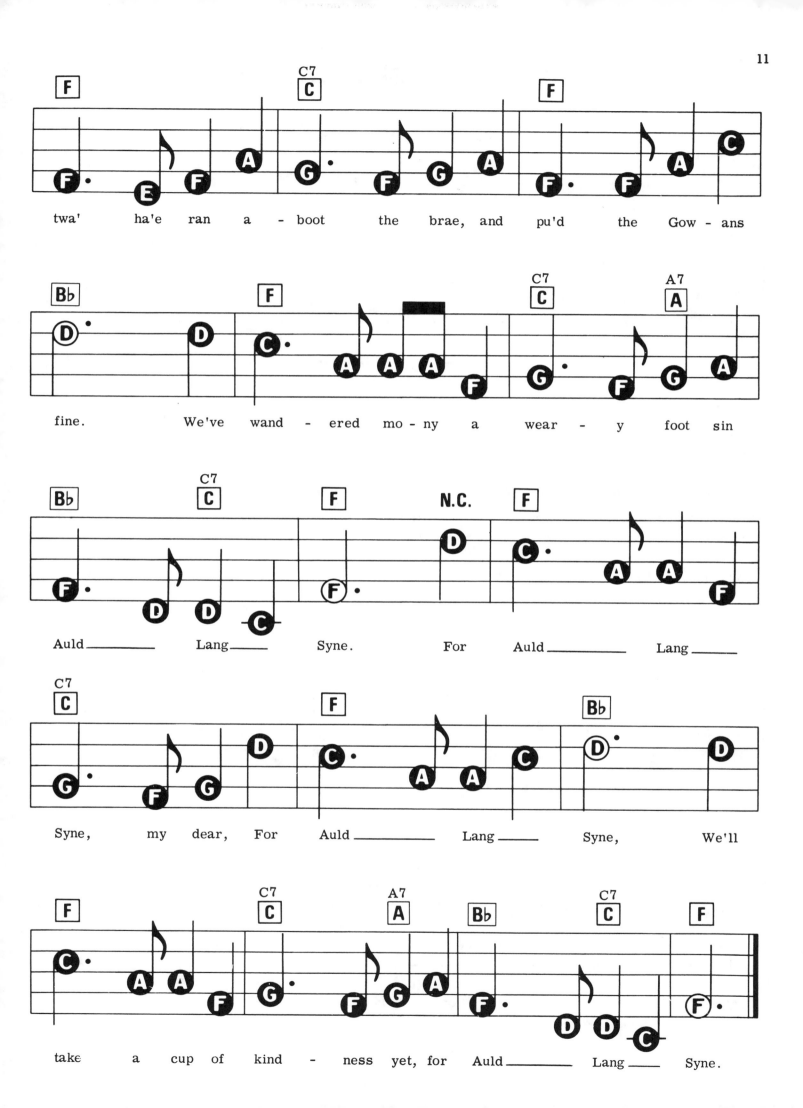

Away In A Manger

Registration 1
Rhythm: Waltz

Luther/Spillman

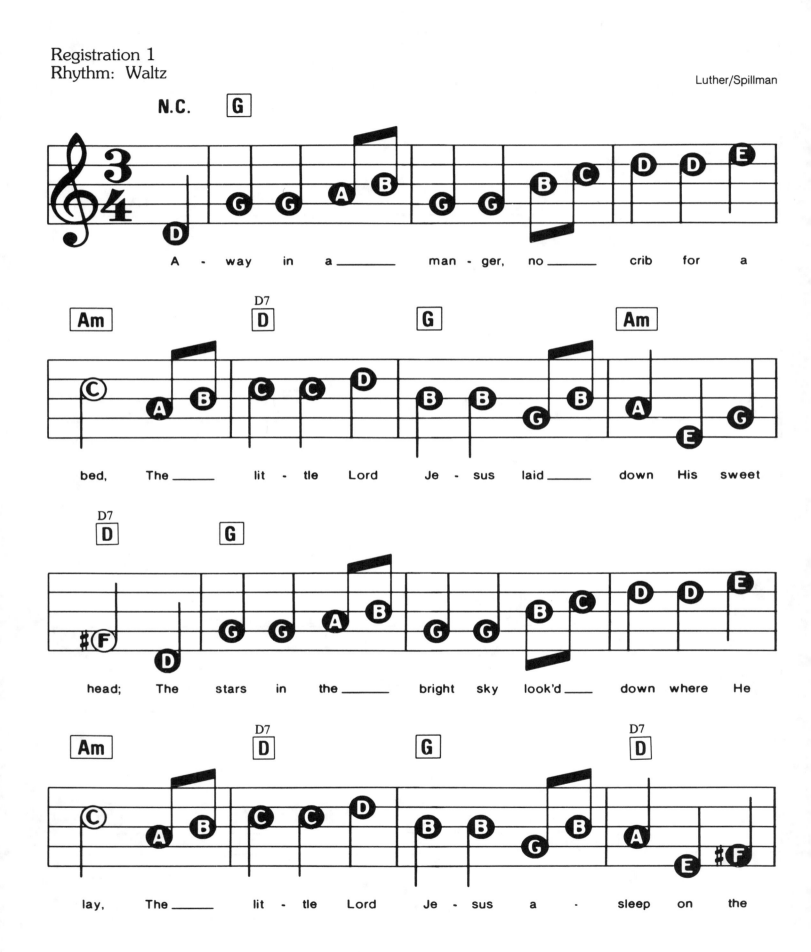

13

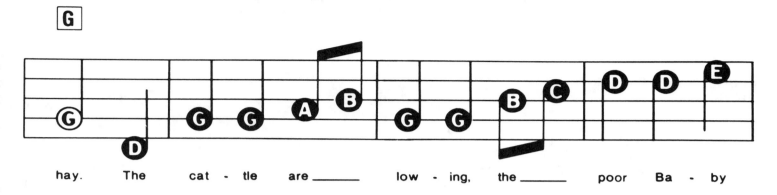

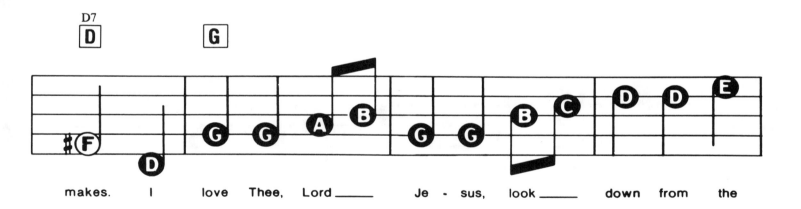

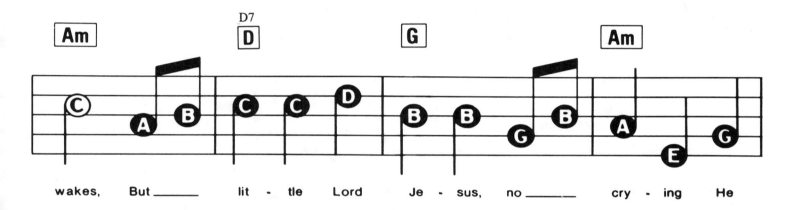

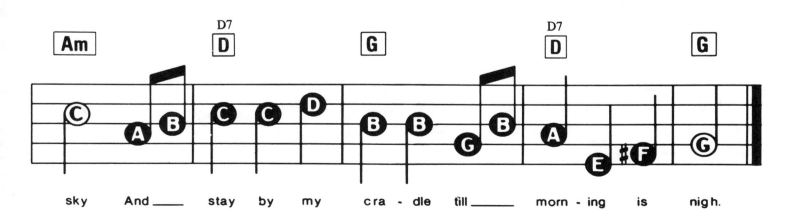

Away In A Manger

Registration 10
Rhythm: None

Mueller

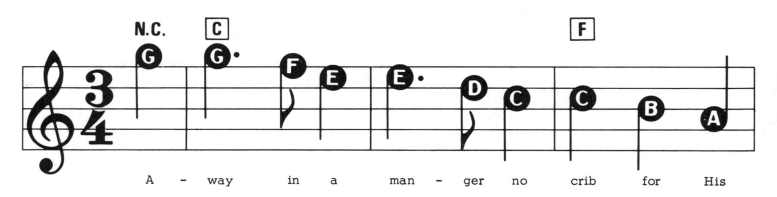

A - way in a man - ger no crib for His

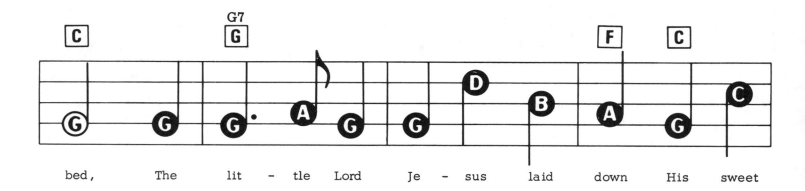

bed, The lit - tle Lord Je - sus laid down His sweet

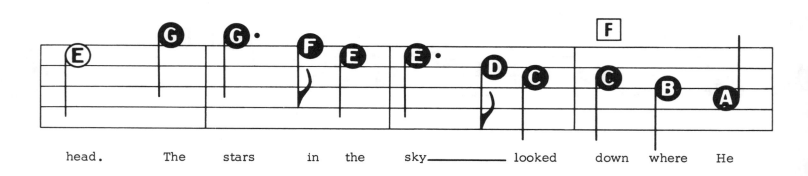

head. The stars in the sky——— looked down where He

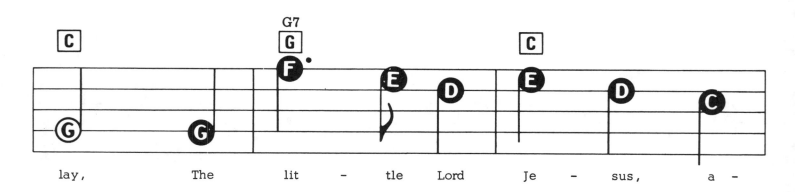

lay, The lit - tle Lord Je - sus, a -

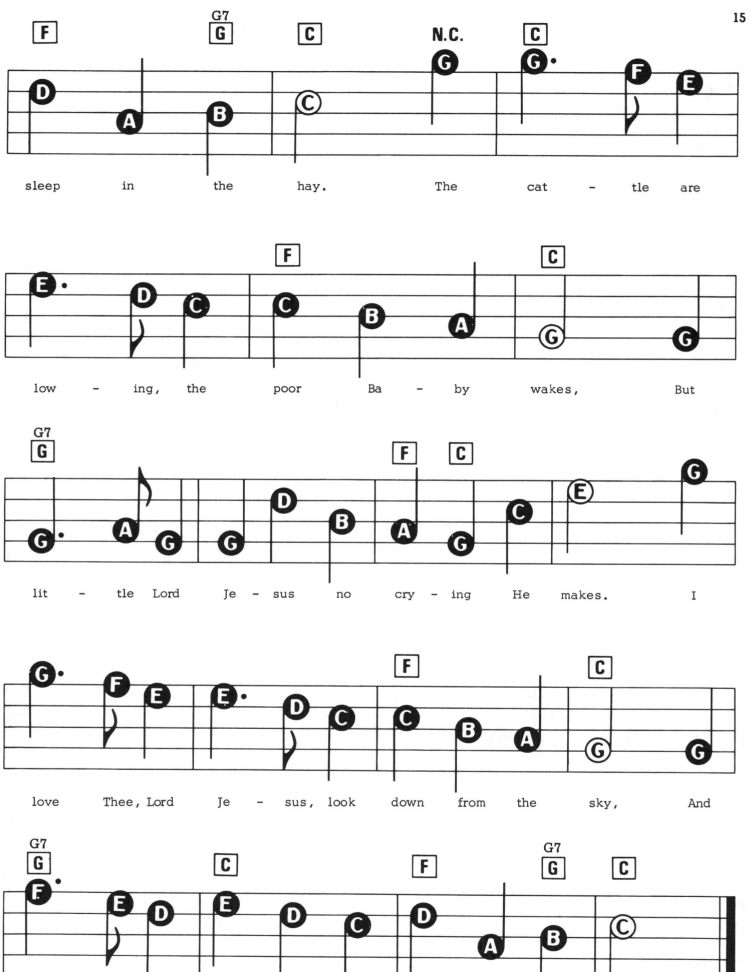

Blue Christmas

Registration 3
Rhythm: Fox Trot or Swing

Words and Music by Billy Hayes
and Jay Johnson

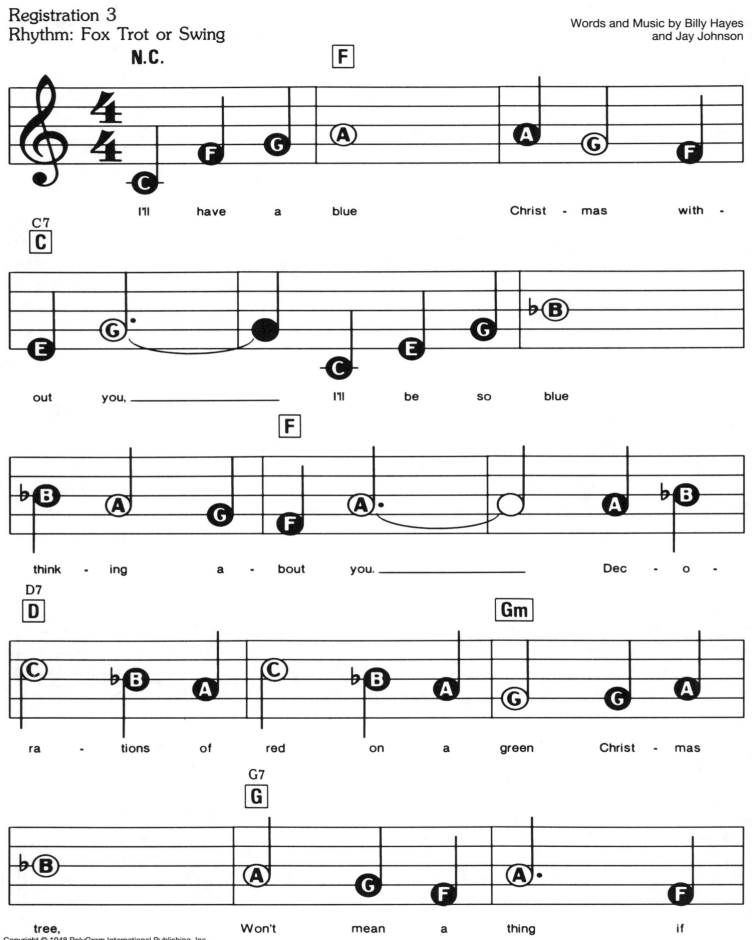

Bring A Torch, Jeanette, Isabella

Registration 3
Rhythm: None

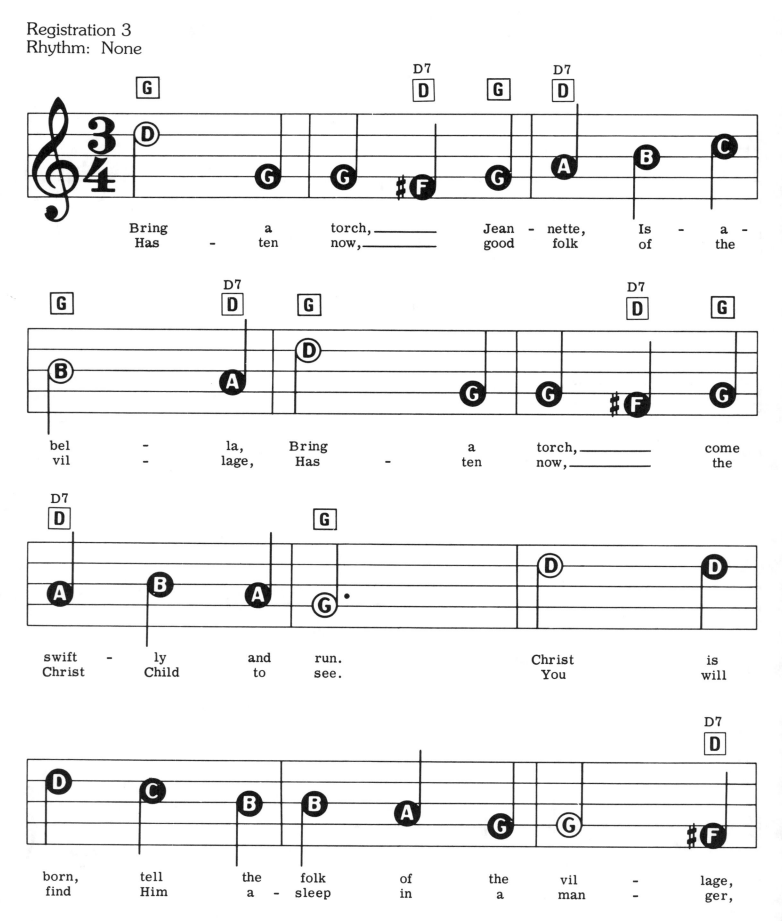

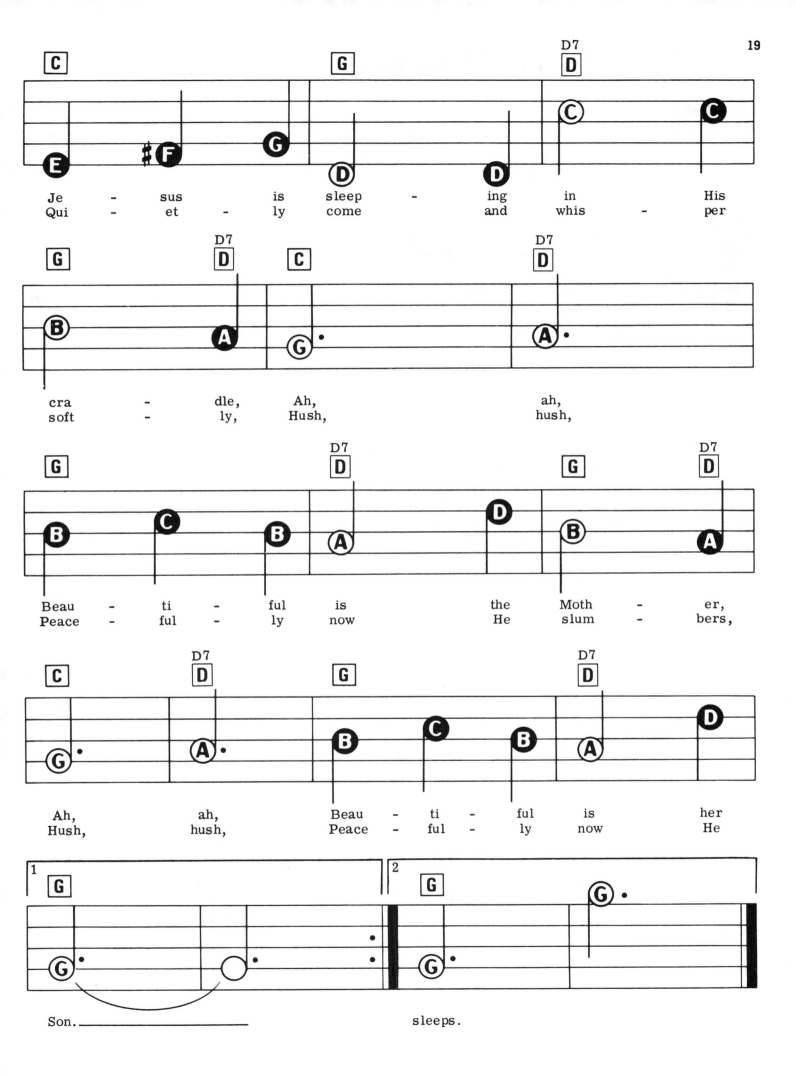

The Chipmunk Song

Registration 3
Rhythm: Waltz

Words and Music by
Ross Bagdasarian

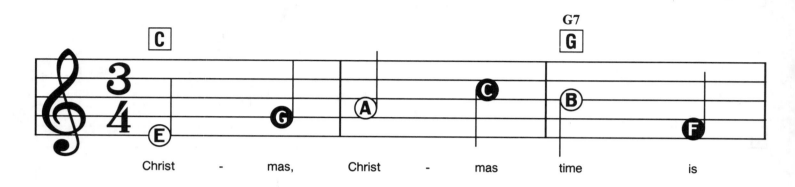

Christ - mas, Christ - mas time is

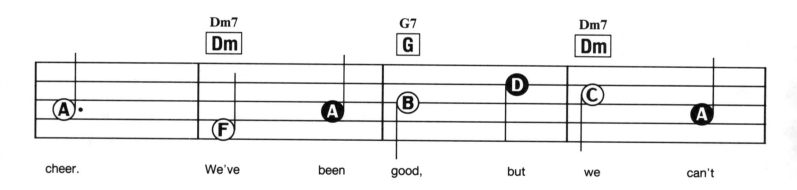

near, Time for toys and time for

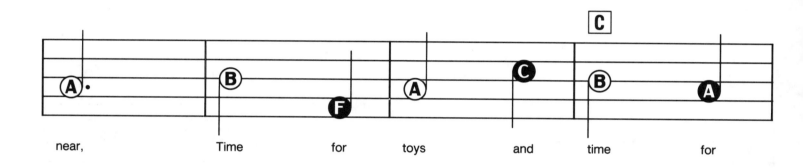

cheer. We've been good, but we can't

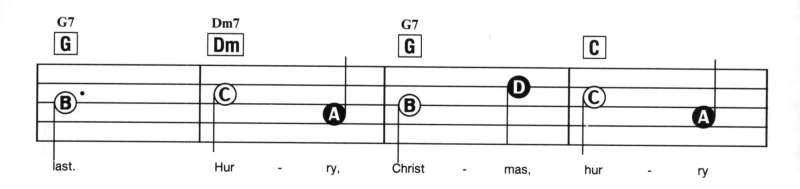

last. Hur - ry, Christ - mas, hur - ry

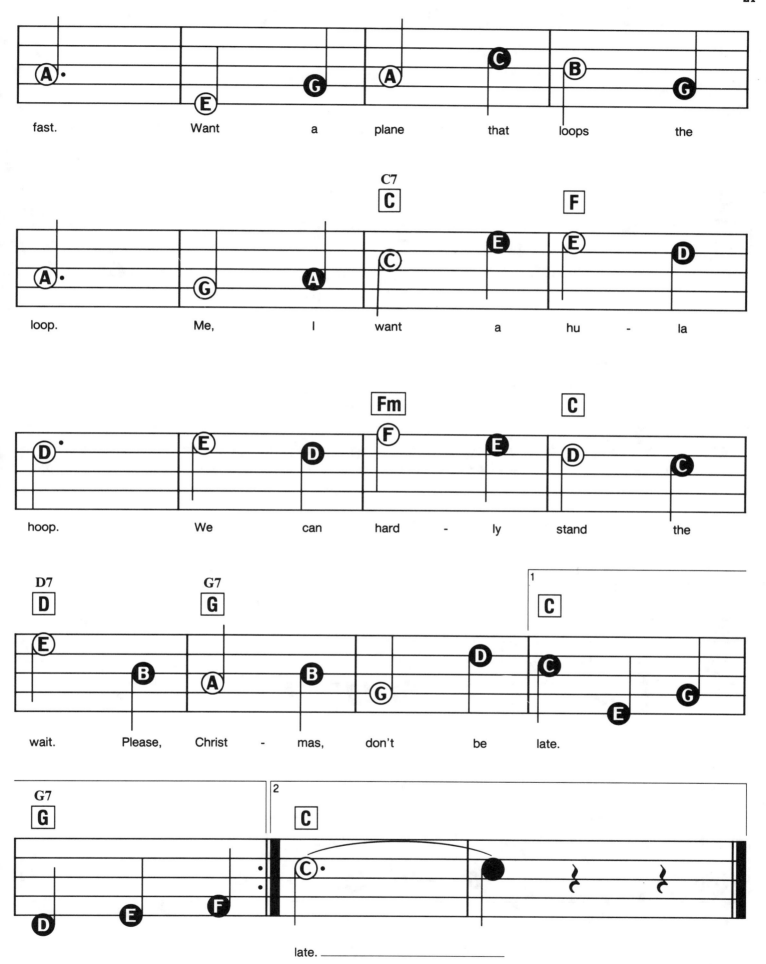

Christ Was Born On Christmas Day

Registration 6
Rhythm: None

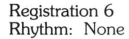

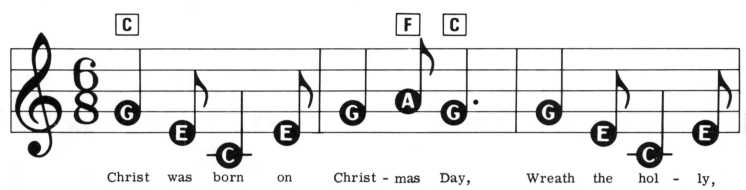

Christ was born on Christ - mas Day, Wreath the hol - ly,

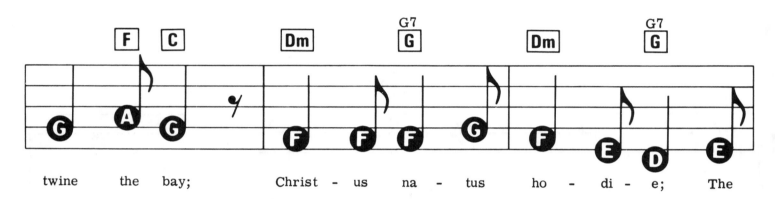

twine the bay; Christ - us na - tus ho - di - e; The

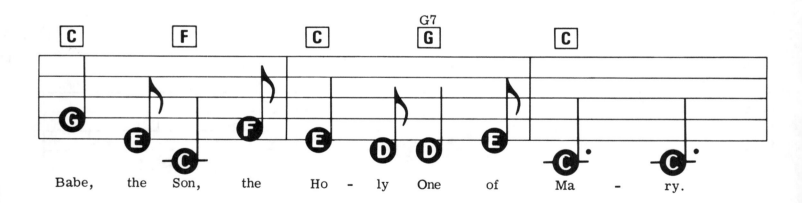

Babe, the Son, the Ho - ly One of Ma - ry.

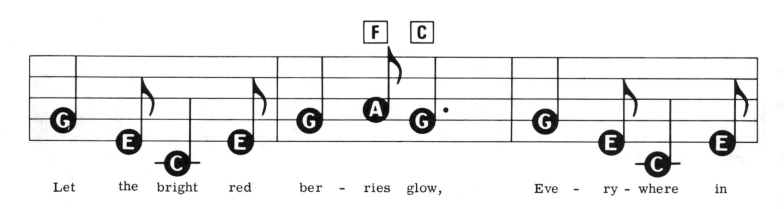

Let the bright red ber - ries glow, Eve - ry - where in

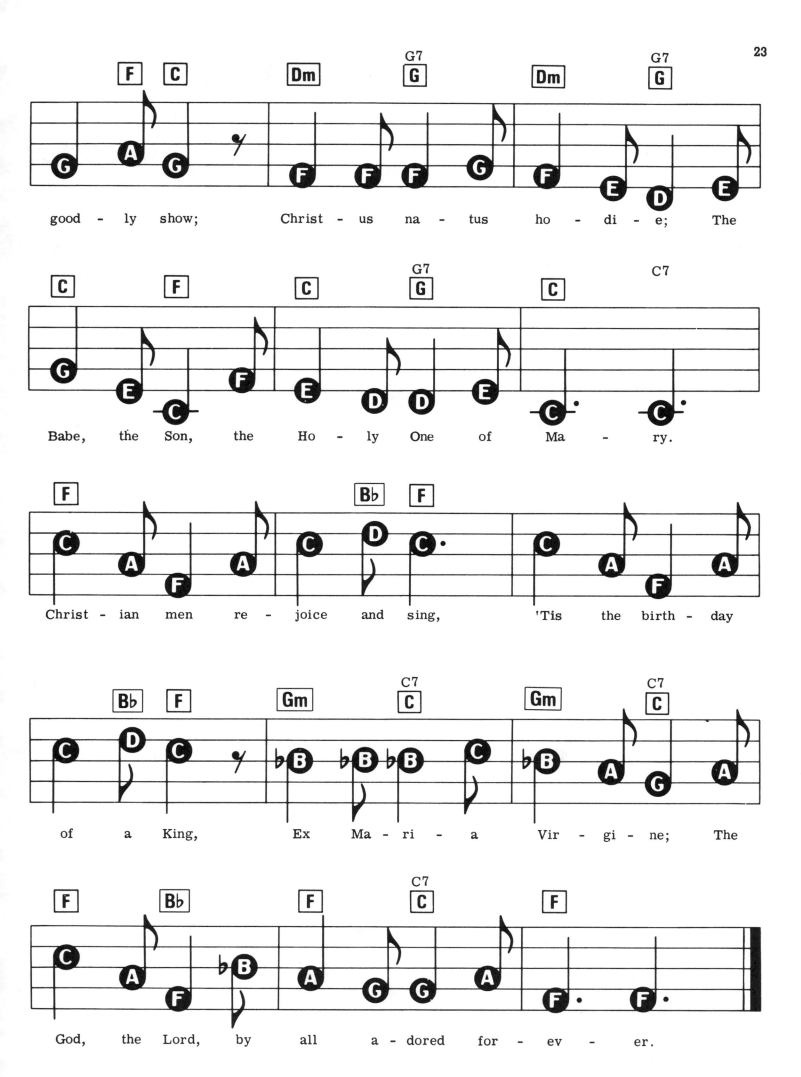

C-H-R-I-S-T-M-A-S

Registration 5
Rhythm: Fox Trot or Ballad

Words by Jenny Lou Carson
Music by Eddy Arnold

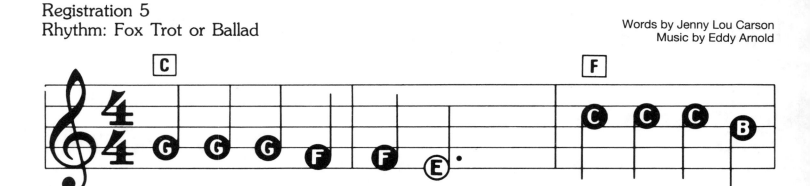

"C" is for the Christ child born up - on this

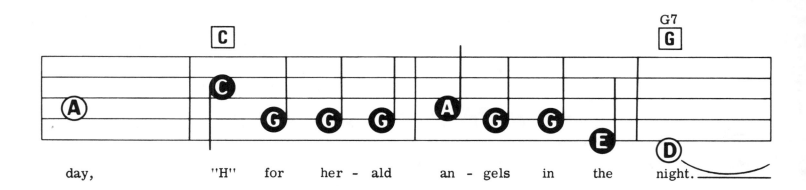

day, "H" for her - ald an - gels in the night.

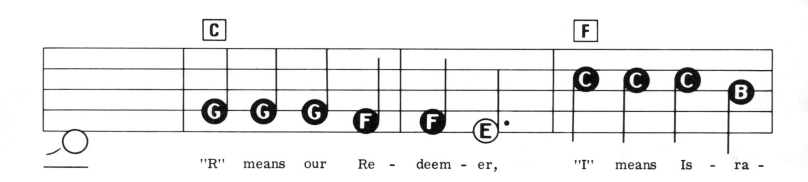

"R" means our Re - deem - er, "I" means Is - ra -

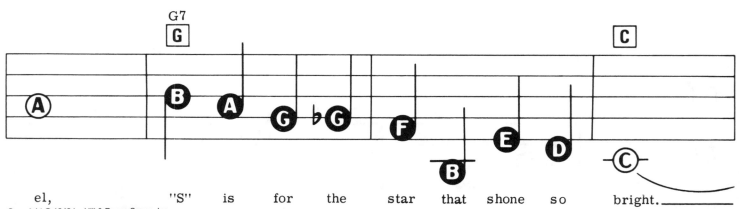

el, "S" is for the star that shone so bright.

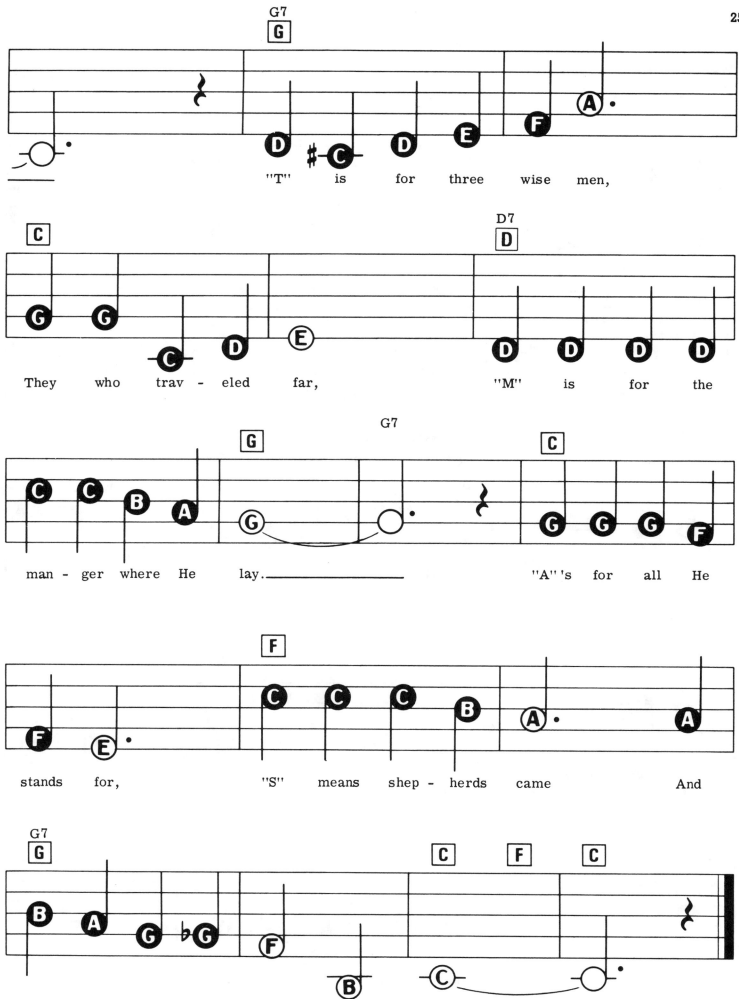

Christmas Is

Registration 10
Rhythm: Fox Trot or Slow Swing

Lyrics by Spence Maxwell
Music by Percy Faith

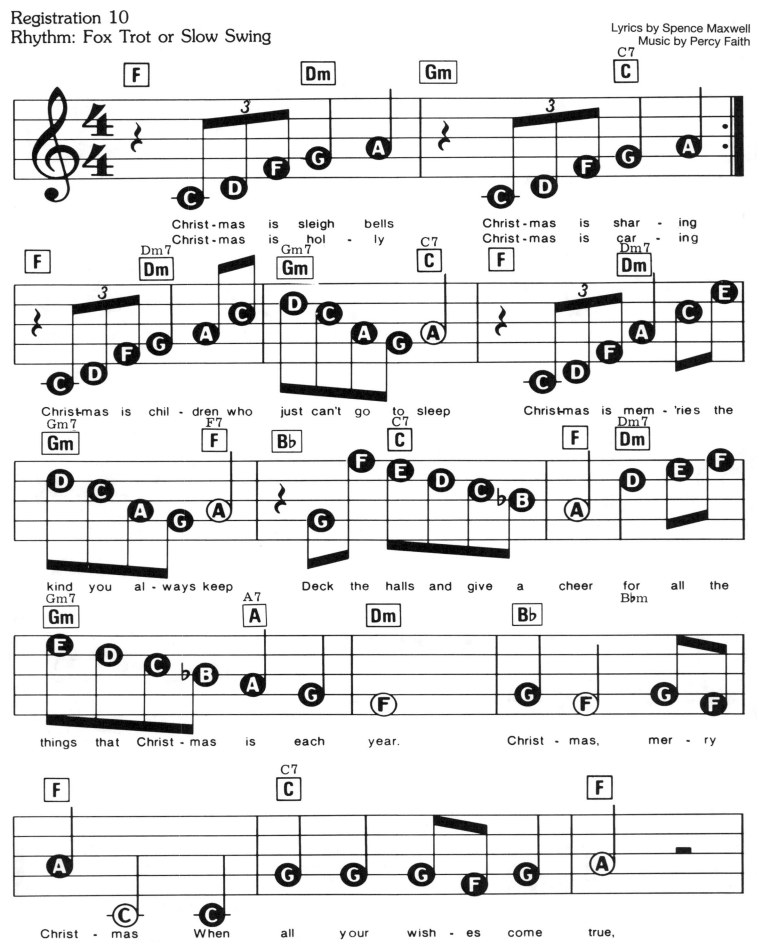

Christ - mas is sleigh bells   Christ - mas is shar - ing
Christ - mas is hol - ly   Christ - mas is car - ing

Christ - mas is chil - dren who just can't go to sleep   Christ - mas is mem - 'ries the

kind you al - ways keep   Deck the halls and give a cheer for all the

things that Christ - mas is each year.   Christ - mas, mer - ry

Christ - mas   When all your wish - es come true,

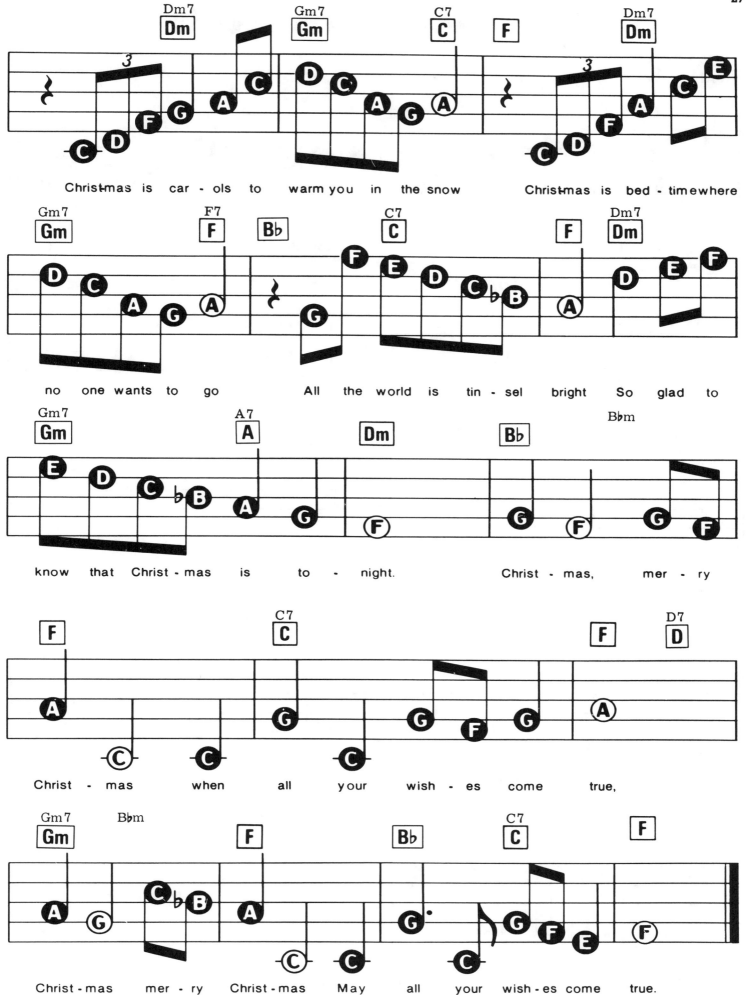

The Christmas Waltz

Registration 2
Rhythm: Waltz

Words by Sammy Cahn
Music by Jule Styne

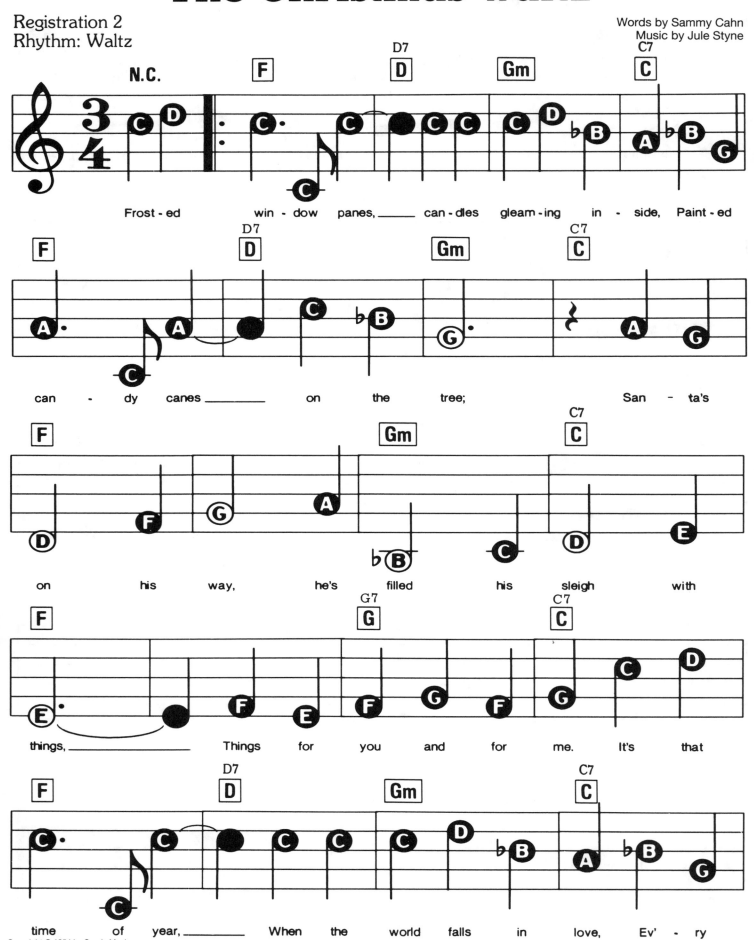

29

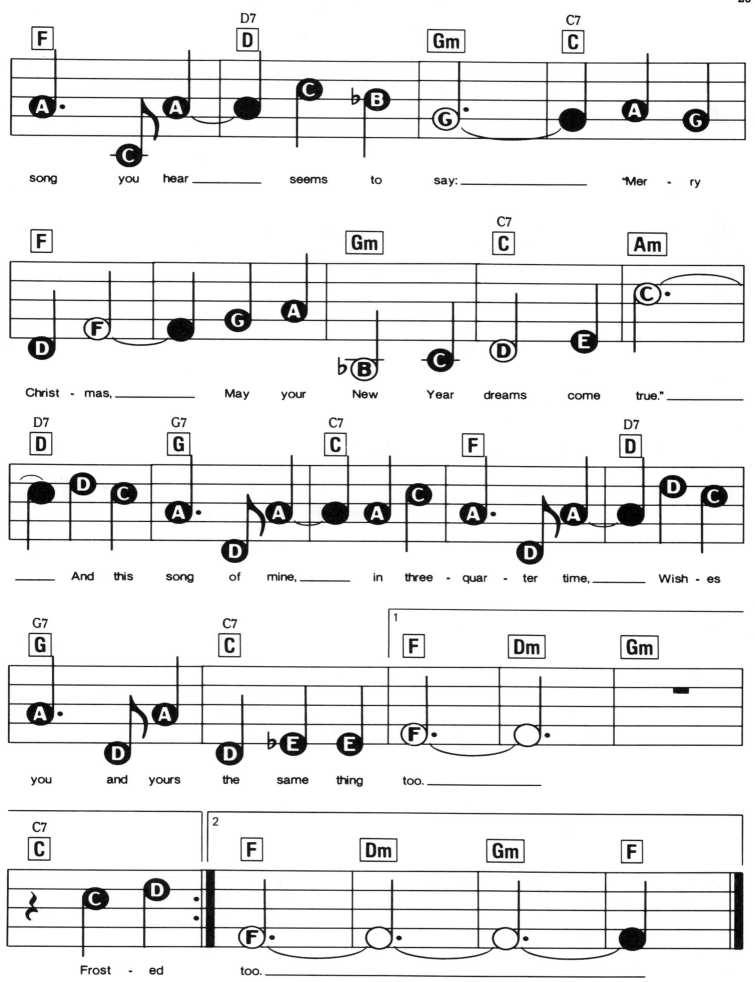

The Coventry Carol

Registration 1
Rhythm: None

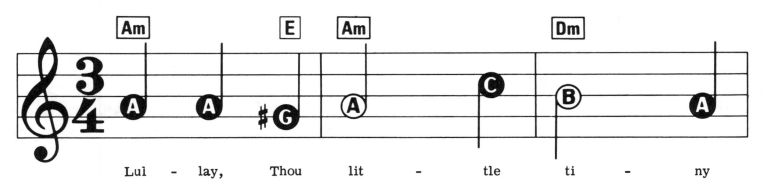

Lul - lay, Thou lit - tle ti - ny

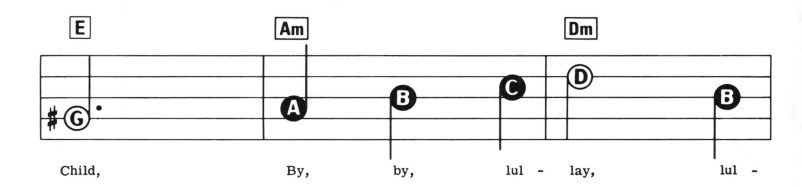

Child, By, by, lul - lay, lul -

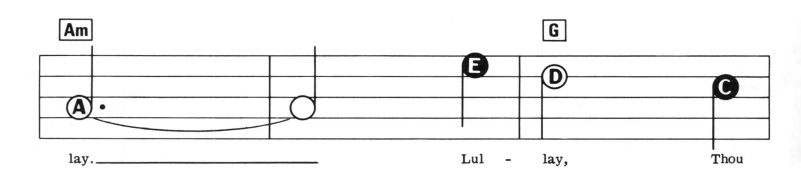

lay._____ Lul - lay, Thou

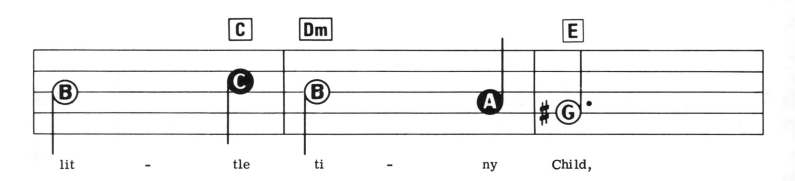

lit - tle ti - ny Child,

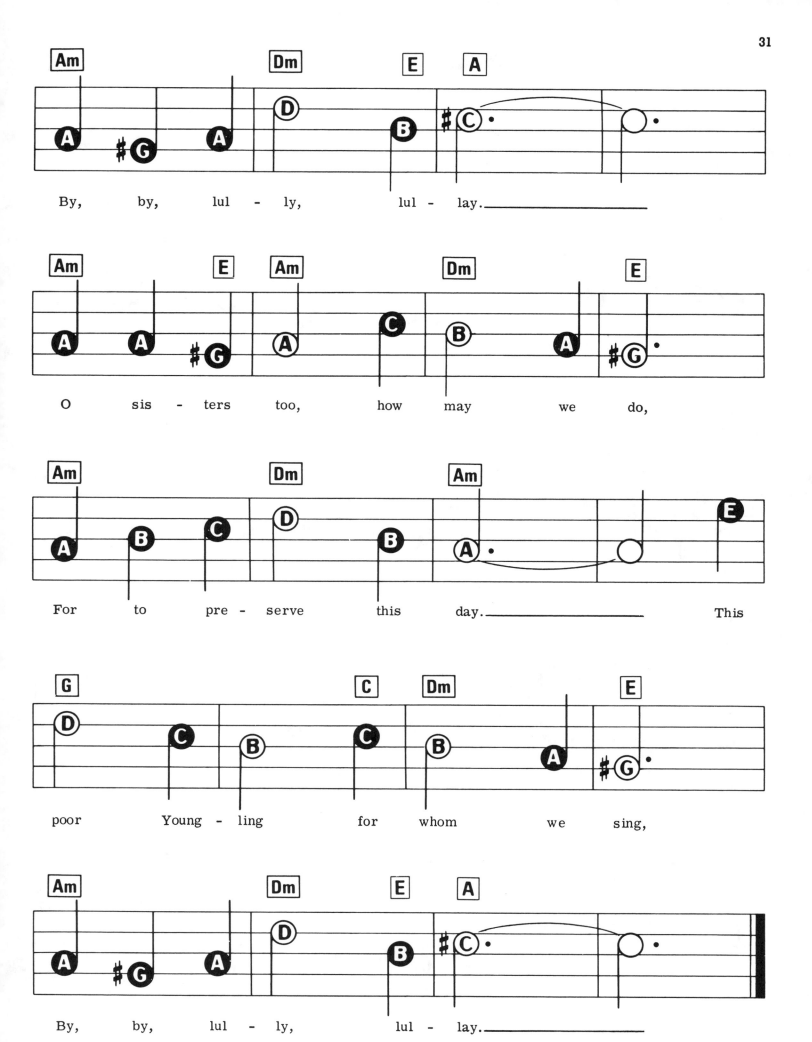

Deck The Hall

Registration 5
Rhythm: None

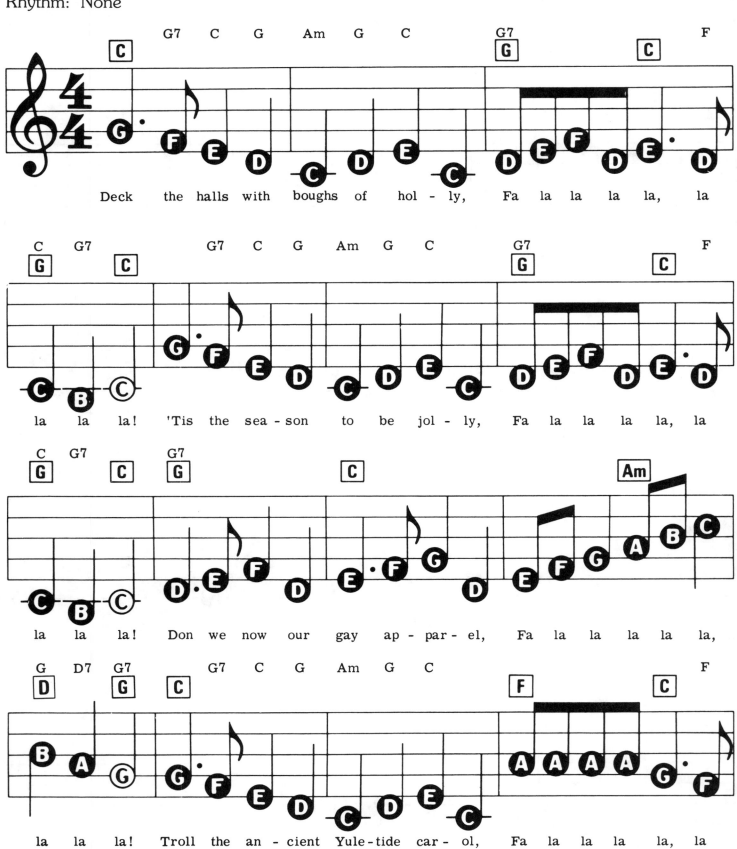

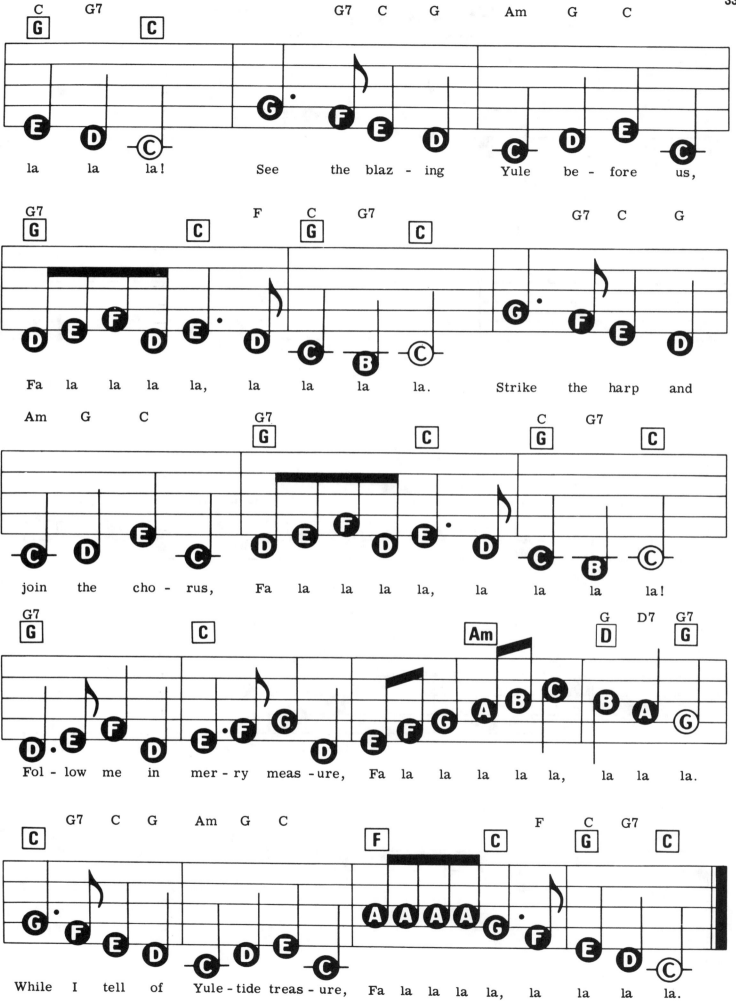

Do They Know It's Christmas?

Registration 1
Rhythm: Latin or Rock

Words and Music by M. Ure
and B. Geldof

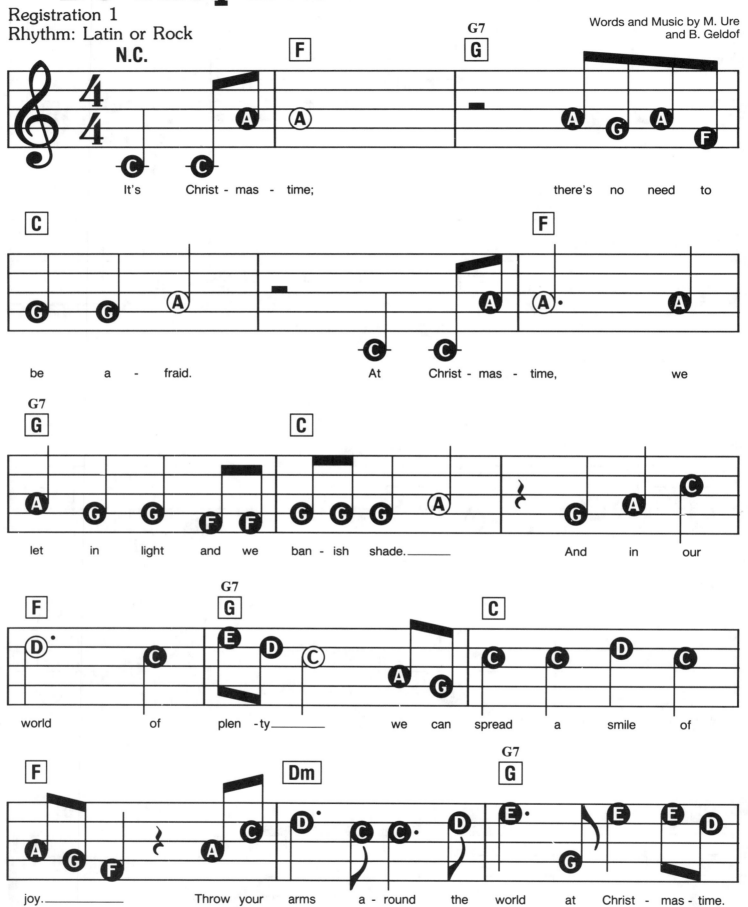

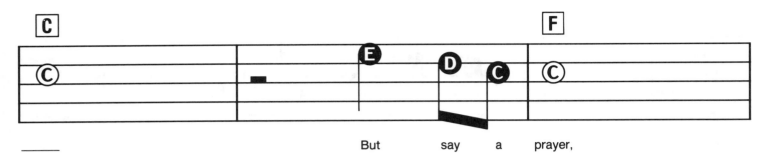

_____

But say a prayer,

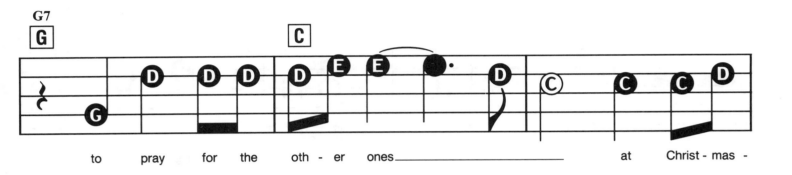

to pray for the oth - er ones_____ at Christ - mas -

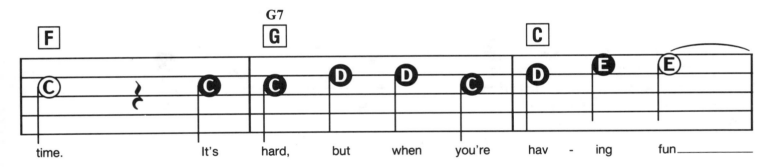

time. It's hard, but when you're hav - ing fun_____

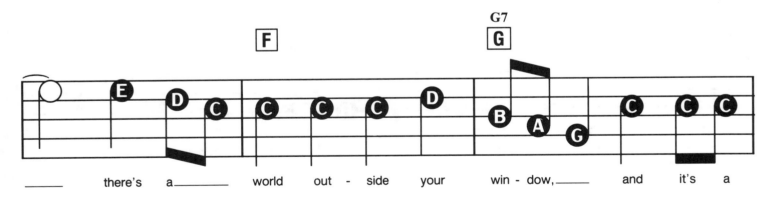

_____ there's a_____ world out - side your win - dow,_____ and it's a

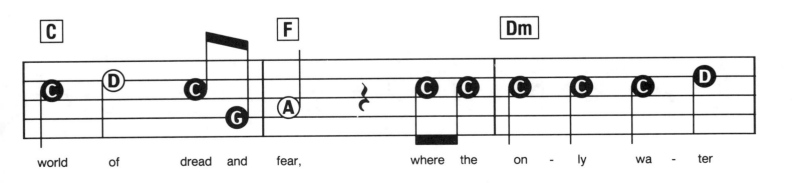

world of dread and fear, where the on - ly wa - ter

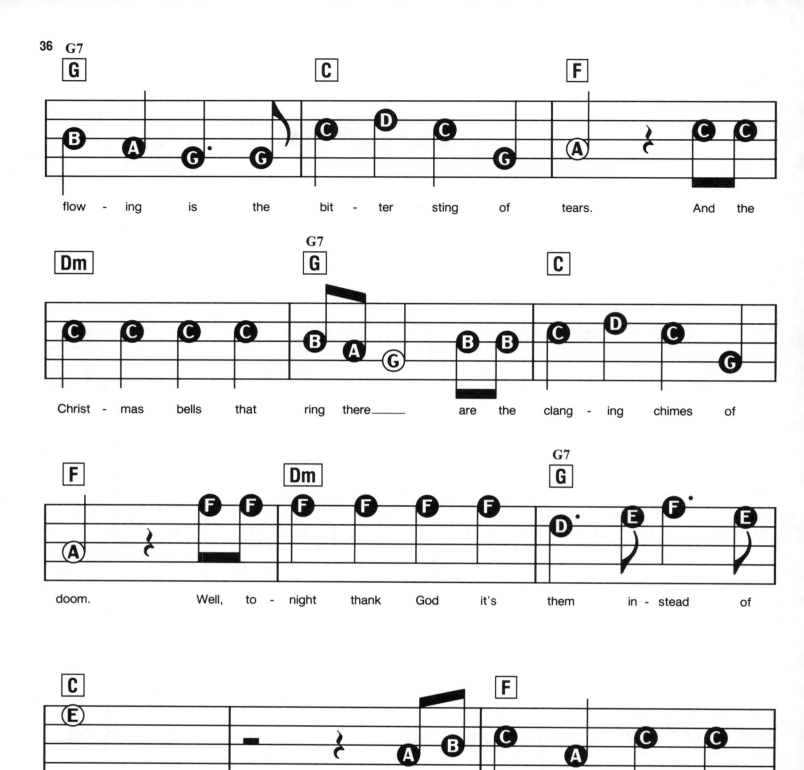

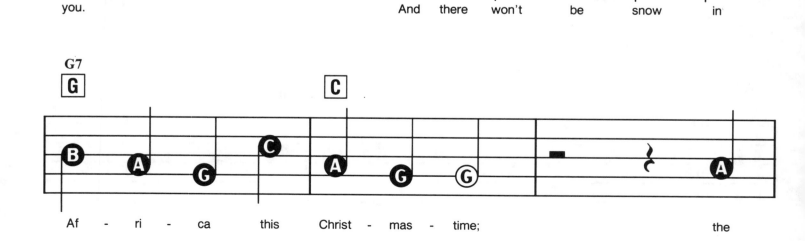

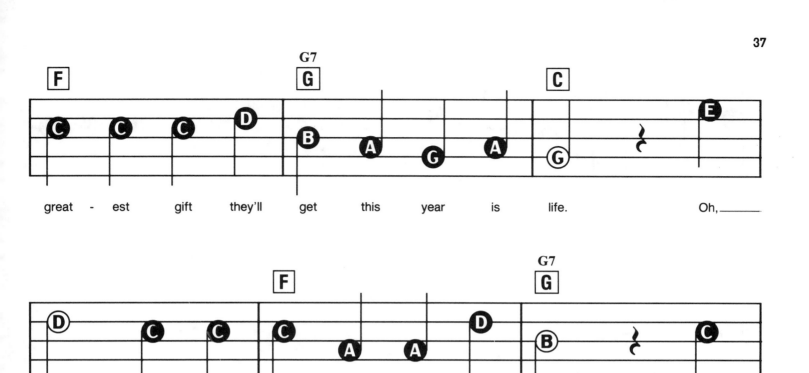

great - est gift they'll get this year is life. Oh,_____

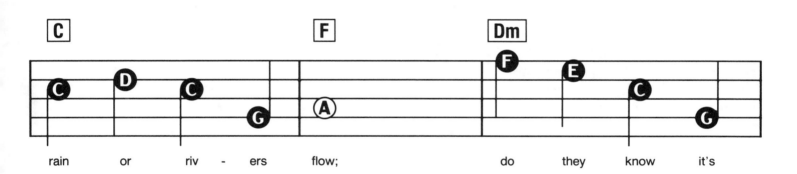

_____ Where noth - ing ev - er grows, no

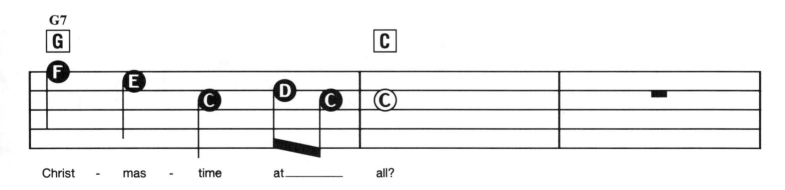

rain or riv - ers flow; do they know it's

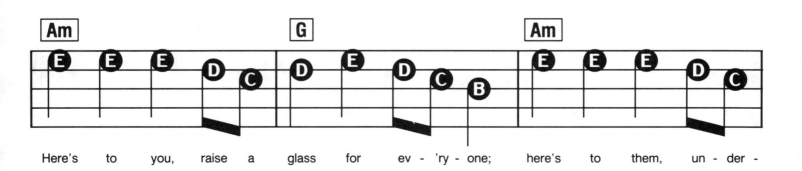

Christ - mas - time at_____ all?

Here's to you, raise a glass for ev - 'ry - one; here's to them, un - der -

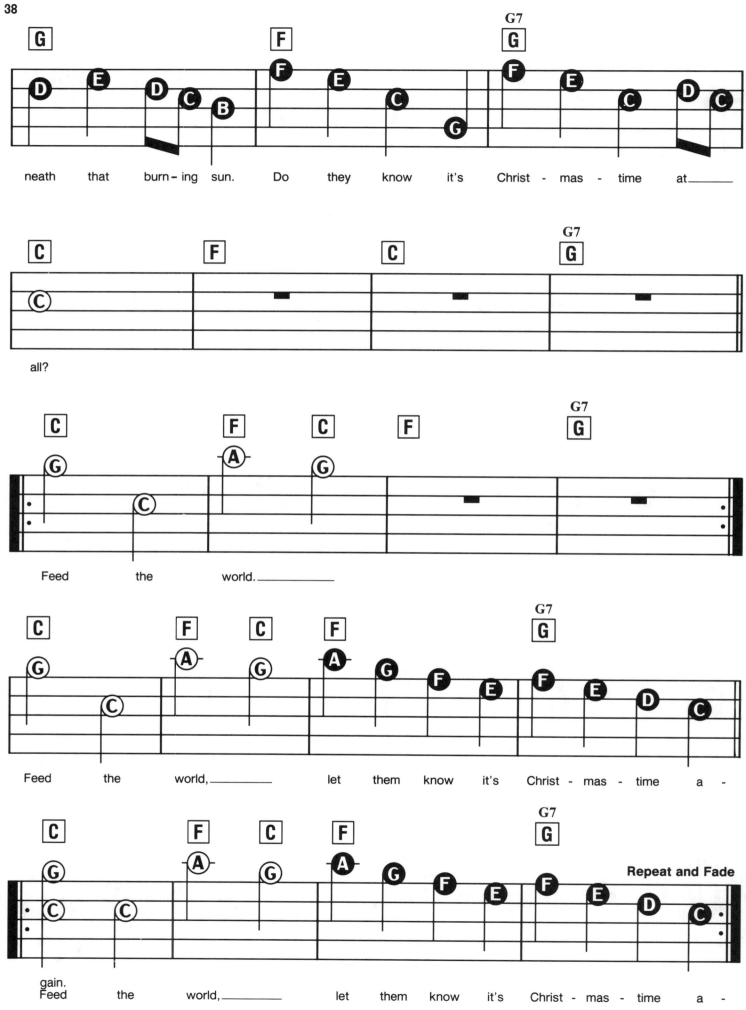

Do You Hear What I Hear

Registration 4
Rhythm: 8 Beat or Pops

Words and Music by Noel Regney
and Gloria Shayne

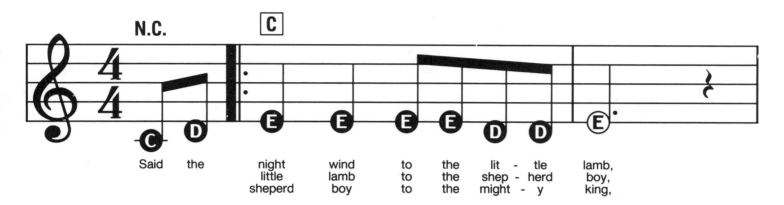

Said the night wind to the lit - tle lamb,
little lamb to the shep - herd boy,
sheperd boy to the might - y king,

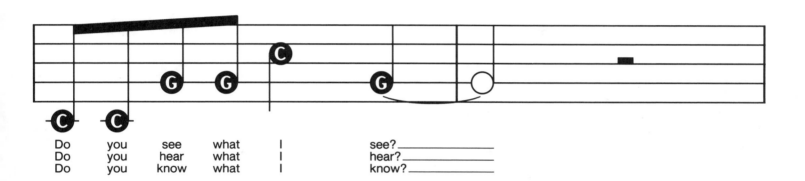

Do you see what I see?
Do you hear what I hear?
Do you know what I know?

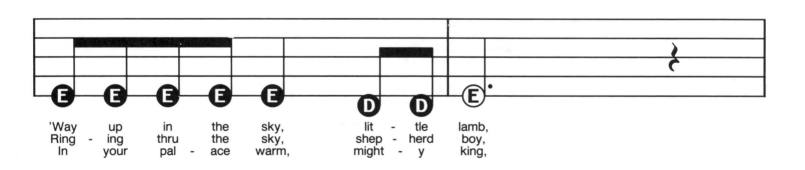

'Way up in the sky, lit - tle lamb,
Ring - ing thru the sky, shep - herd boy,
In your pal - ace warm, might - y king,

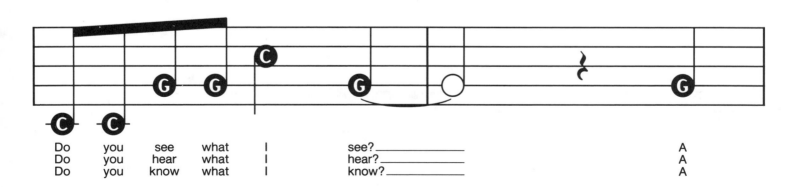

Do you see what I see?
Do you hear what I hear? A
Do you know what I know? A

40

_____ Pray for peace, peo - ple ev' - ry -

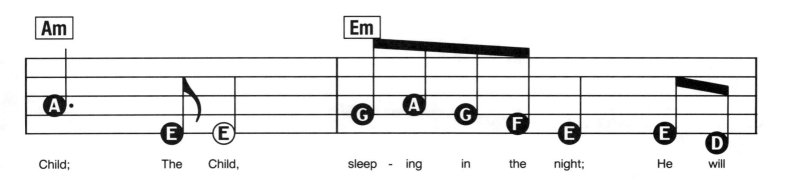

where, Lis - ten to what I say!_____ The

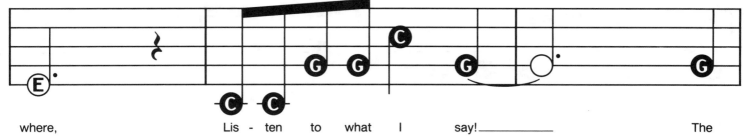

Am   **Em**

Child; The Child, sleep - ing in the night; He will

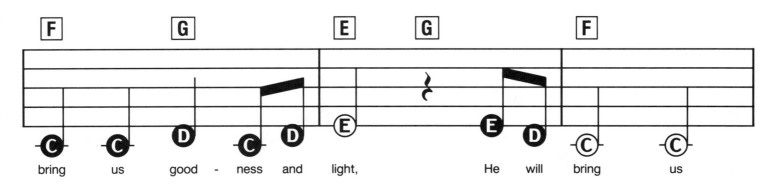

F   **G**   **E**   **G**   **F**

bring us good - ness and light, He will bring us

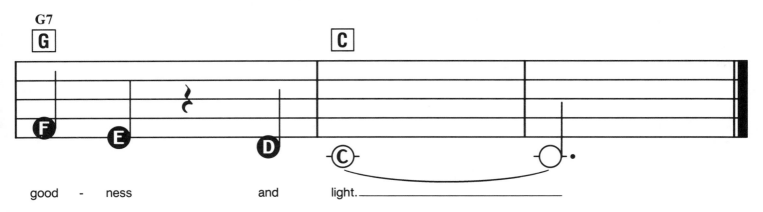

G7
G   **C**

good - ness and light._____

Because It's Christmas

Registration 2
Rhythm: Swing

Music by Barry Manilow
Lyric by Bruce Sussman and Jack Feldman

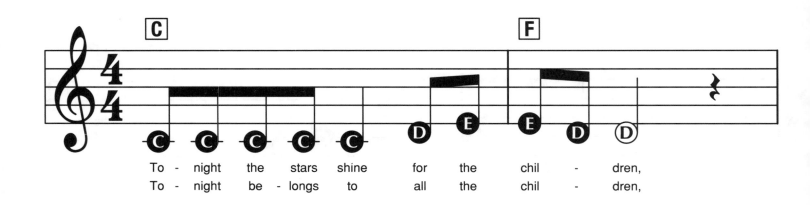

To - night the stars shine for the chil - dren,
To - night be - longs to all the chil - dren,

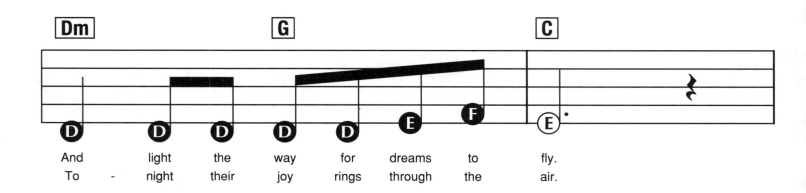

And light the way for dreams to fly.
To - night their joy rings through the air.

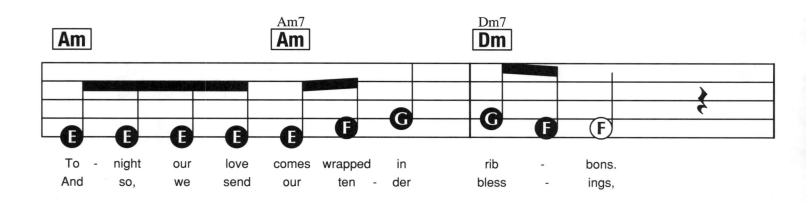

To - night our love comes wrapped in rib - bons.
And so, we send our ten - der bless - ings,

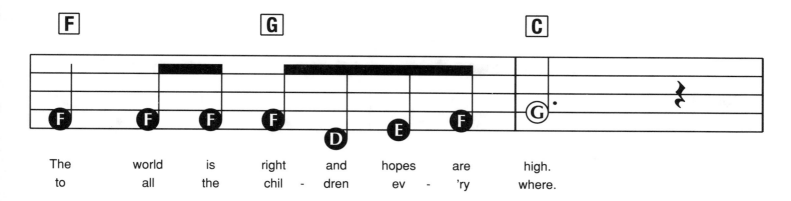

The world is right and hopes are high.
to all the right chil - dren ev - 'ry where.

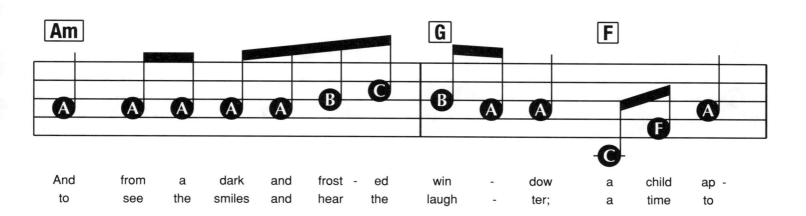

And from a dark and frost - ed win - dow a child ap -
to see the smiles and hear the laugh - ter; a time to

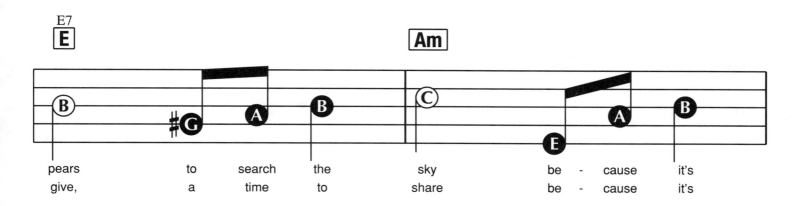

pears to search the sky be - cause it's
give, a time to share be - cause it's

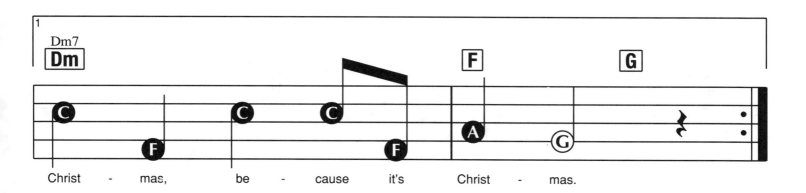

Christ - mas, be - cause it's Christ - mas.

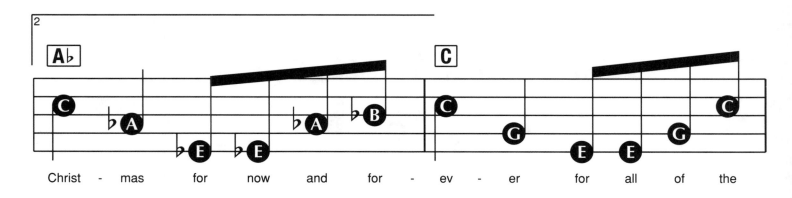

Christ - mas for now and for - ev - er for all of the

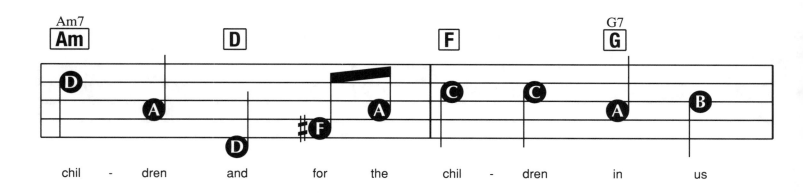

chil - dren and for the chil - dren in us

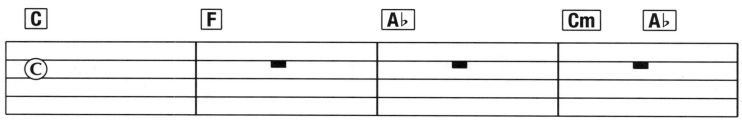

all.

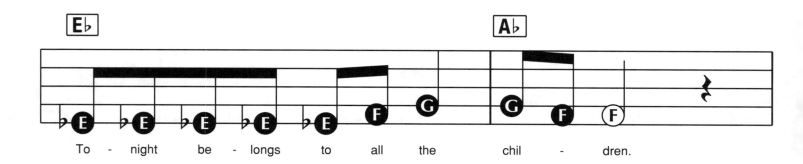

To - night be - longs to all the chil - dren.

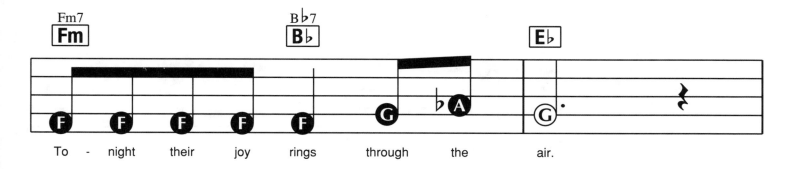

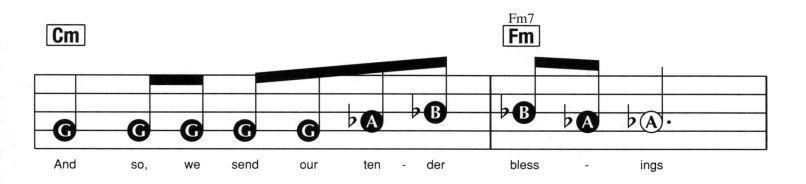

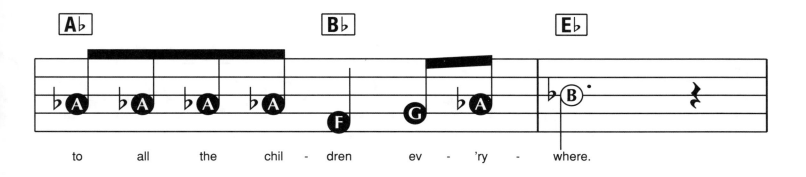

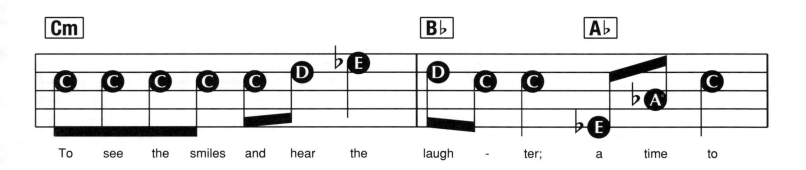

45

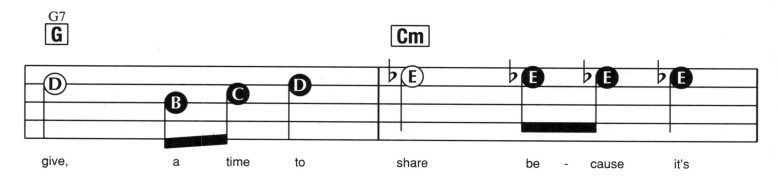

give,   a   time   to   share   be - cause   it's

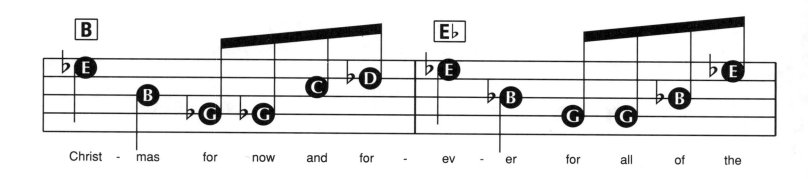

Christ - mas   for   now   and   for - ev - er   for   all   of   the

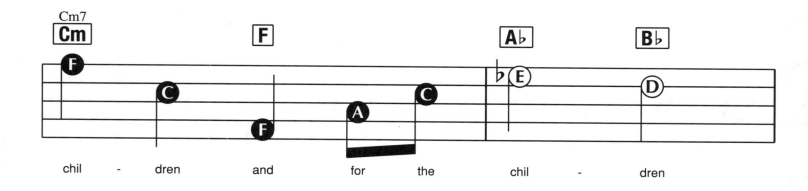

chil - dren   and   for   the   chil - dren

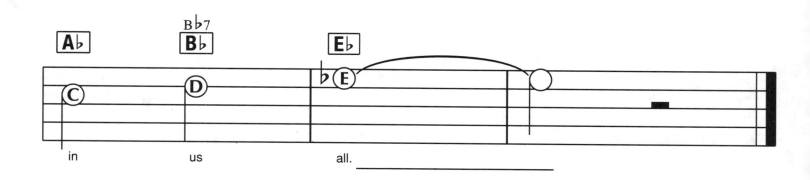

in   us   all.

Feliz Navidad

Registration 1
Rhythm: Latin or Bossa Nova

Words and Music by
Jose Feliciano

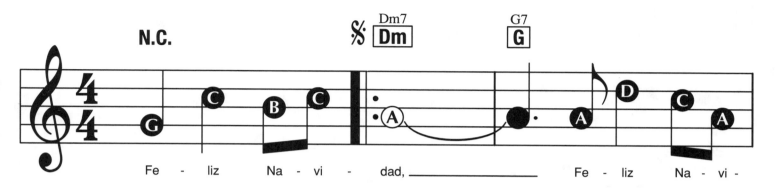

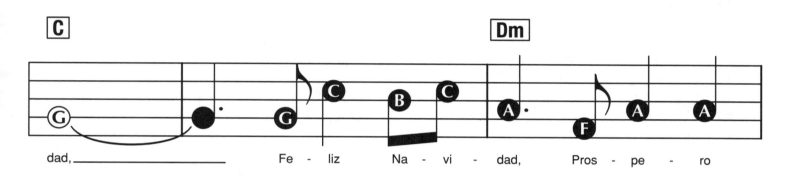

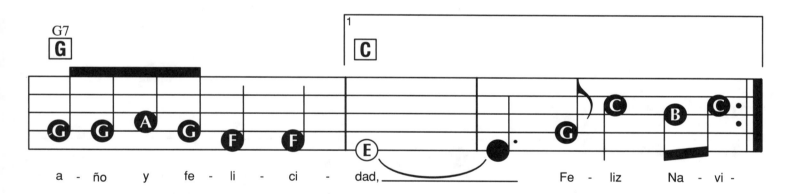

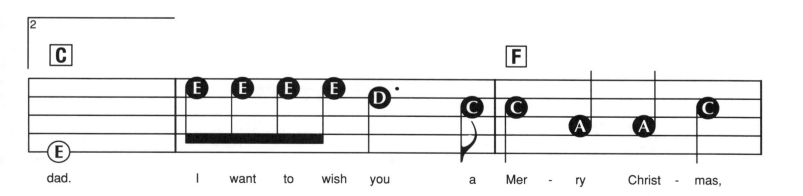

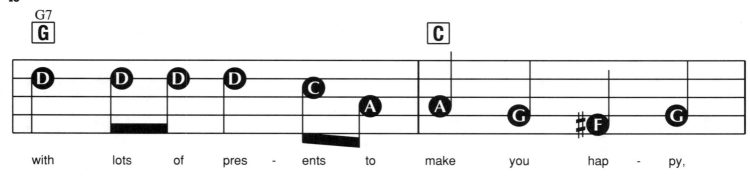

with lots of pres - ents to make you hap - py,

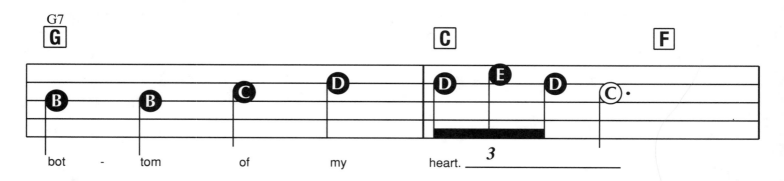

I want to wish you a mer - ry Christ - mas from the

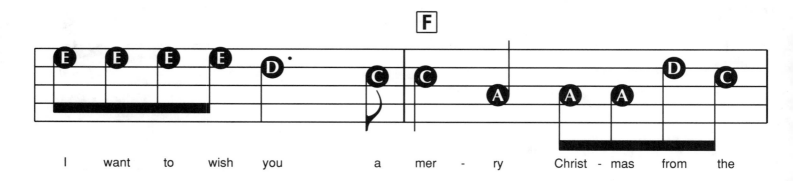

bot - tom of my heart. _____

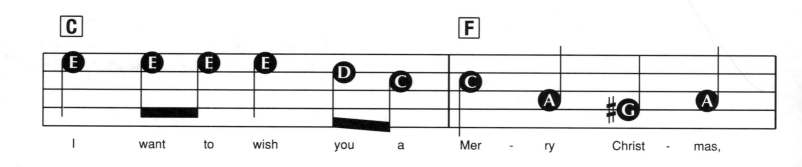

I want to wish you a Mer - ry Christ - mas,

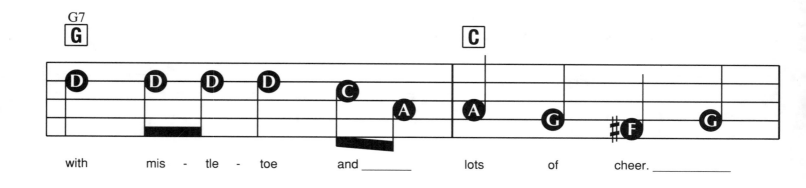

with mis - tle - toe and _____ lots of cheer. _____

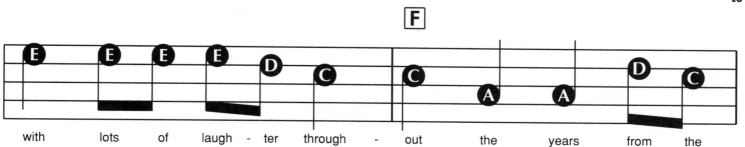

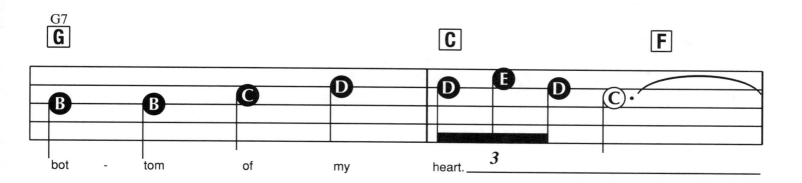

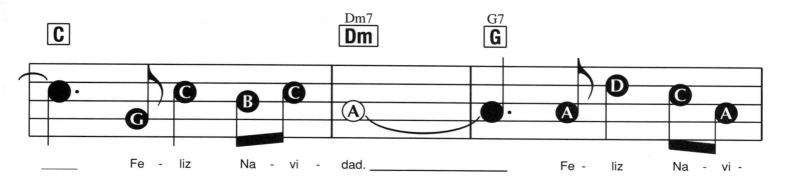

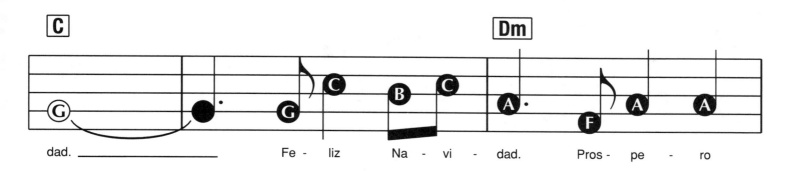

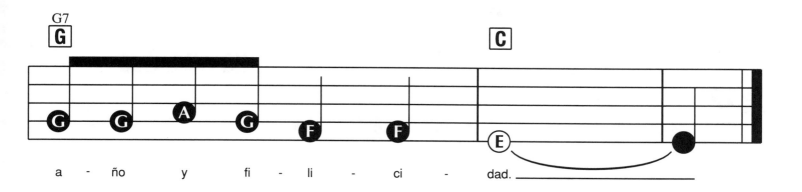

The First Noel

Registration 9
Rhythm: None

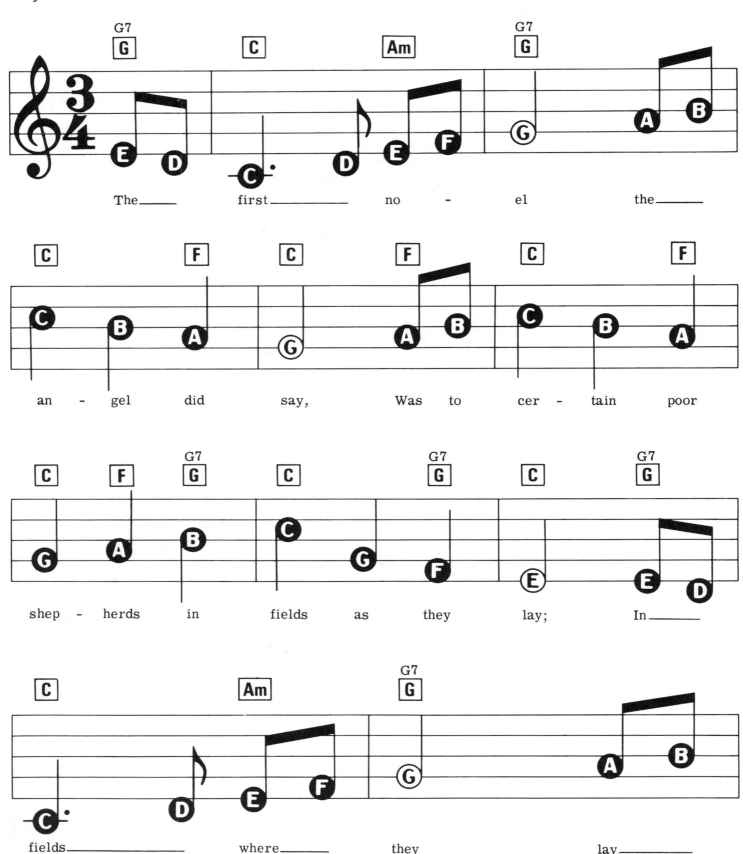

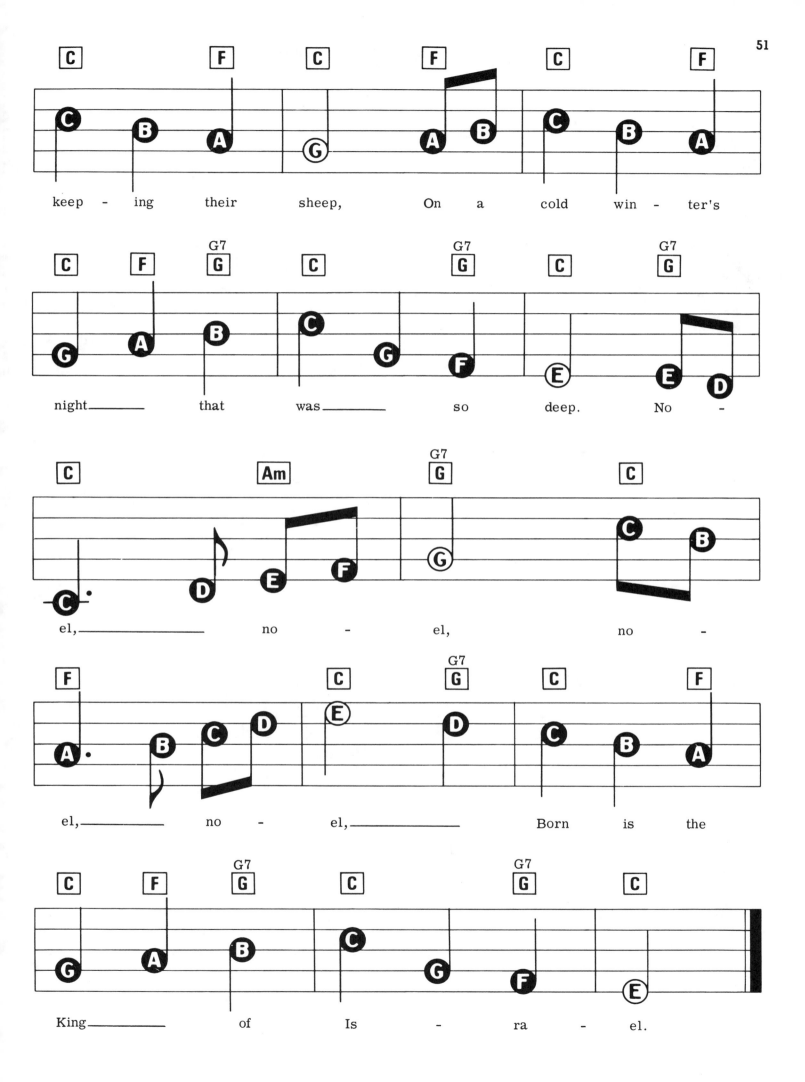

The Friendly Beasts

Registration 2
Rhythm: None

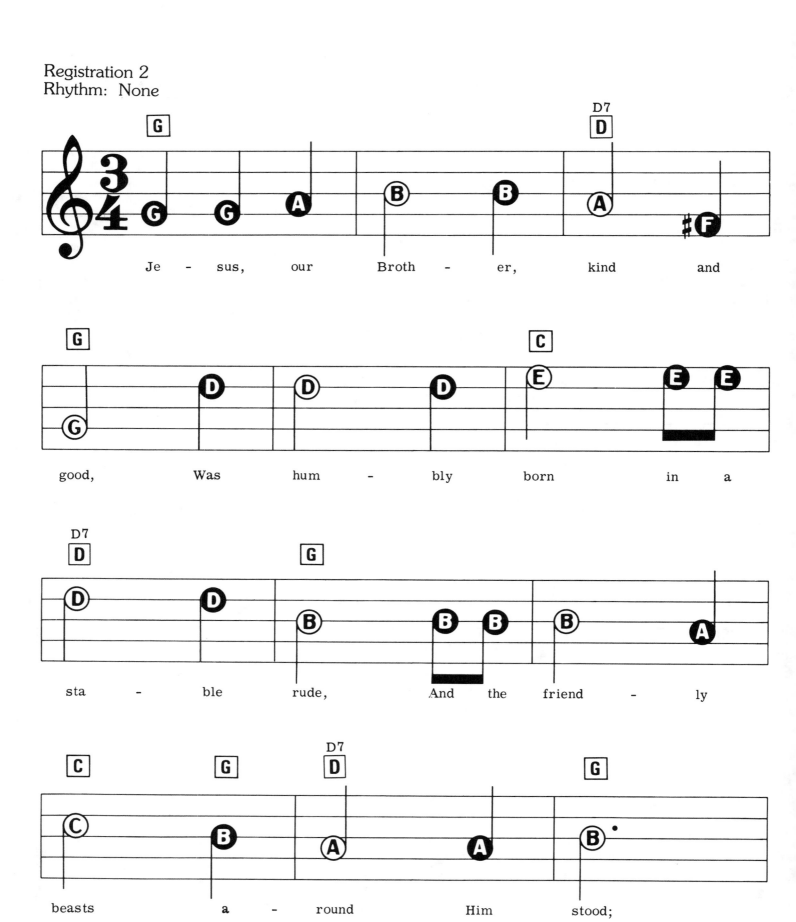

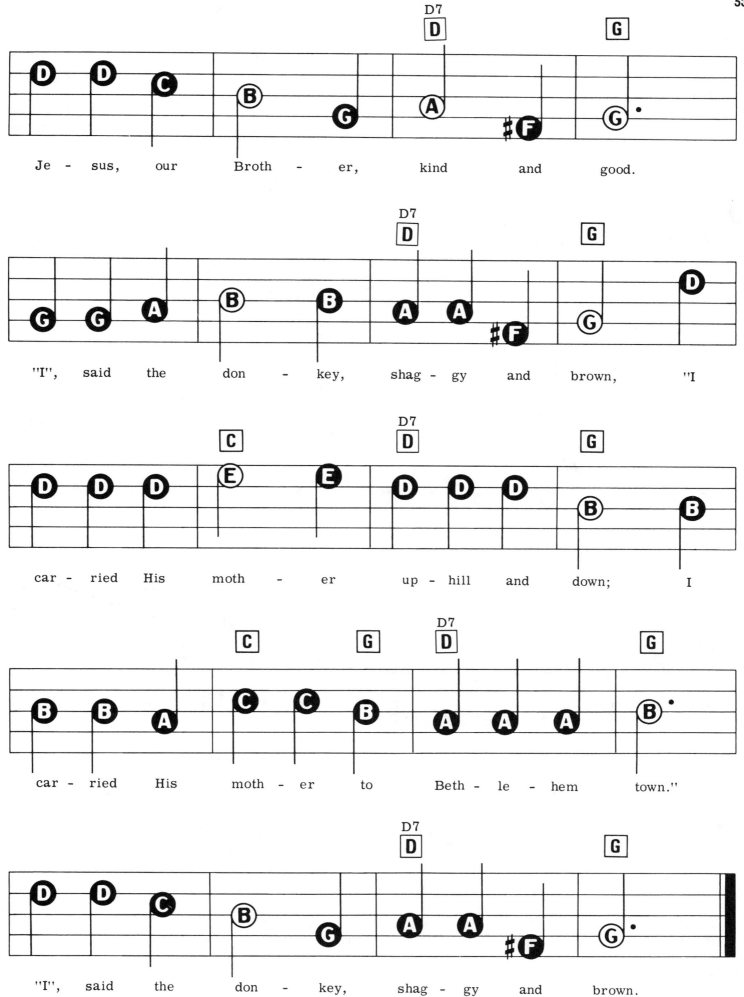

53

Frosty The Snowman

Registration 2
Rhythm: Fox Trot or Swing

Words and Music by Steve Nelson
and Jack Rollins

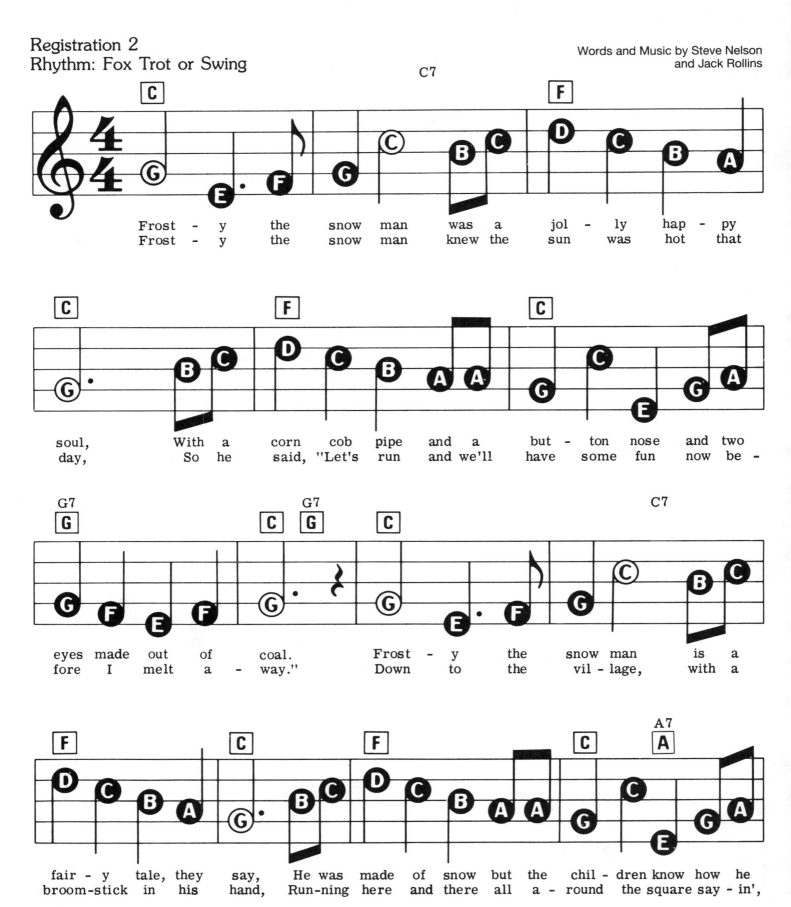

God Rest Ye Merry, Gentlemen

Registration 6
Rhythm: Fox Trot or March

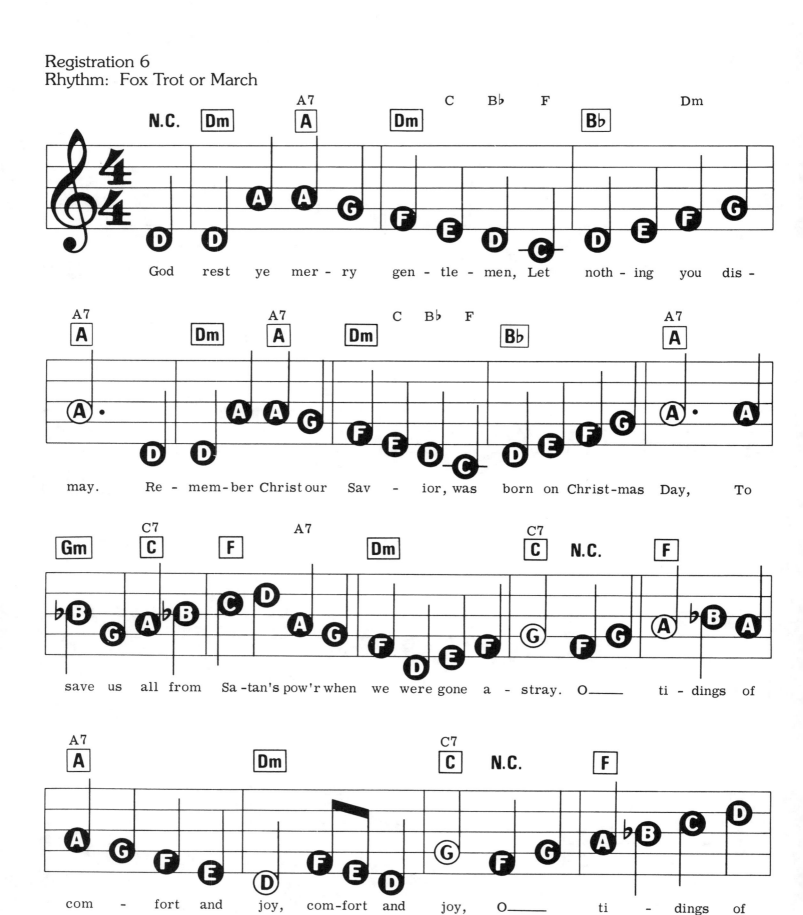

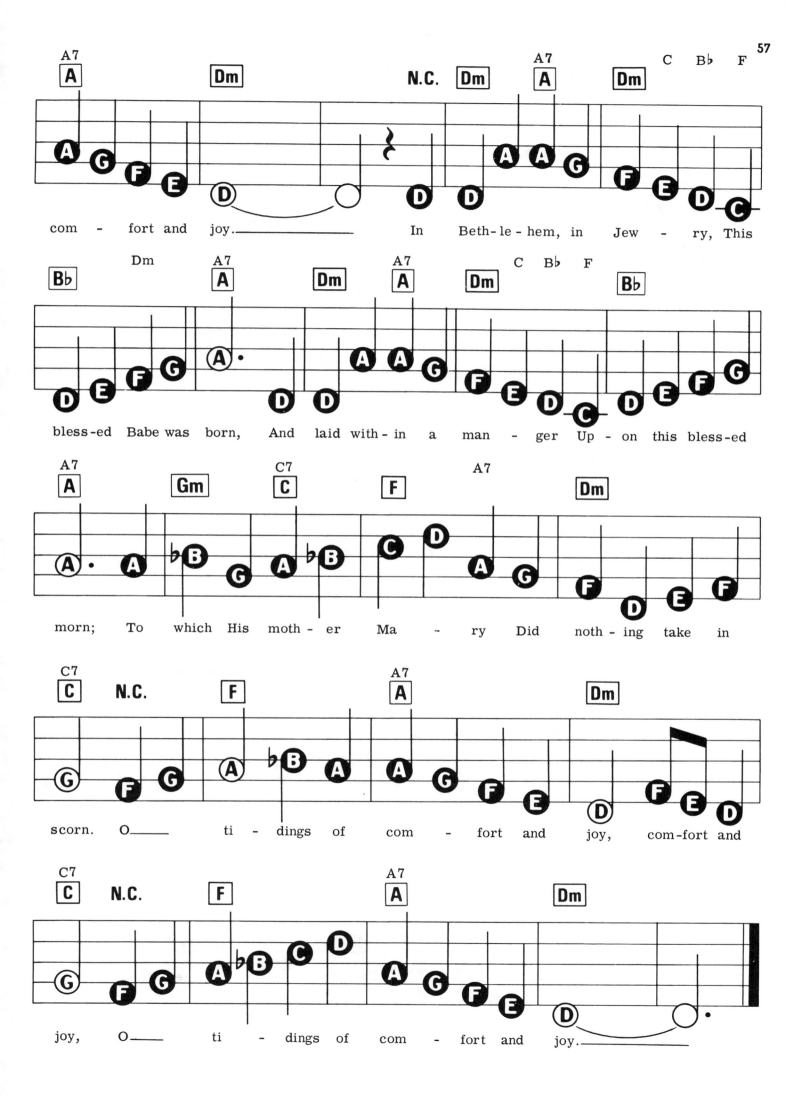

Good Christian Men, Rejoice

Registration 6
Rhythm: None

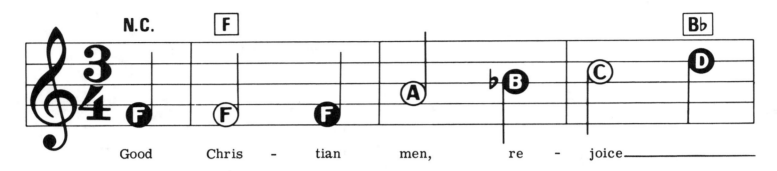

Good Chris - tian men, re - joice

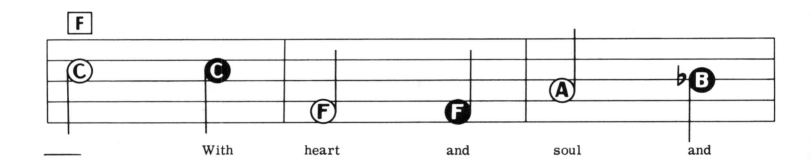

With heart and soul and

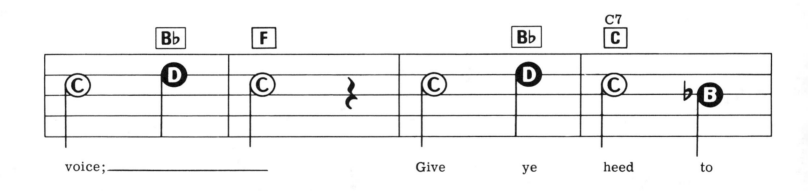

voice; Give ye heed to

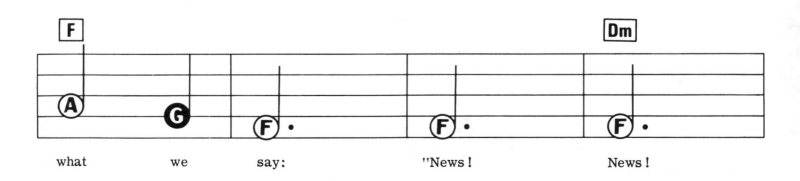

what we say: "News! News!

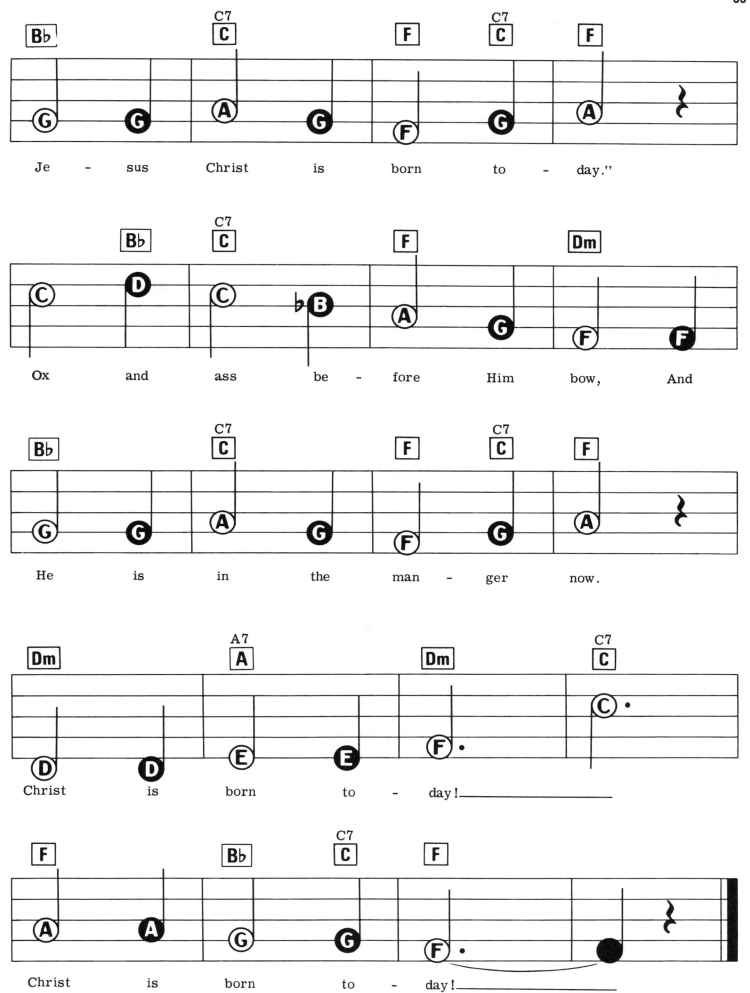

Good King Wenceslas

Registration 4
Rhythm: March, Polka or Fox Trot

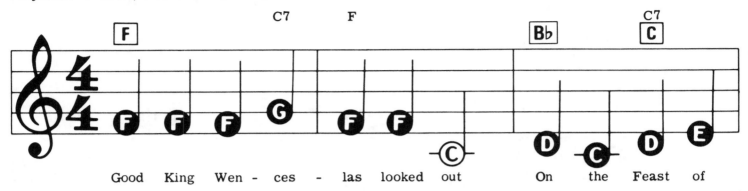

Good King Wen - ces - las looked out   On the Feast of

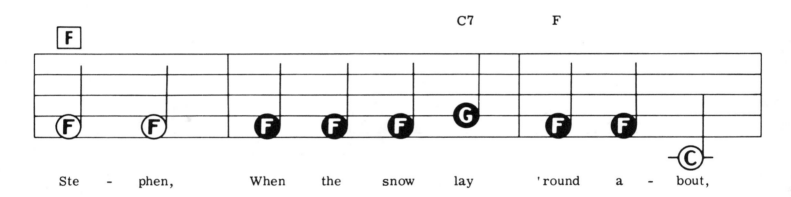

Ste - phen,   When the snow lay 'round a - bout,

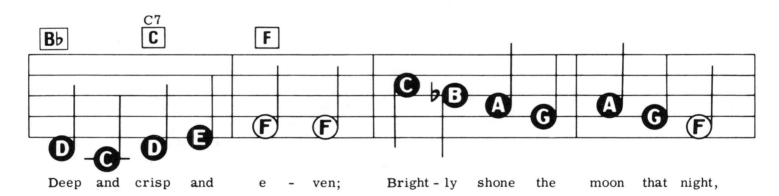

Deep and crisp and e - ven;   Bright - ly shone the moon that night,

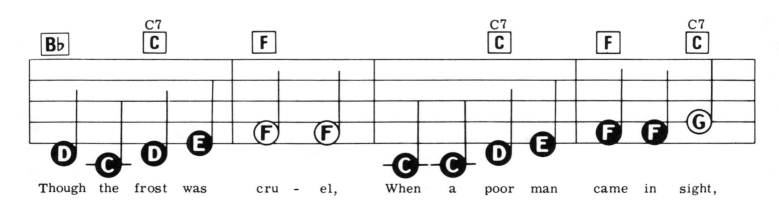

Though the frost was cru - el,   When a poor man came in sight,

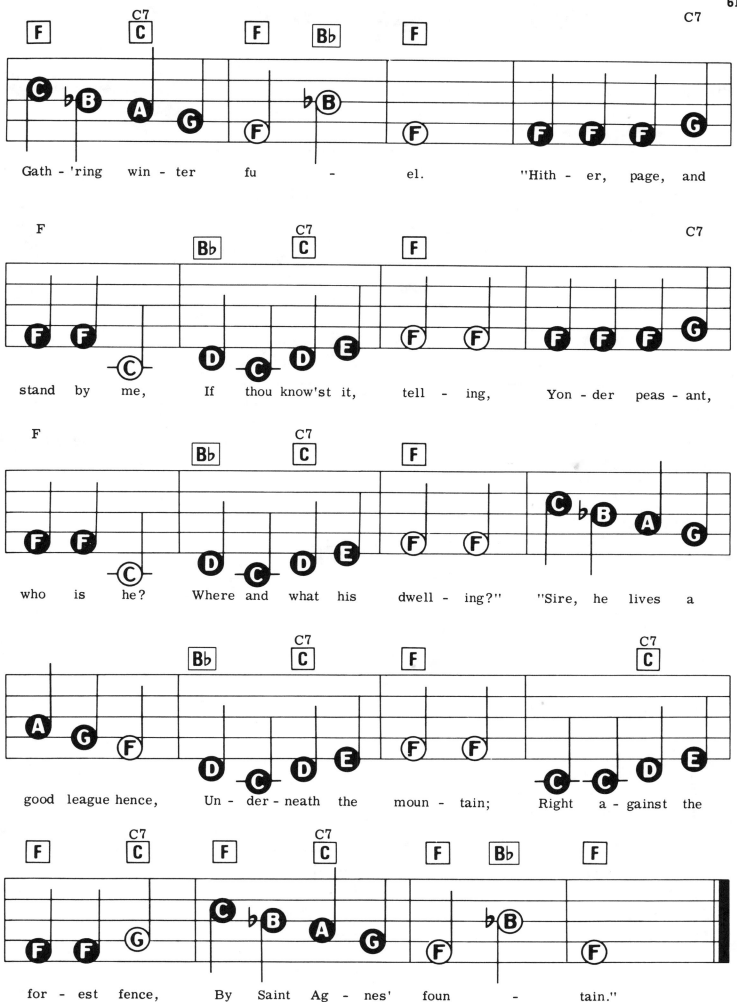

Giving (Santa's Theme)

Registration 2
Rhythm: Fox Trot or Swing

Music by Henry Mancini
Lyrics by Leslie Bricusse

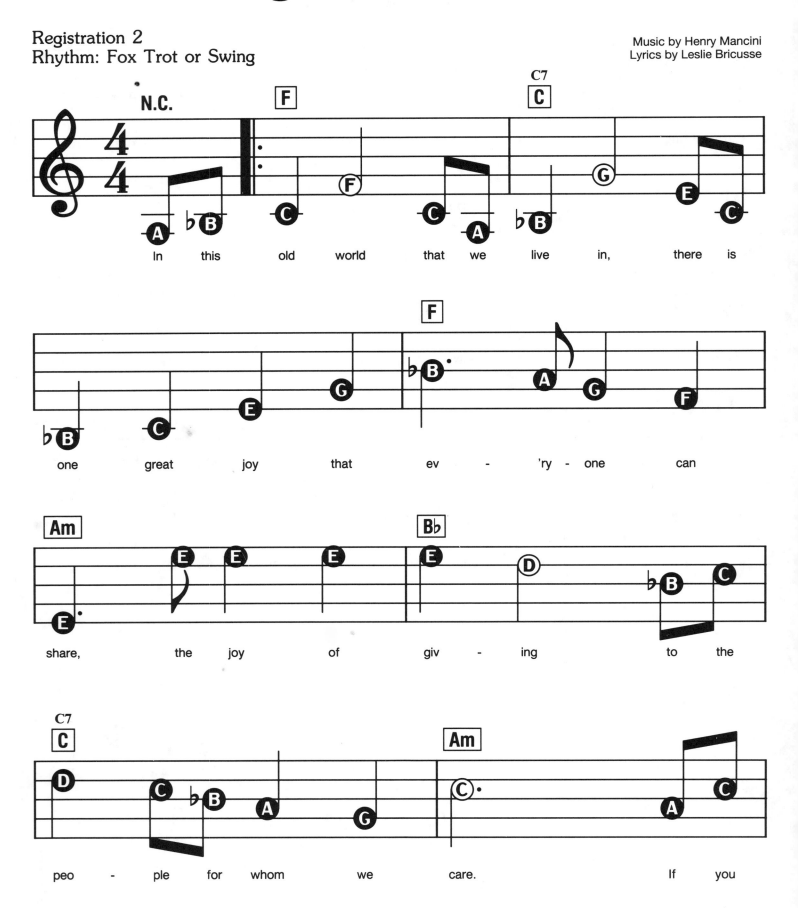

63

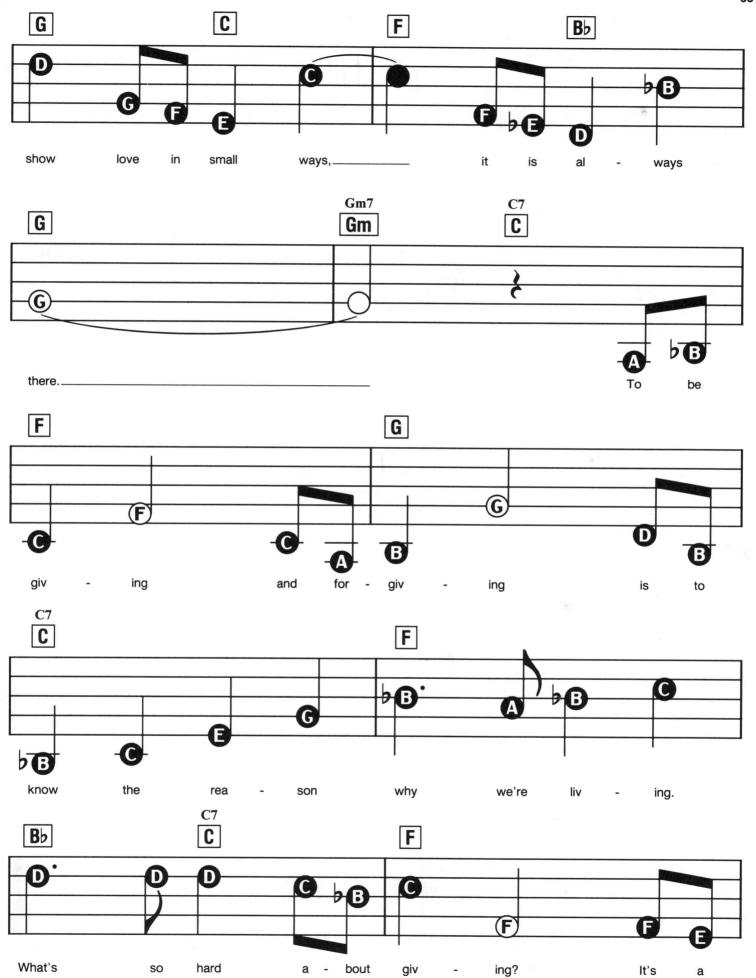

per - fect - ly sim - ple art.   The

trick   is   to   live   with   love   from   the   start,   and   to

give   with   an   o   -   pen

heart._____

In   this   heart._____

Grandma Got Run Over By A Reindeer

Registration 2
Rhythm: Swing

Words and Music by
Randy Brooks

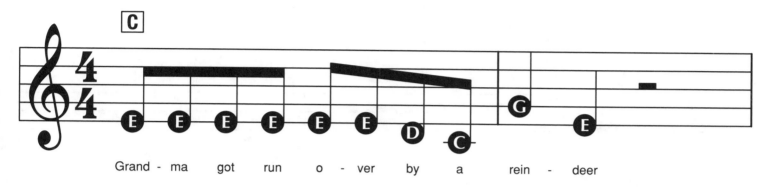

Grand - ma got run o - ver by a rein - deer

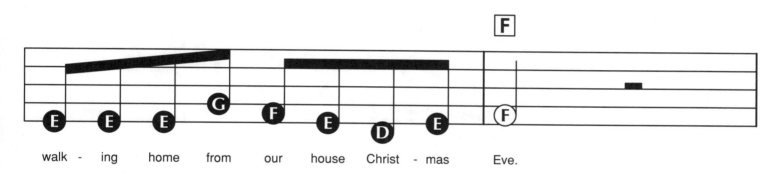

walk - ing home from our house Christ - mas Eve.

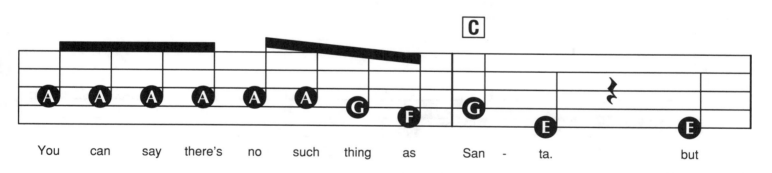

You can say there's no such thing as San - ta. but

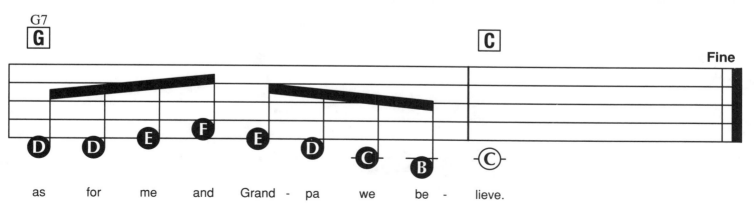

as for me and Grand - pa we be - lieve.

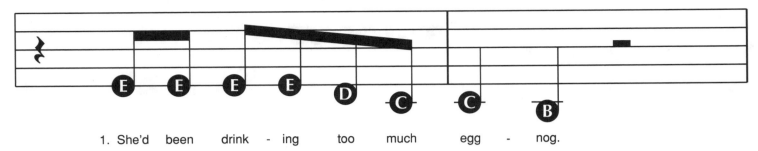

1. She'd been drink - ing too much egg - nog.

2. 3. *(See additional lyrics)*

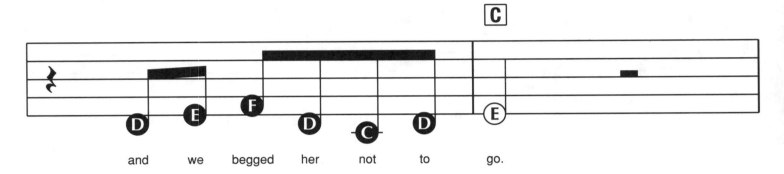

and we begged her not to go.

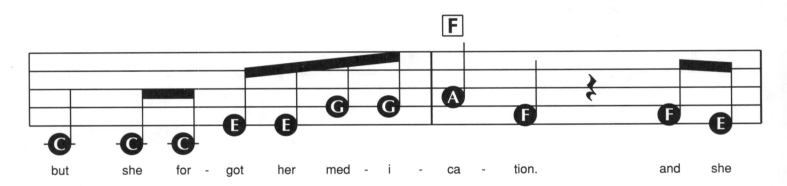

but she for - got her med - i - ca - tion. and she

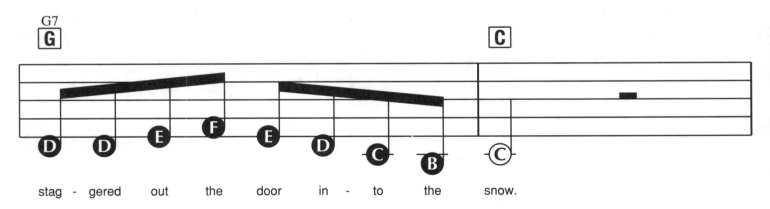

stag - gered out the door in - to the snow.

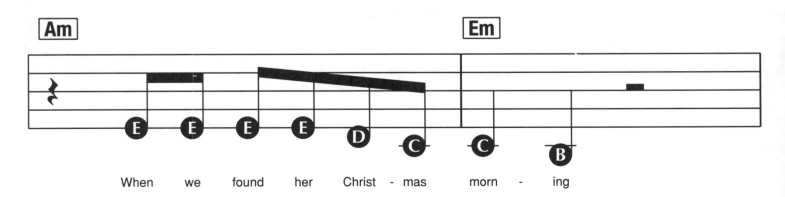

When we found her Christ - mas morn - ing

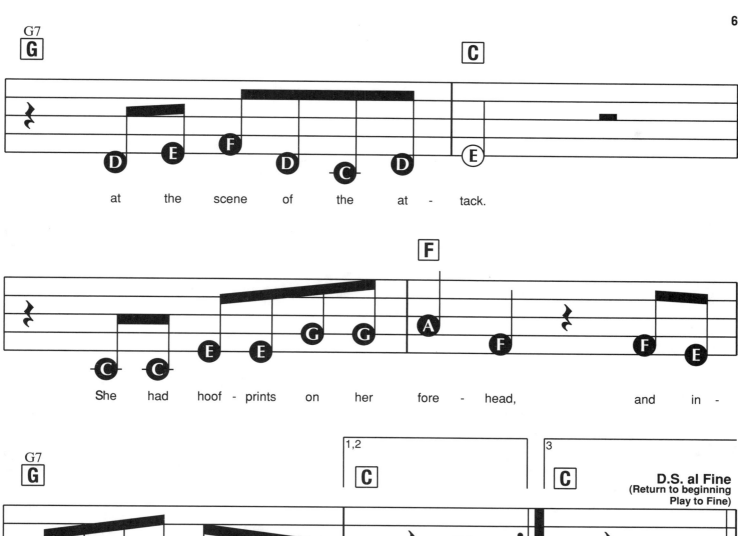

Additional Lyrics

2. Now we're all so proud of Grandpa,
He's been taking this so well.
See him in there watching football,
Drinking beer and playing cards with Cousin Mel.
It's not Christmas without Grandma.
All the family's dressed in black,
And we just can't help but wonder:
Should we open up her gifts or send them back? *(To Chorus:)*

3. Now the goose is on the table,
And the pudding made of fig,
And the blue and silver candles,
That would just have matched the hair in Grandma's wig.
I've warned all my friends and neighbors,
Better watch out for yourselves.
They should never give a license
To a man who drives a sleigh and plays with elves. *(To Chorus:)*

The Greatest Gift Of All

Registration 4
Rhythm: Shuffle or Country

Words and Music by
John Jarvis

Dawn is slow - ly break - ing our friends have all gone home. You and I are wait - ing for San - ta Claus to come. There's a pres - ent by the tree, stock - ings on the

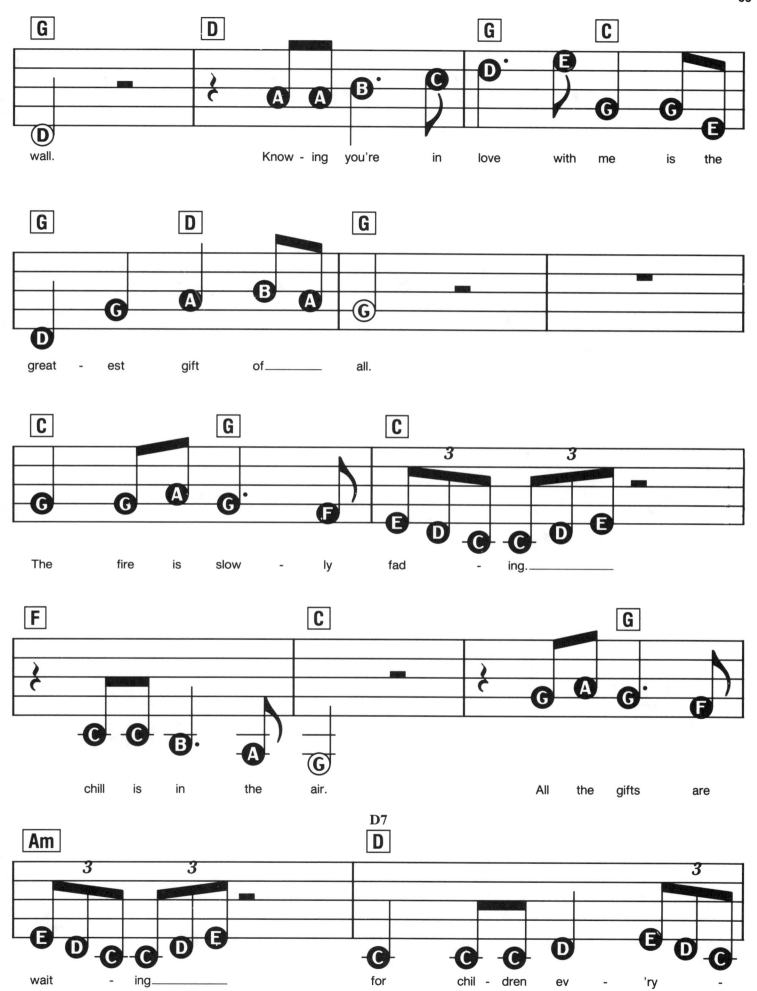

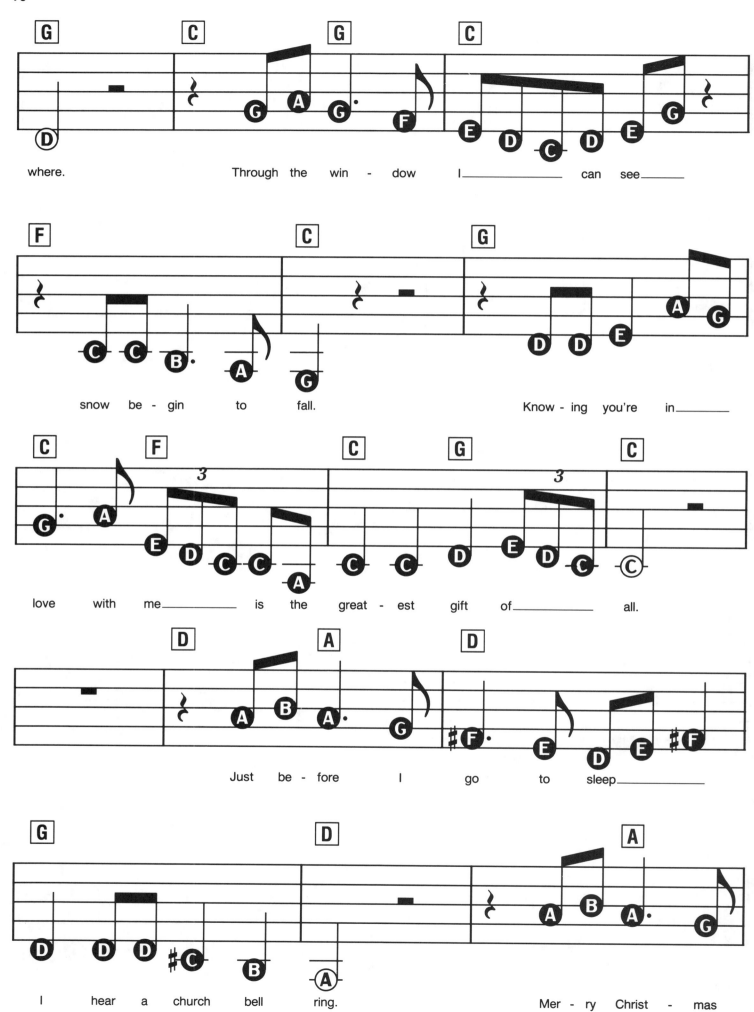

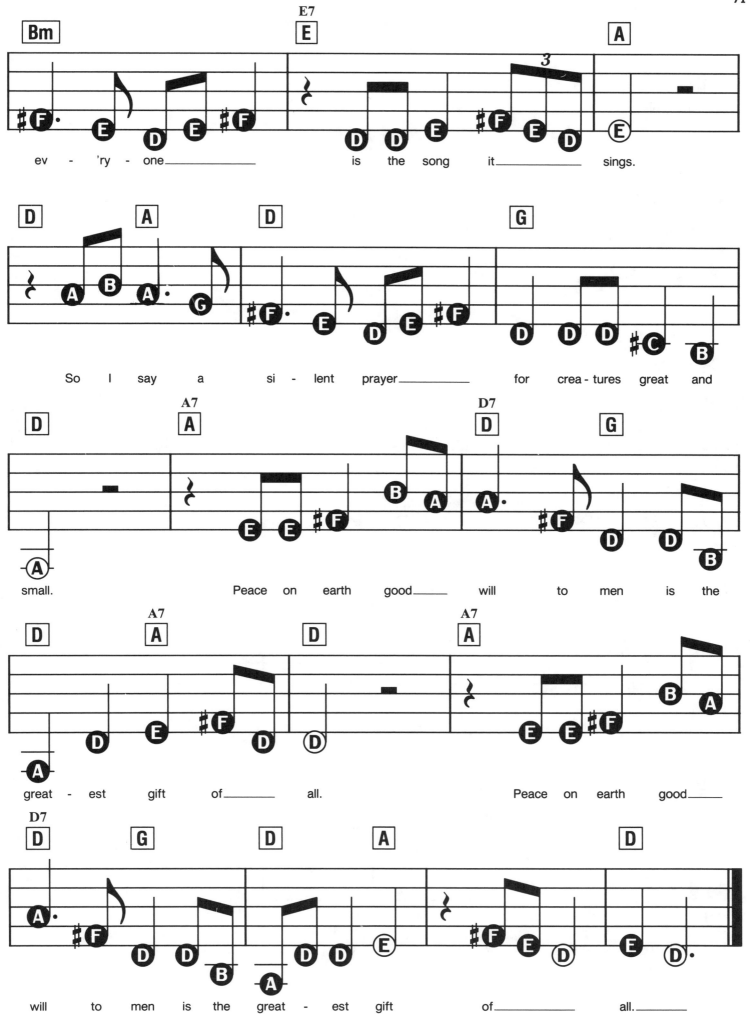

Hark! The Herald Angels Sing

Registration 5
Rhythm: None

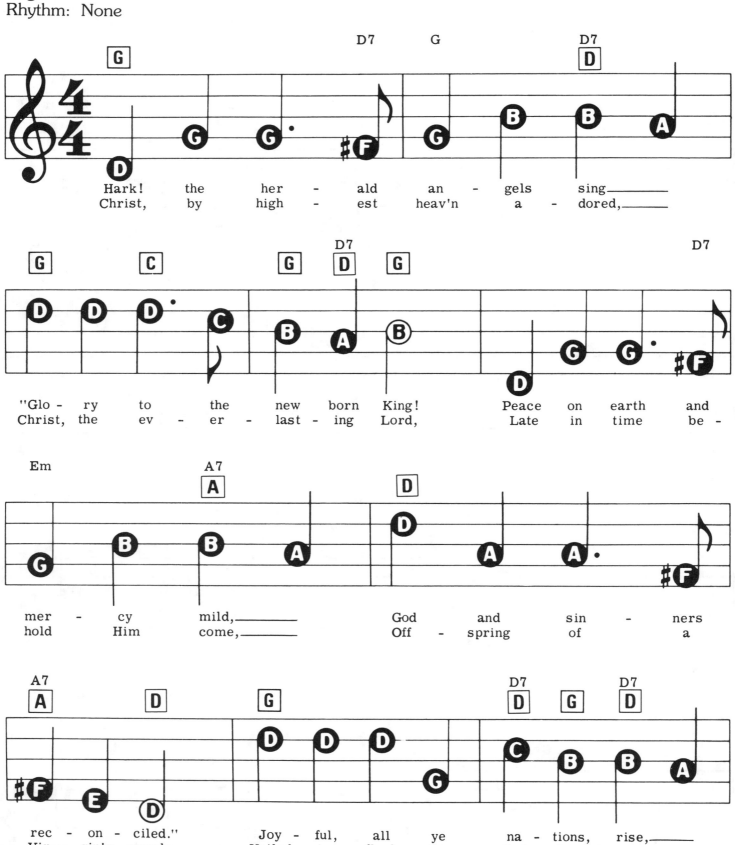

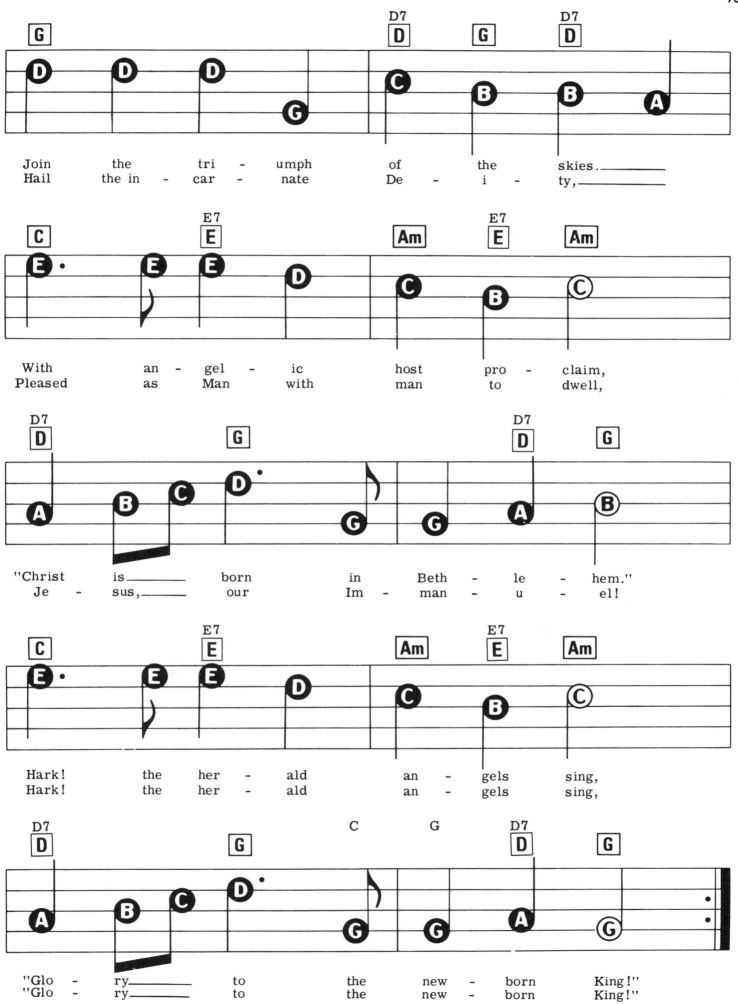

Hard Candy Christmas

Registration 4
Rhythm: Country or Shuffle

Words and Music by
Carol Hall

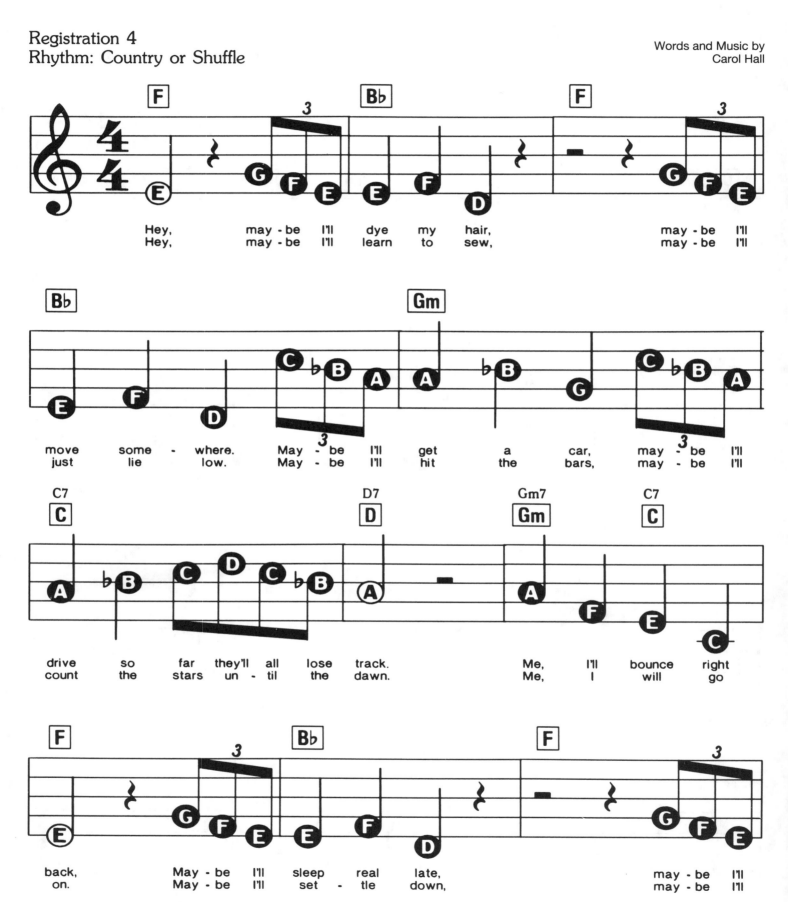

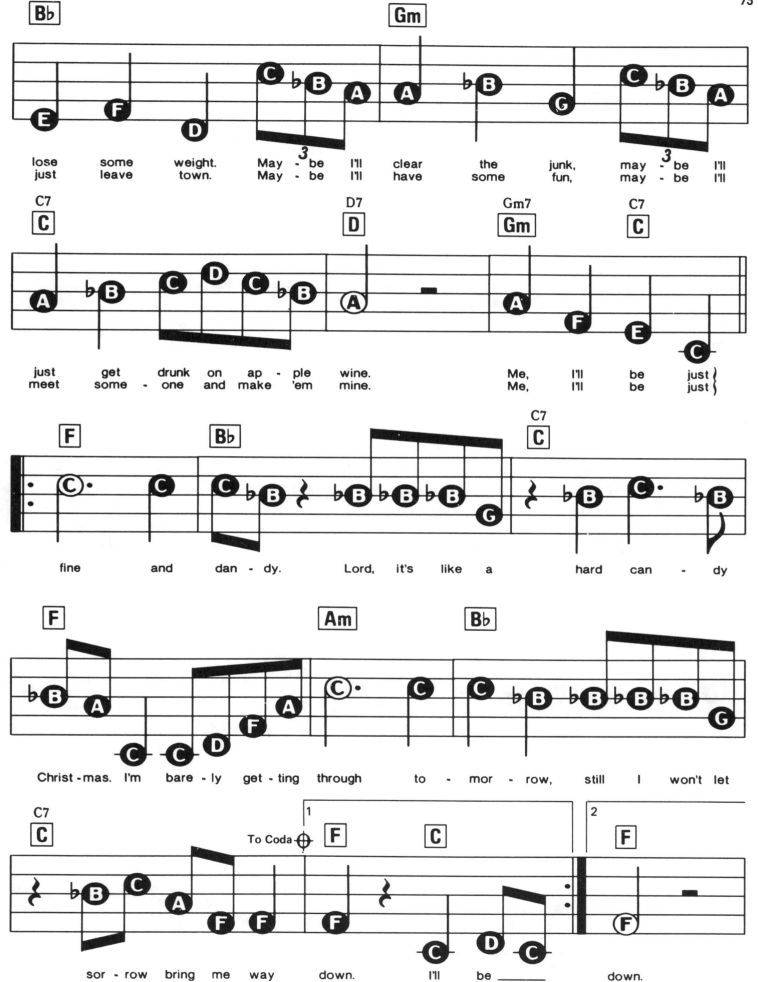

Have Yourself A Merry Little Christmas

Registration 7
Rhythm: Swing or Big Band

By Ralph Blane
and Hugh Martin

Have your-self a mer-ry lit-tle Christ-mas let your heart be

light, Next year all our trou-bles will be out of sight.____

____ Have your-self a mer-ry lit-tle Christ-mas,

make your Yule-tide gay, Next year all our

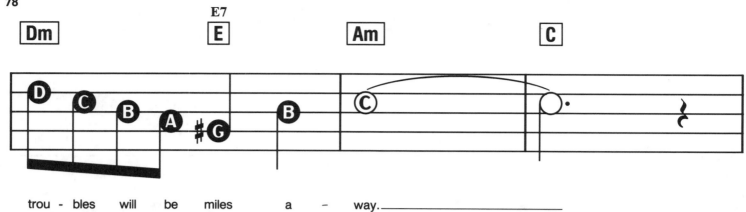

trou - bles will be miles a - way.

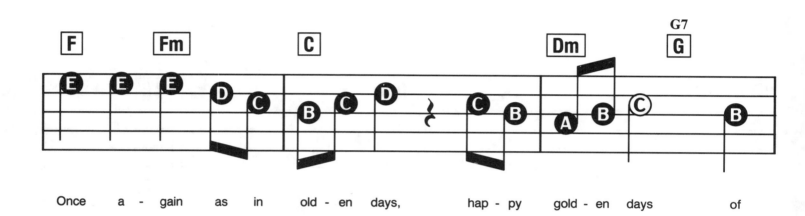

Once a - gain as in old - en days, hap - py gold - en days of

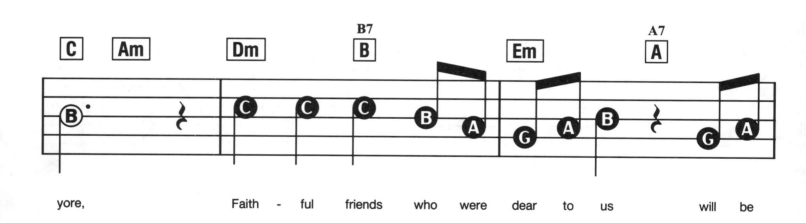

yore, Faith - ful friends who were dear to us will be

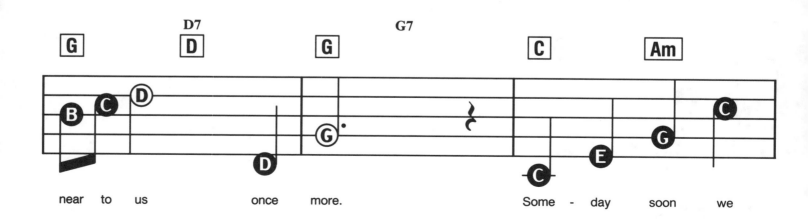

near to us once more. Some - day soon we

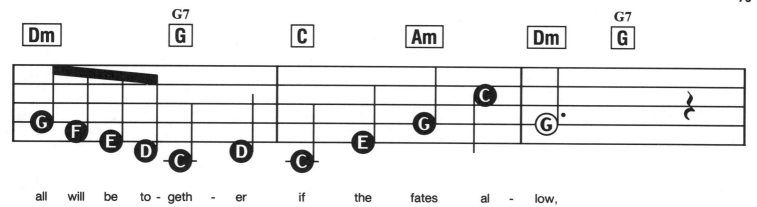

all will be to-geth - er   if   the   fates   al - low,

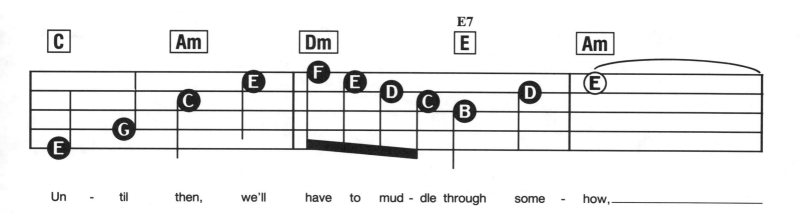

Un - til   then,   we'll   have to mud - dle through   some - how,_____

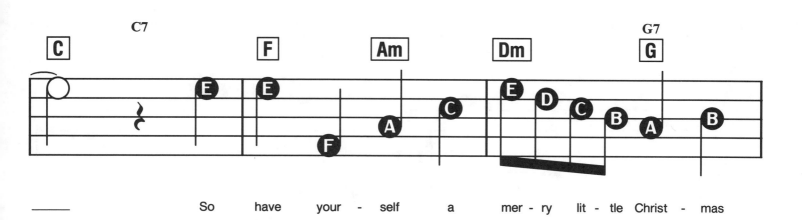

_____   So   have   your - self   a   mer - ry lit - tle Christ - mas

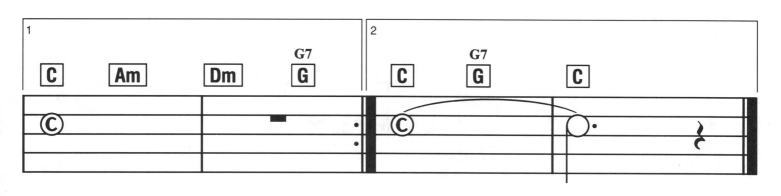

now.   now._____

Here We Come A-Wassailing

Registration 3
Rhythm: None

81

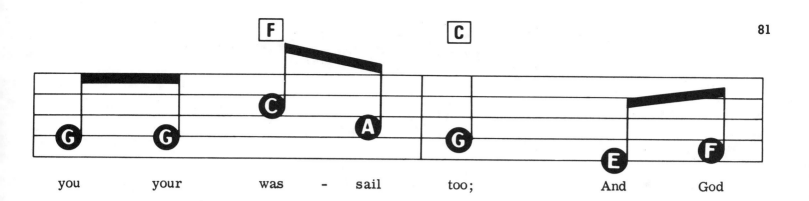

you your was - sail too; And God

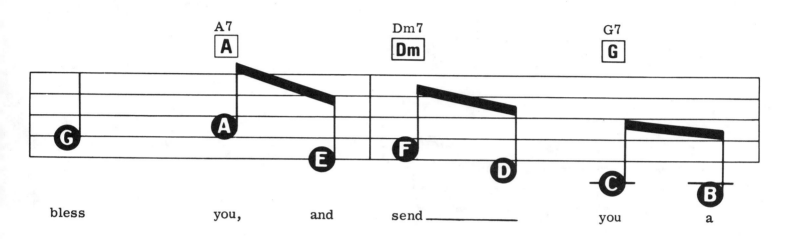

bless you, and send _____ you a

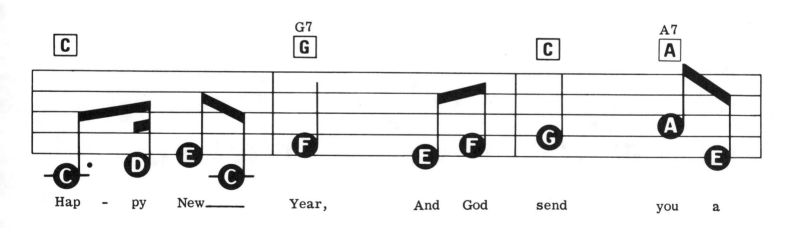

Hap - py New___ Year, And God send you a

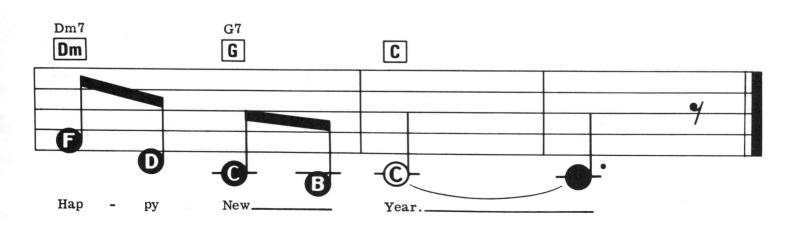

Hap - py New_____ Year._____

The Holly And The Ivy

Registration 1
Rhythm: None

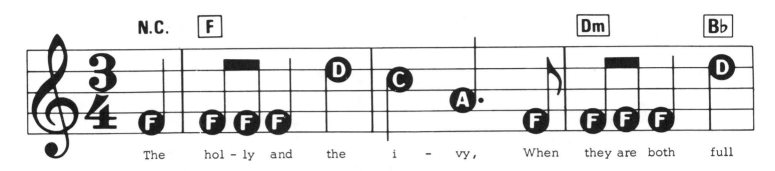

The hol-ly and the i-vy, When they are both full

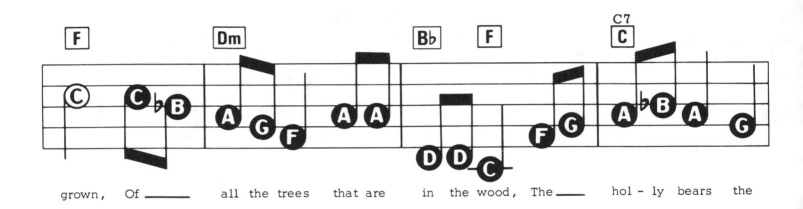

grown, Of _____ all the trees that are in the wood, The_____ hol-ly bears the

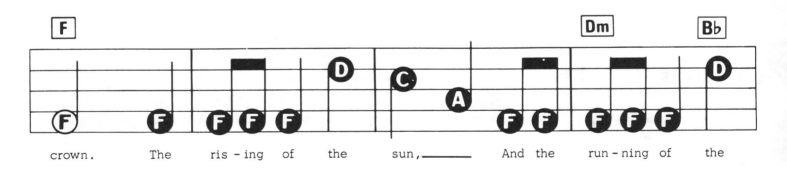

crown. The ris-ing of the sun,_____ And the run-ning of the

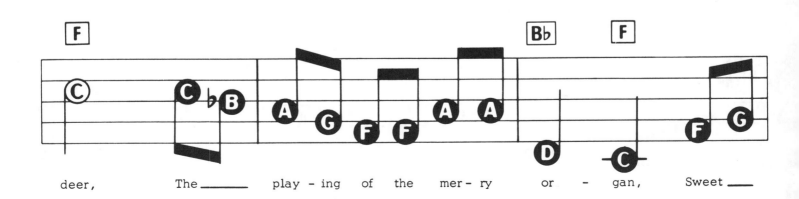

deer, The_____ play-ing of the mer-ry or-gan, Sweet_____

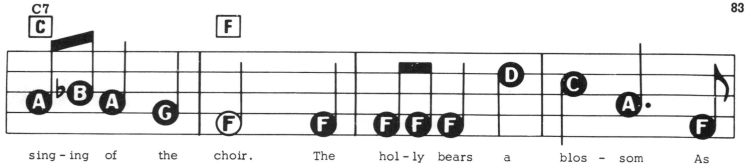

sing – ing of the choir. The hol – ly bears a blos – som As

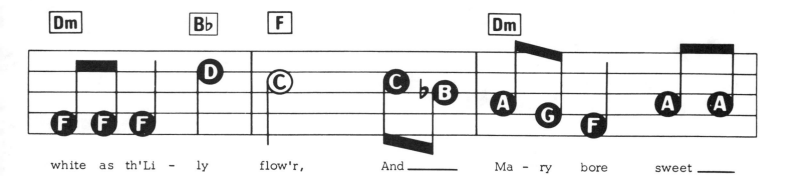

white as th'Li – ly flow'r, And＿ Ma – ry bore sweet＿

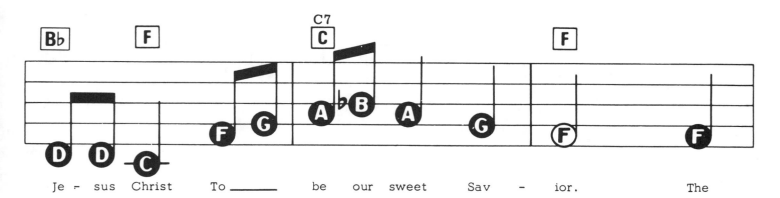

Je – sus Christ To ＿ be our sweet Sav – ior. The

ris – ing of the sun,＿ And the run–ning of the deer, The＿

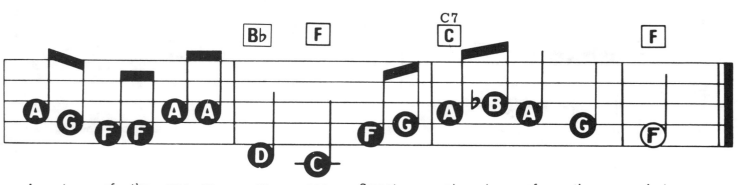

play – ing of the mer – ry or – gan, Sweet ＿ sing – ing of the choir.

A Holly Jolly Christmas

Registration 9
Rhythm: Swing

Words and Music by
Johnny Marks

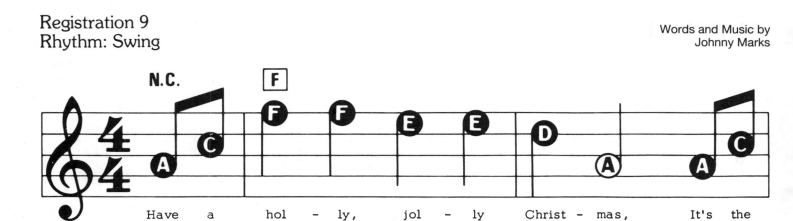

Have a hol - ly, jol - ly Christ - mas, It's the

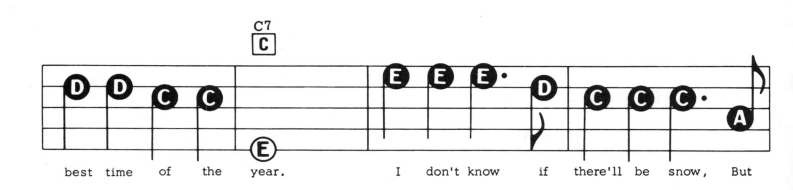

best time of the year. I don't know if there'll be snow, But

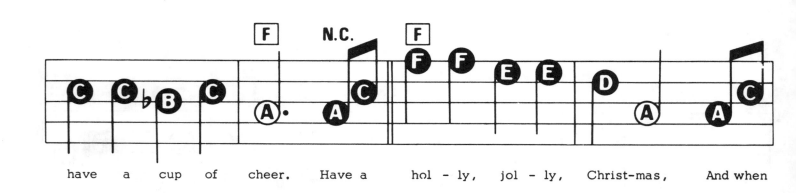

have a cup of cheer. Have a hol - ly, jol - ly, Christ-mas, And when

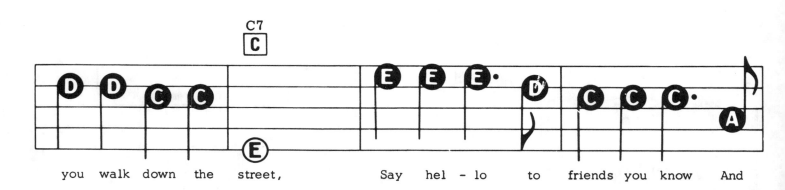

you walk down the street, Say hel - lo to friends you know And

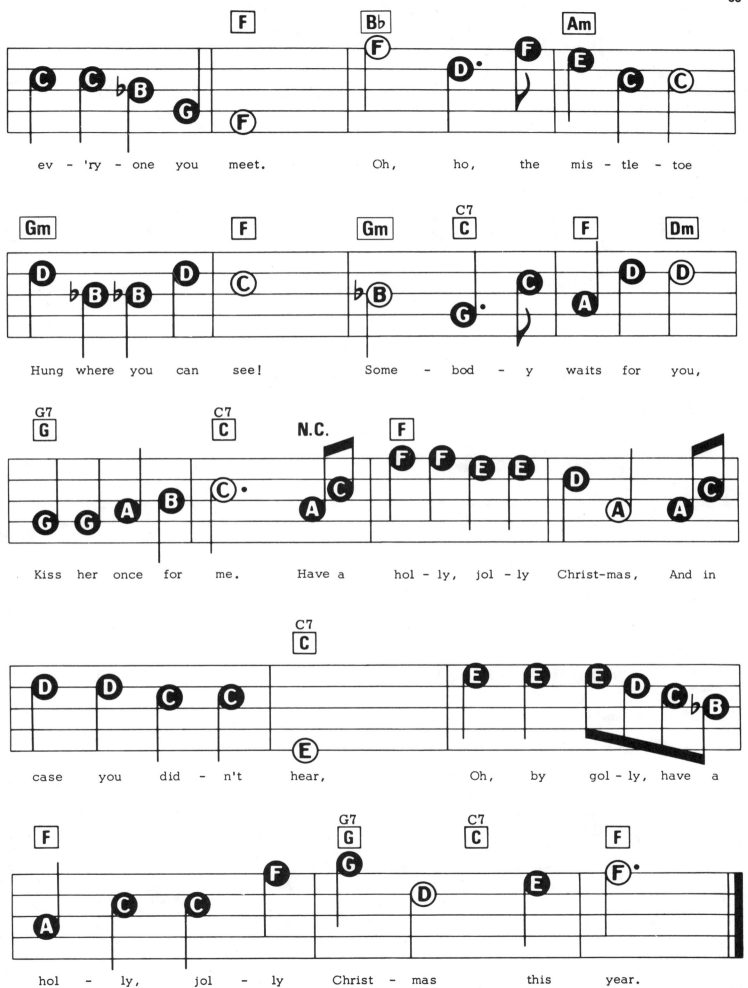

(There's No Place Like)
Home For The Holidays

Registration 5
Rhythm: Fox Trot or Swing

Words by Al Stillman
Music by Robert Allen

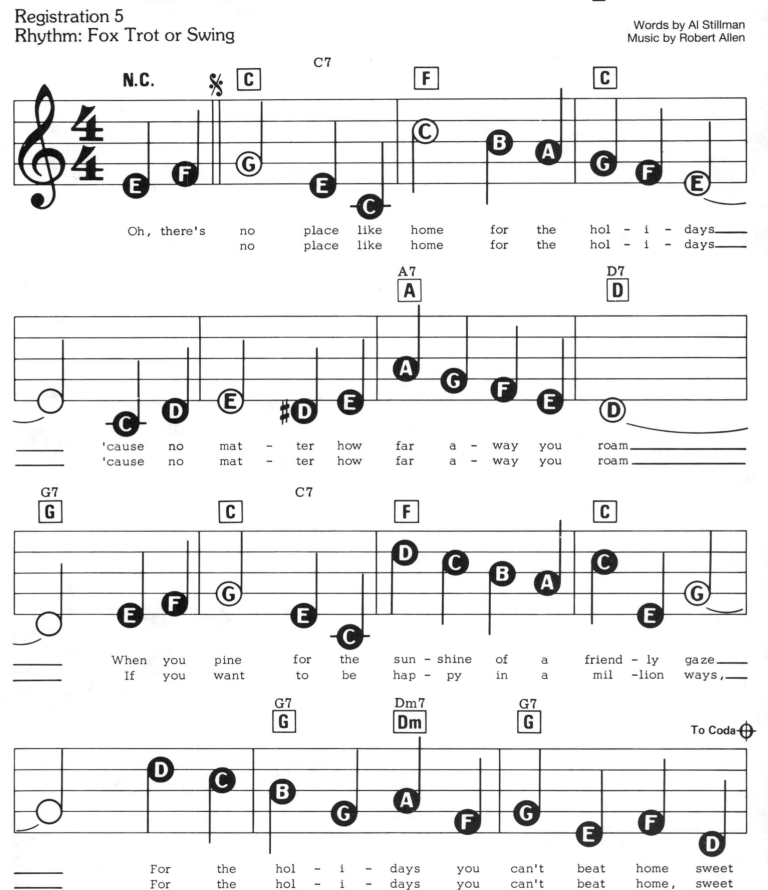

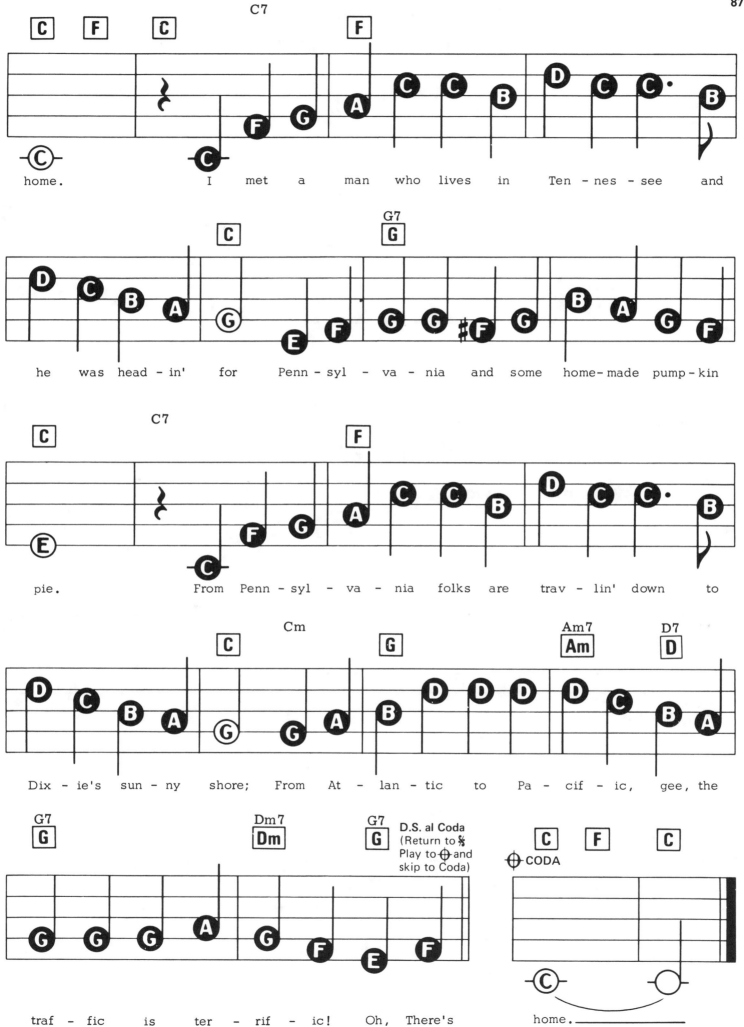

Here Comes Santa Claus
(Right Down Santa Claus Lane)

Registration 4
Rhythm: Swing

Words and Music by Gene Autry
and Oakley Haldeman

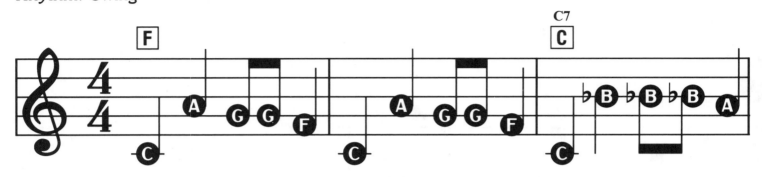

Here comes San-ta Claus! Here comes San-ta Claus! Right down San-ta Claus

Lane!

1. Vix-en and Blitz-en and all his rein-deer are
2. He's got a bag that is all filled with toys for the

pull-ing on the rein. Bells are ring-ing,
boys and girls a-gain. Hear those sleigh-bells

chil-dren sing-ing, all is mer-ry and bright.
jin-gle jan-gle, what a beau-ti-ful sight.

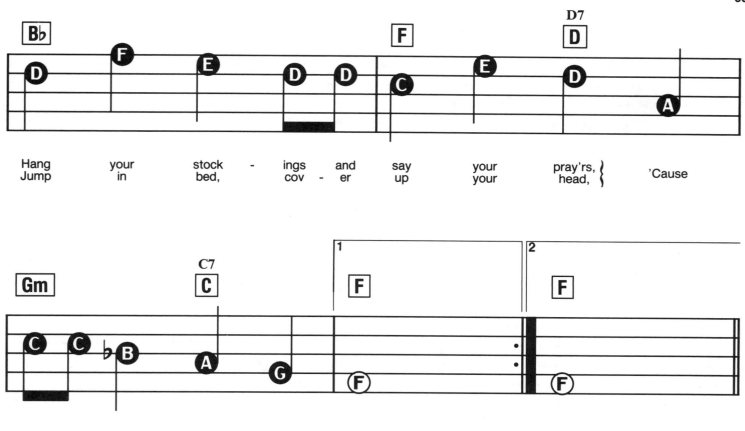

Hang your stock - ings and say your pray'rs, } 'Cause
Jump in bed, cov - er up your head, }

San - ta Claus comes to - night. night.

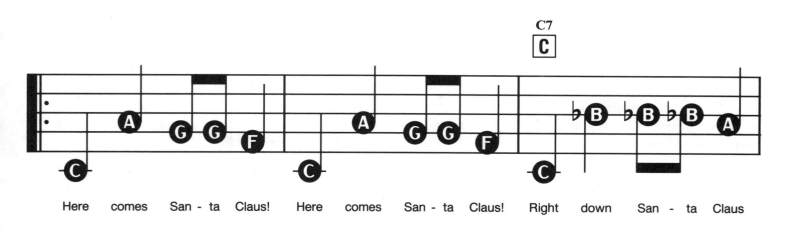

Here comes San - ta Claus! Here comes San - ta Claus! Right down San - ta Claus

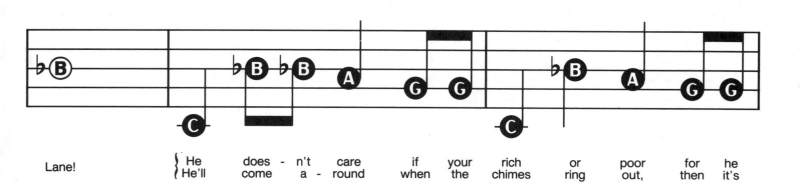

Lane! {He does - n't care if your rich or poor, for he
{He'll come a - round when the chimes ring out, then it's

It's Just Another New Year's Eve

Registration 2
Rhythm: Swing

Music by Barry Manilow
Lyric by Marty Panzer

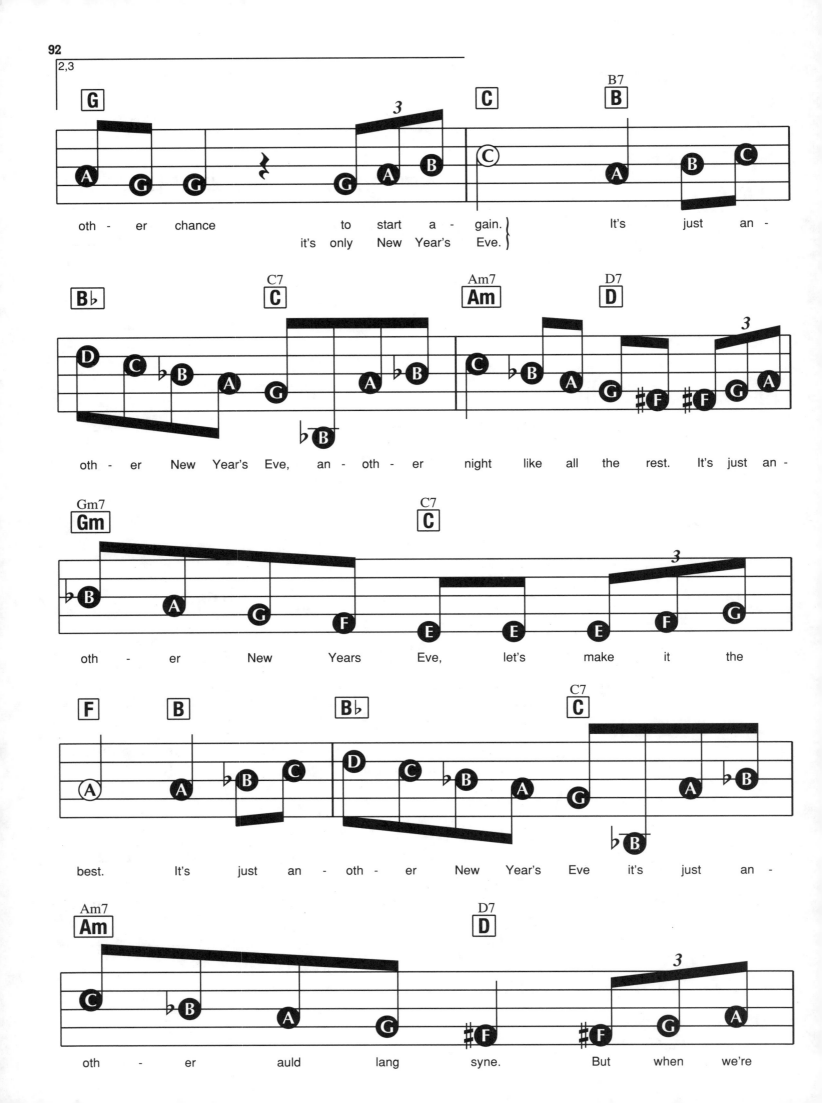

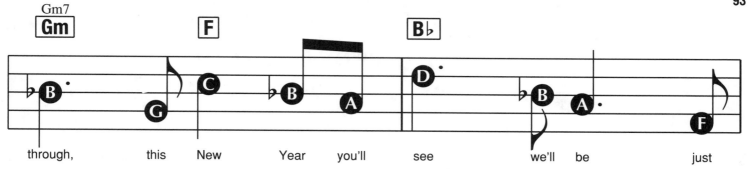

through,   this   New   Year   you'll   see   we'll   be   just

D.S. al Coda
(Return to %
Play to ⊕
Skip to Coda)

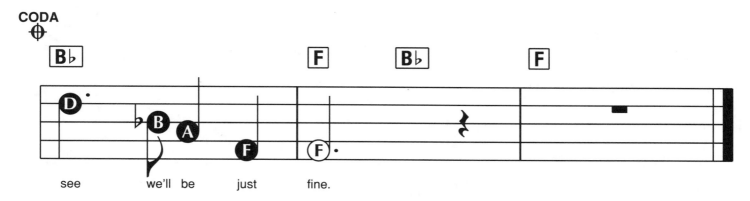

fine.   We're   not   a -

CODA
⊕

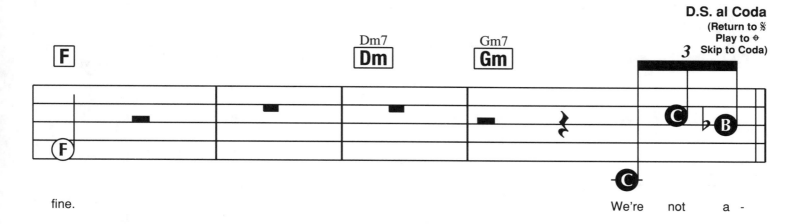

see   we'll   be   just   fine.

Additional Lyrics

3. We're not alone,
    We've got the world, you know.
    And it won't let us down,
    Just wait and see.
    And we'll grow old,
    But think how wise we'll grow,
    There's more you know,
    It's only New Year's Eve.

    (Chorus)

I Heard The Bells On Christmas Day

Words by Henry Longfellow
Adapted by Johnny Marks
Music by Johnny Marks

Registration 9
Rhythm: 8 Beat or Pops

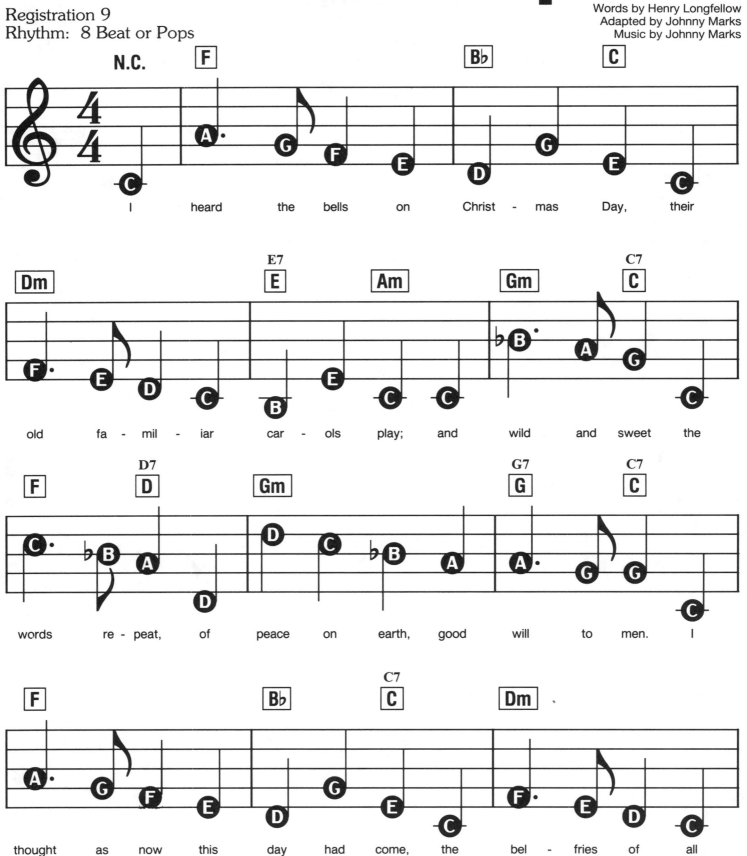

I Heard The Bells On Christmas Day

Registration 7
Rhythm: Ballad or Fox Trot

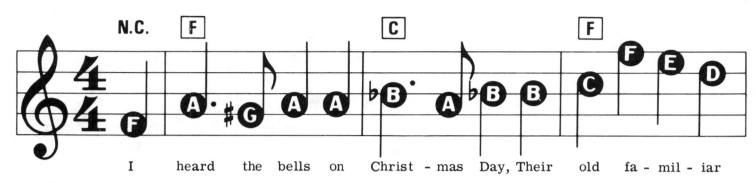

I heard the bells on Christ - mas Day, Their old fa - mil - iar

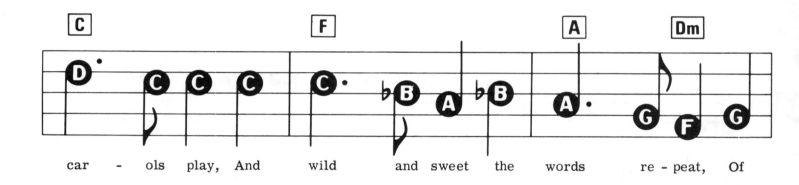

car - ols play, And wild and sweet the words re - peat, Of

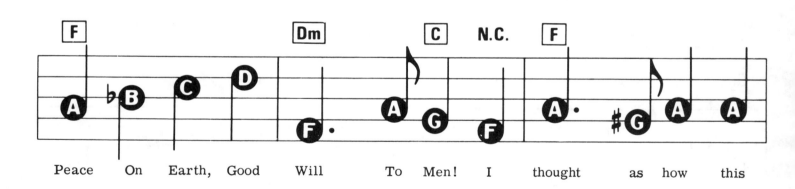

Peace On Earth, Good Will To Men! I thought as how this

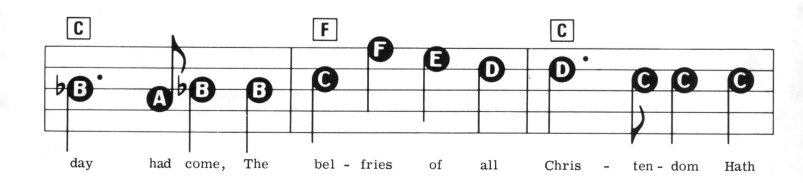

day had come, The bel - fries of all Chris - ten - dom Hath

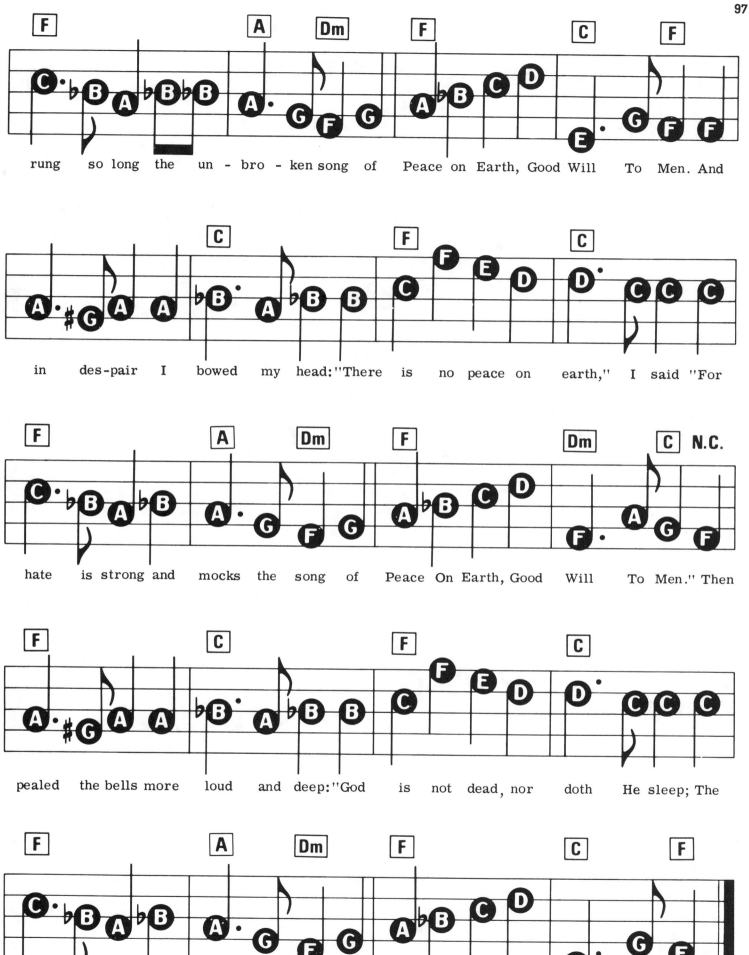

I Saw Mommy Kissing Santa Claus

Registration 5
Rhythm: Fox Trot or Swing

Words and Music by
Tommie Connor

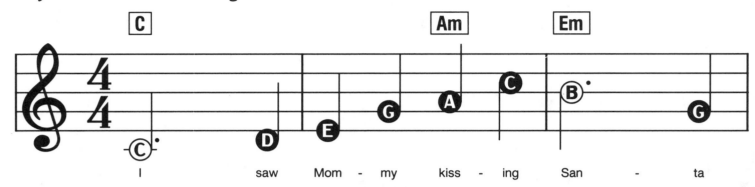

I saw Mom - my kiss - ing San - ta

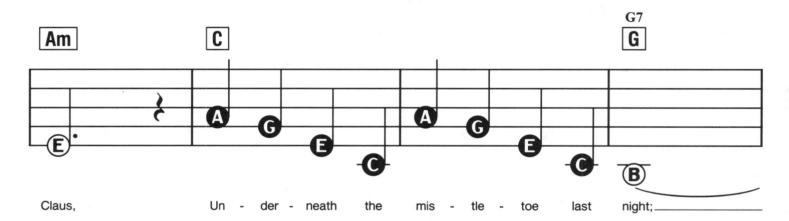

Claus, Un - der - neath the mis - tle - toe last night;

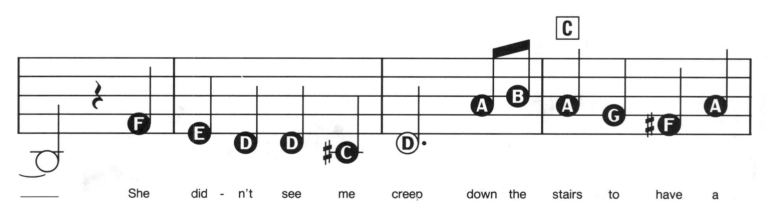

She did - n't see me creep down the stairs to have a

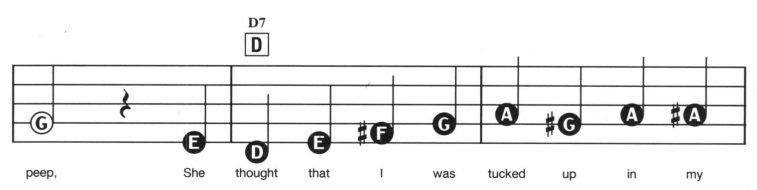

peep, She thought that I was tucked up in my

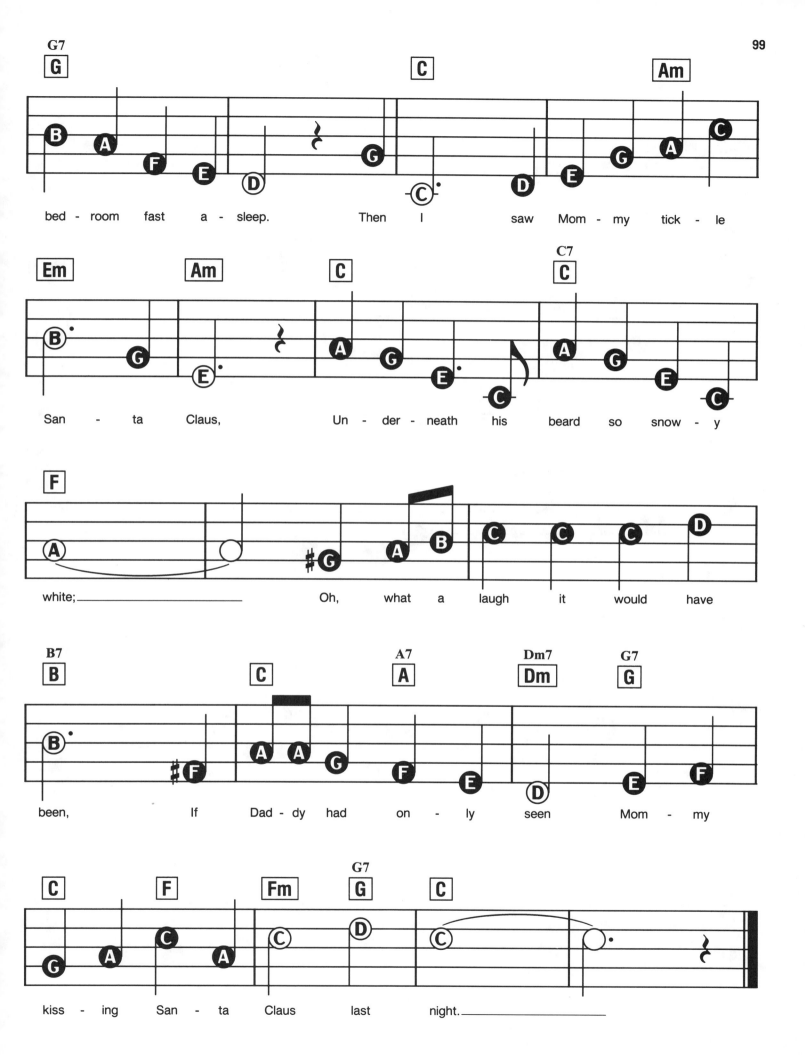

I Saw Three Ships

Registration 2
Rhythm: 6/8 March or Waltz

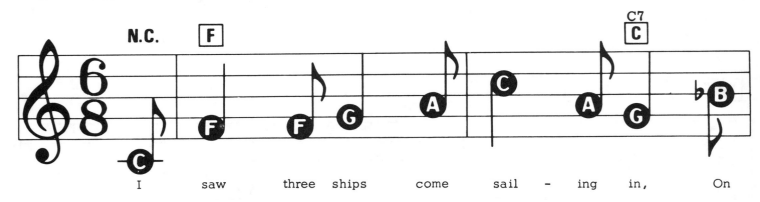

I saw three ships come sail - ing in, On

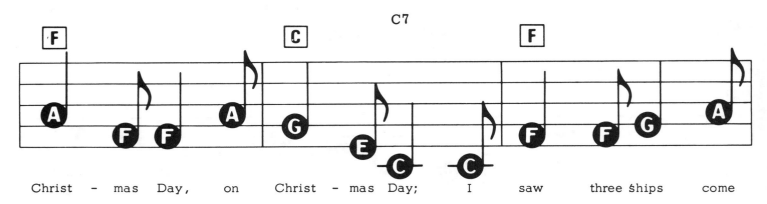

Christ - mas Day, on Christ - mas Day; I saw three ships come

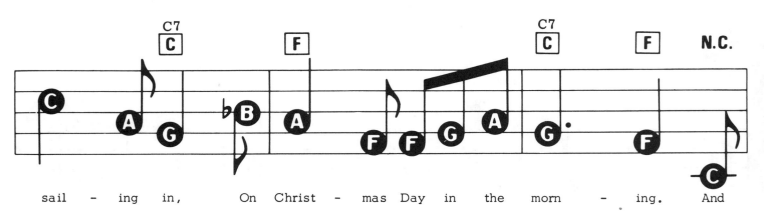

sail - ing in, On Christ - mas Day in the morn - ing. And

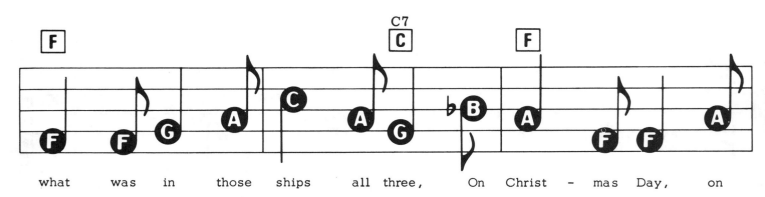

what was in those ships all three, On Christ - mas Day, on

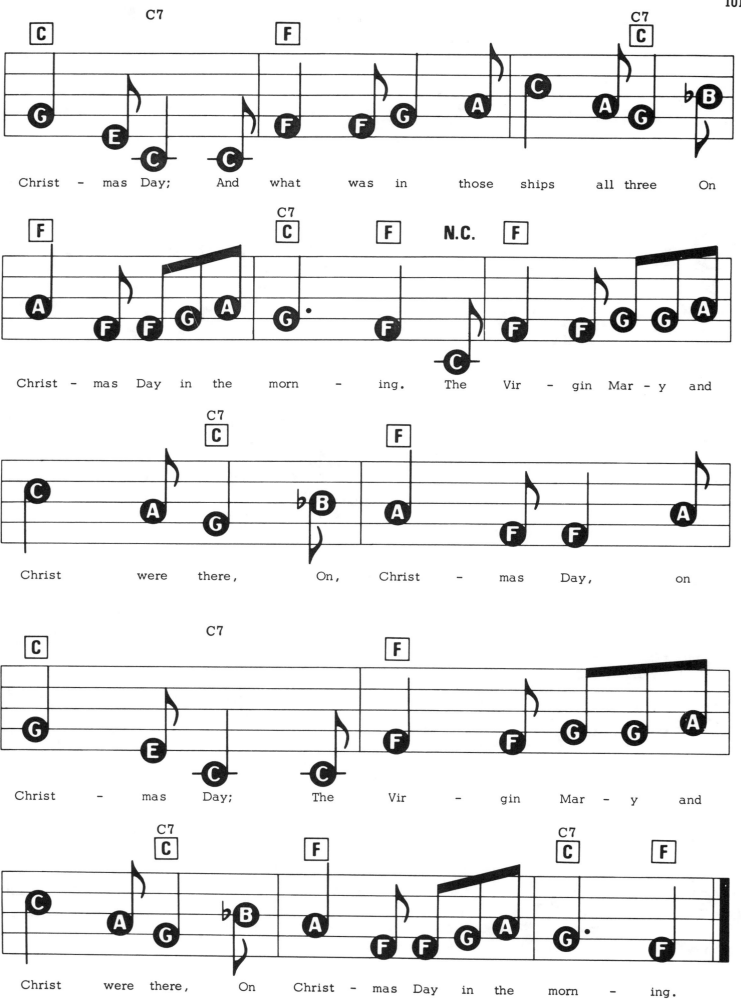

I'll Be Home For Christmas

Registration 1
Rhythm: Fox Trot

Words and Music by Kim Gannon
and Walter Kent

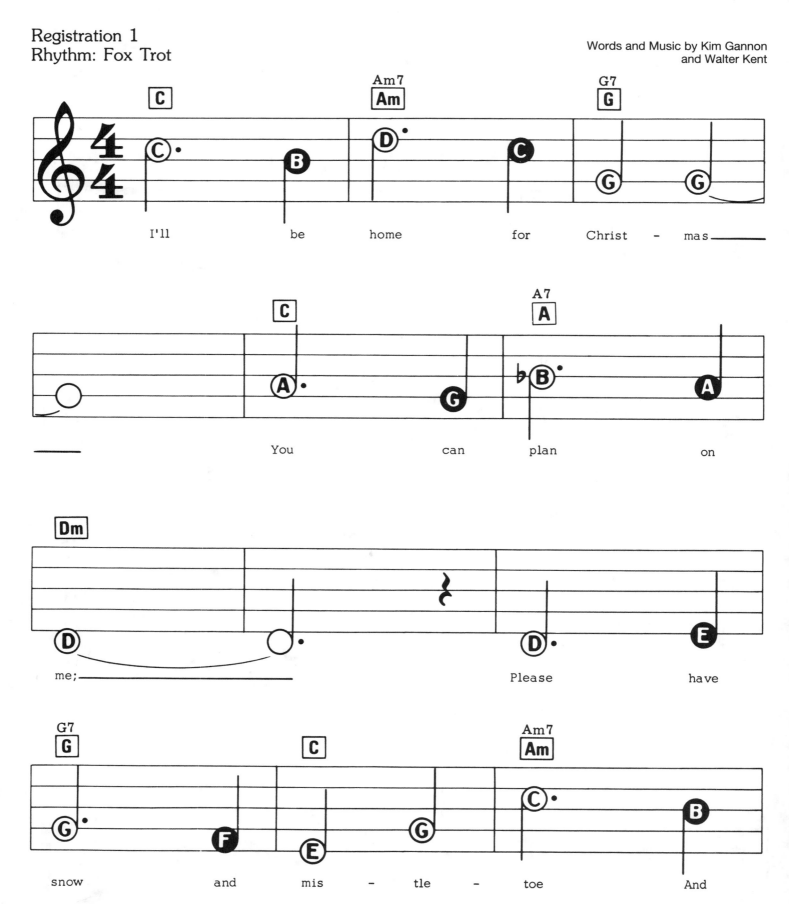

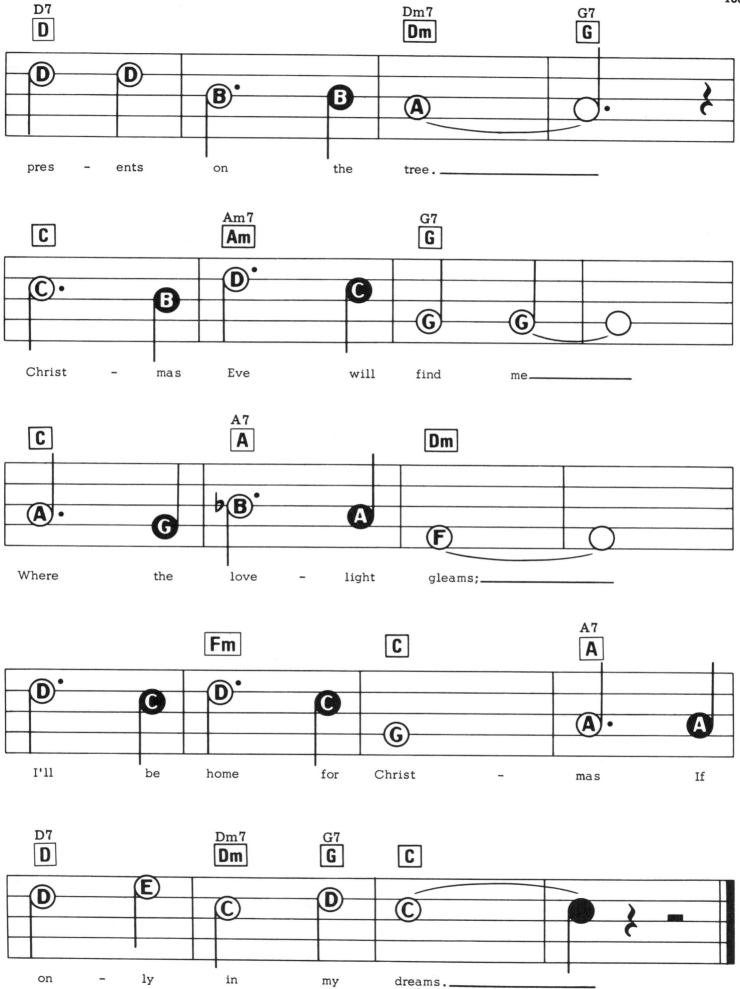

It Came Upon The Midnight Clear

Registration 1
Rhythm: None

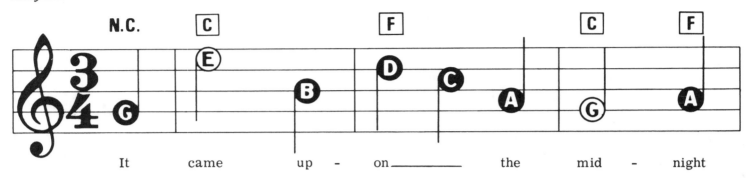

It came up - on_____ the mid - night

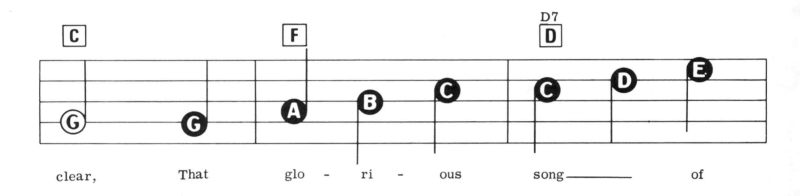

clear, That glo - ri - ous song_____ of

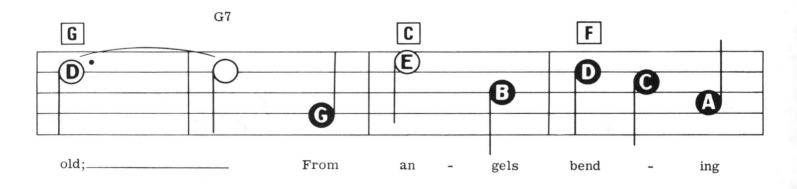

old;_____ From an - gels bend - ing

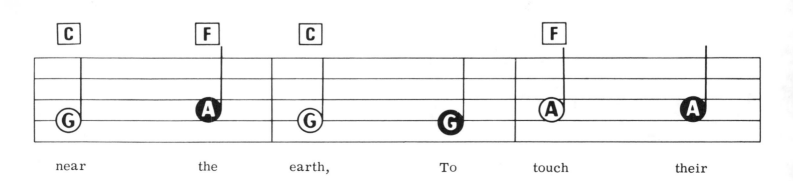

near the earth, To touch their

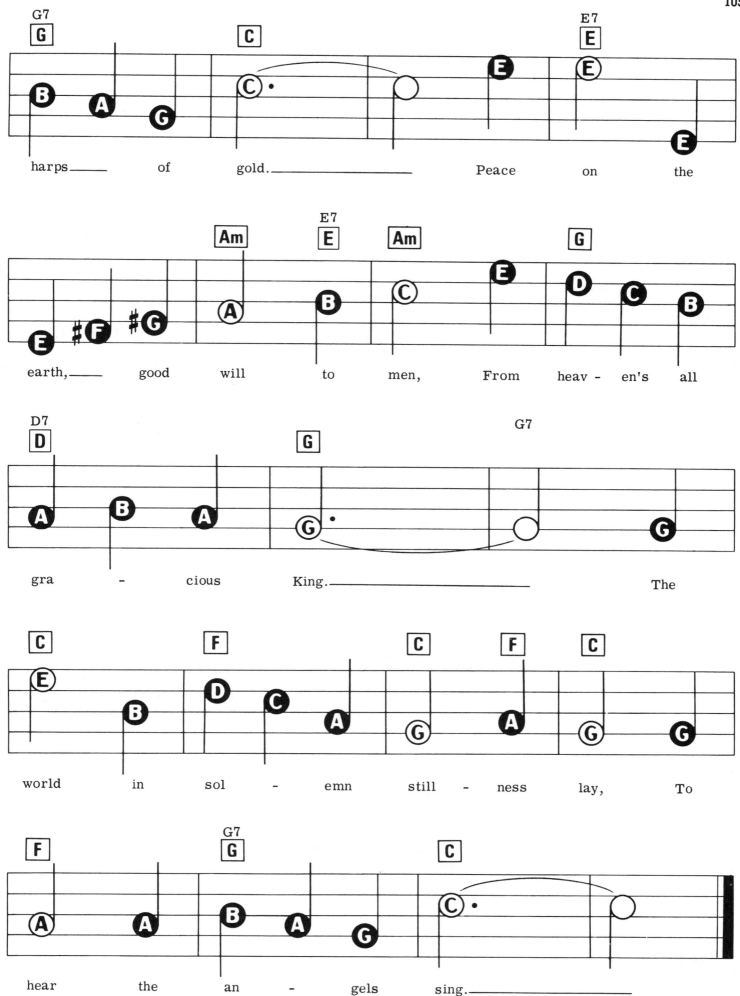

Jingle-Bell Rock

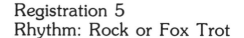

Registration 5
Rhythm: Rock or Fox Trot

Words and Music by Joe Beal
and Jim Boothe

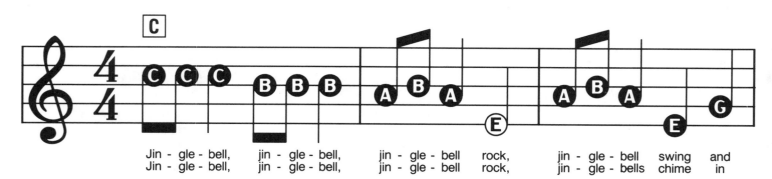

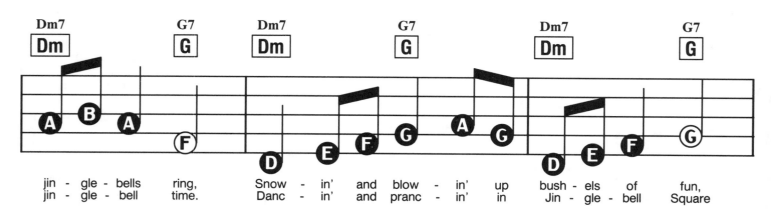

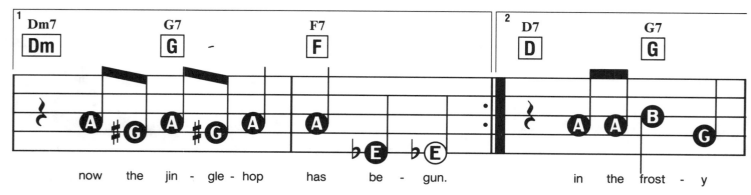

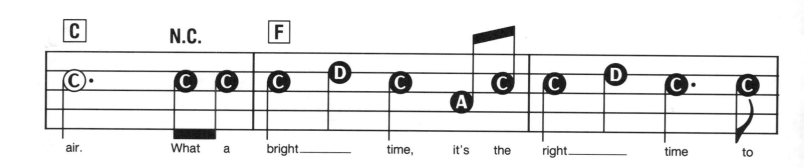

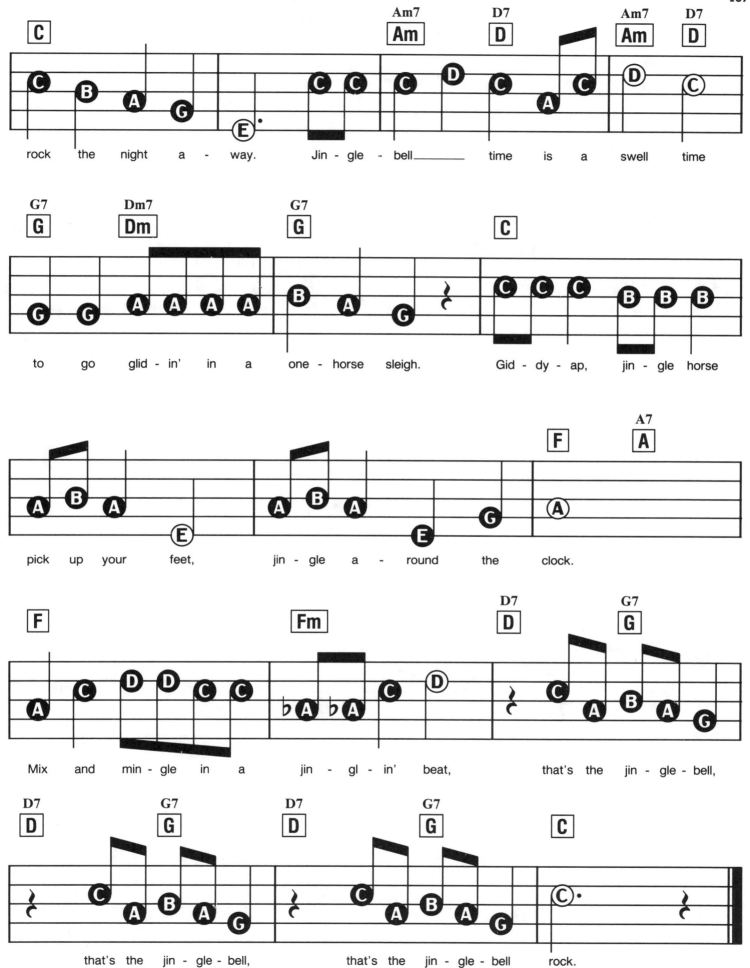

Jingle Bells

Registration 5
Rhythm: Fox Trot or Swing

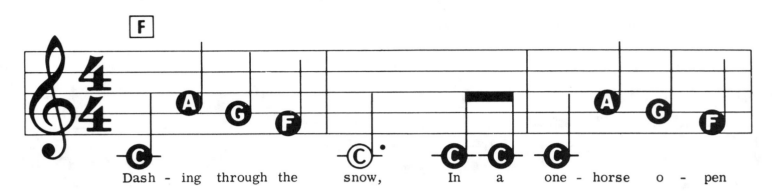

Dash - ing through the snow, In a one-horse o - pen

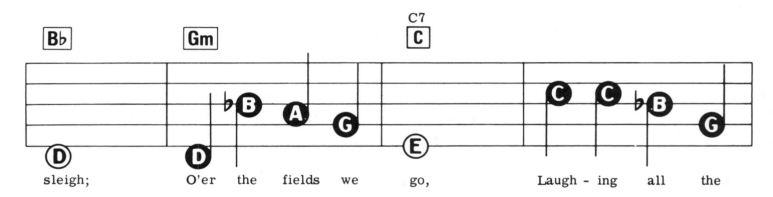

sleigh; O'er the fields we go, Laugh - ing all the

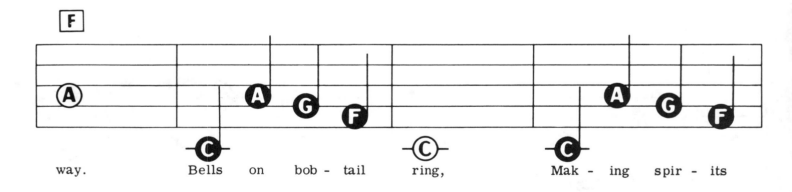

way. Bells on bob - tail ring, Mak - ing spir - its

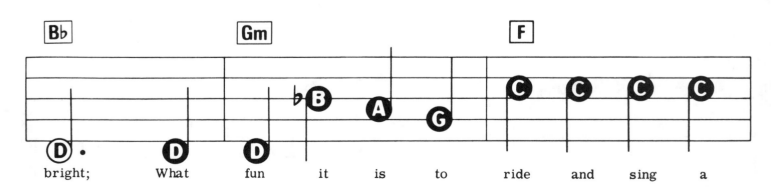

bright; What fun it is to ride and sing a

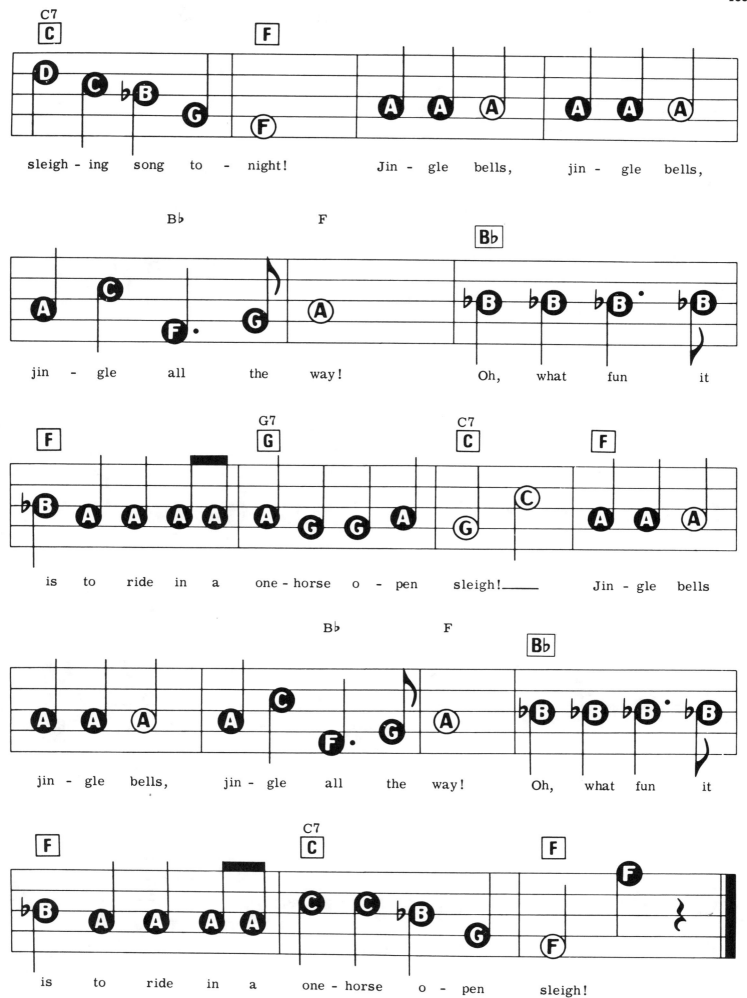

Jolly Old St. Nicholas

Registration 2
Rhythm: Fox Trot or Swing

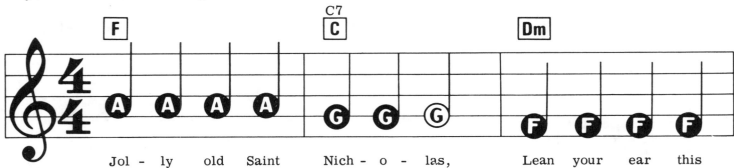

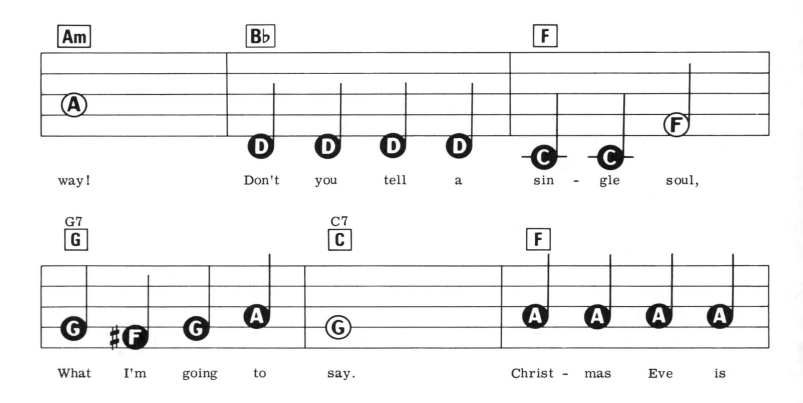

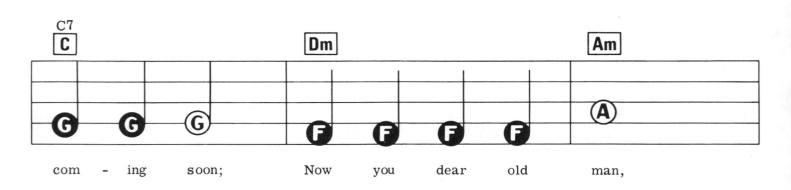

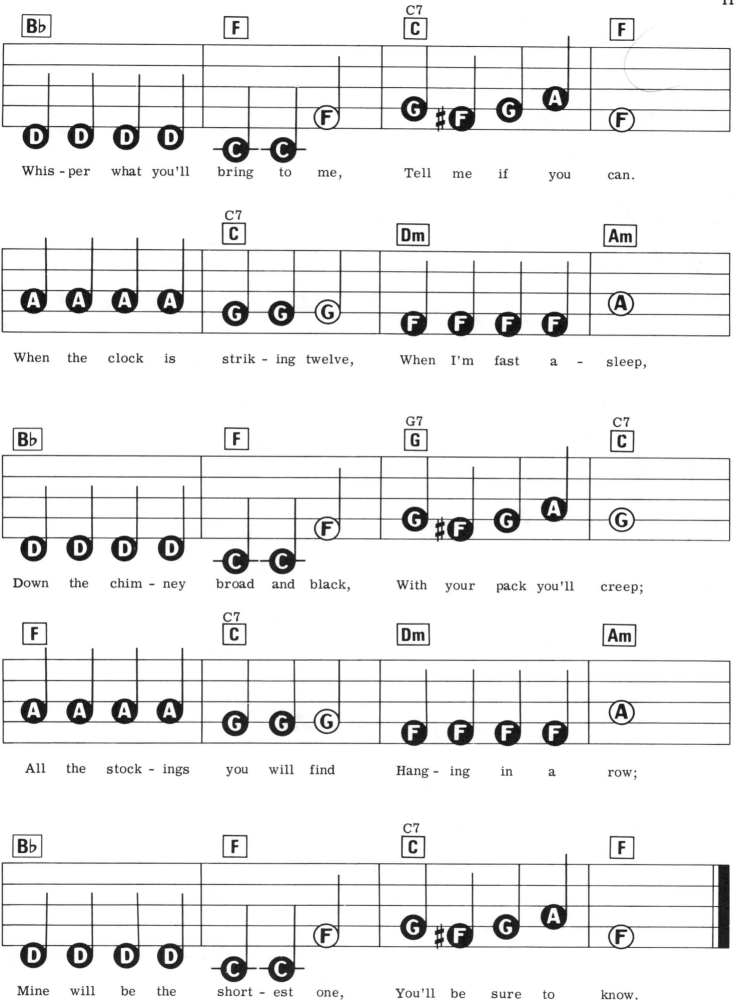

Joy To The World

Registration 2
Rhythm: March or Pops

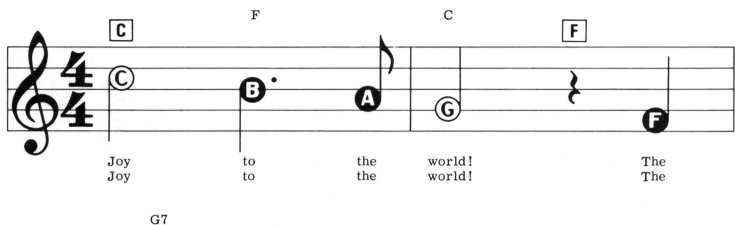

Joy   to   the world!   The
Joy   to   the world!   The

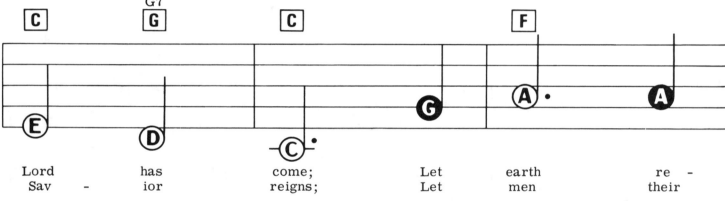

Lord   has   come;   Let   earth   re -
Sav - ior   reigns;   Let   men   their

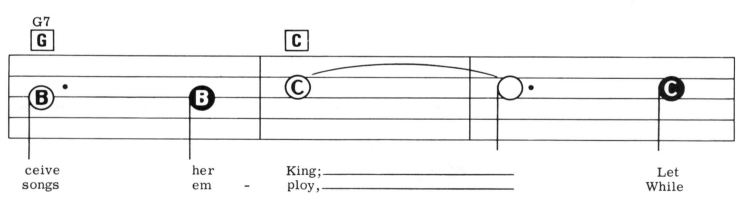

ceive   her   King;_____   Let
songs   em - ploy,_____   While

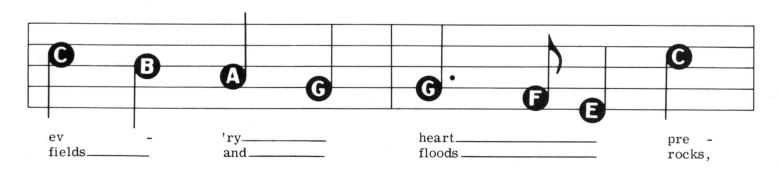

ev - 'ry_____   heart_____   pre -
fields_____ and_____   floods_____   rocks,

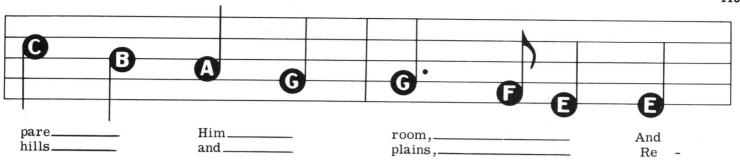

pare _____ Him _____ room, _____ And
hills _____ and _____ plains, _____ Re -

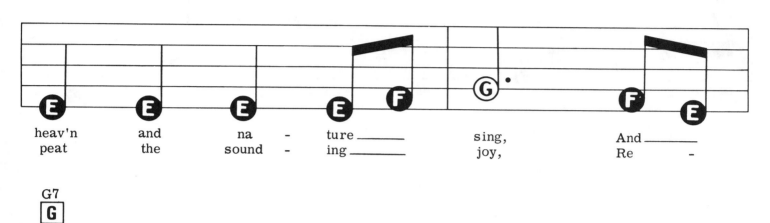

heav'n and na - ture _____ sing, And _____
peat the sound - ing _____ joy, Re -

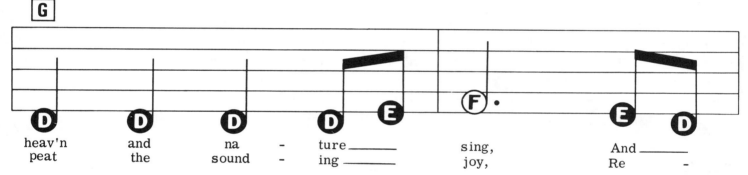

heav'n and na - ture _____ sing, And _____
peat the sound - ing _____ joy, Re -

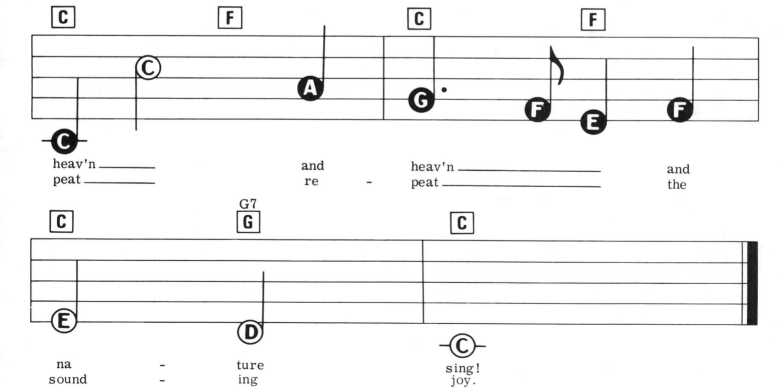

heav'n _____ and heav'n _____ and
peat _____ re - peat _____ the

na - ture sing!
sound - ing joy.

The Last Month Of The Year
(What Month Was Jesus Born In?)

Registration 10
Rhythm: Pops or Country

Words and Music by Vera Hall
Adapted and Arranged by Ruby Pickens Tartt
and Alan Lomax

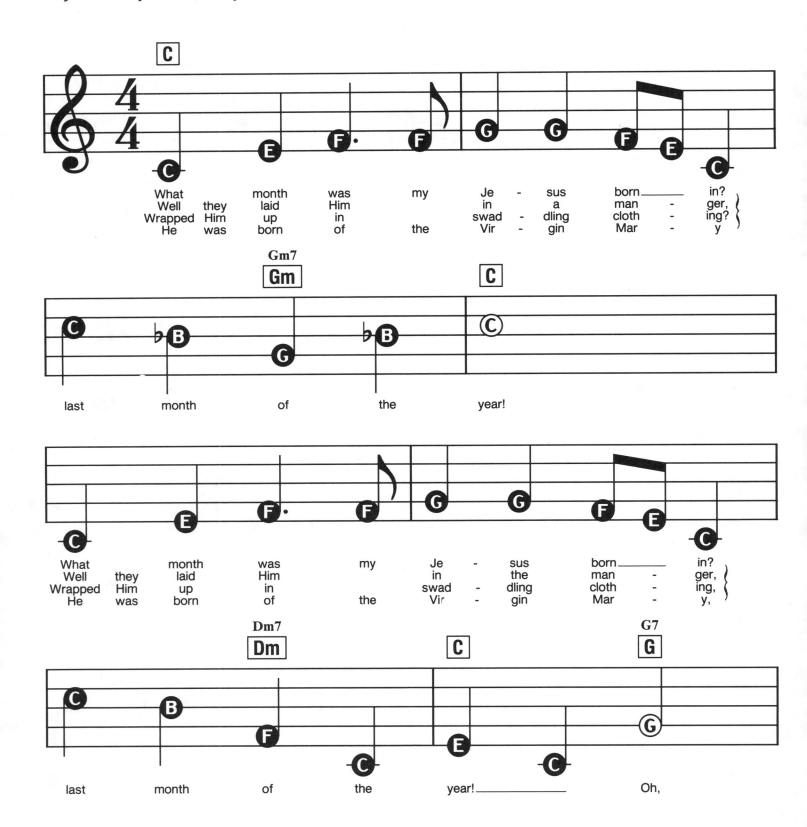

115

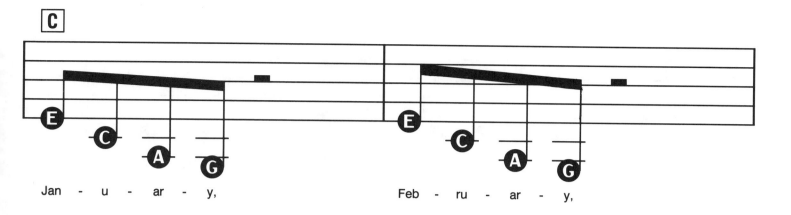

Jan - u - ar - y,   Feb - ru - ar - y,

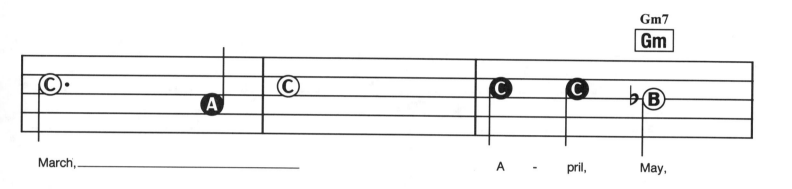

March,   A - pril,   May,

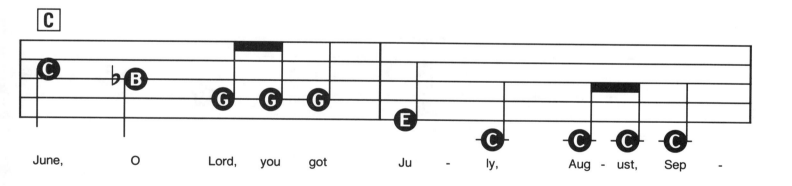

June,   O   Lord, you   got   Ju - ly,   Aug - ust,   Sep -

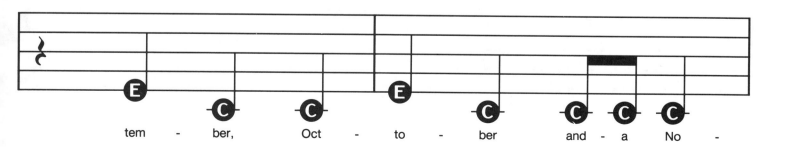

tem - ber,   Oct - to - ber   and - a   No -

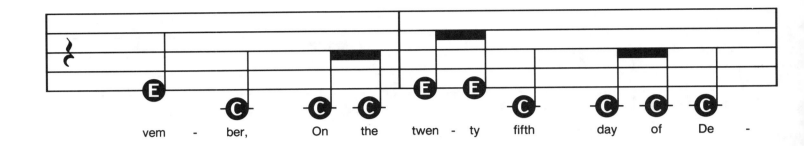

vem - ber, On the twen - ty fifth day of De -

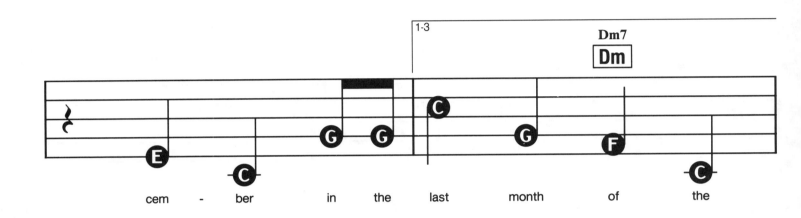

cem - ber in the last month of the

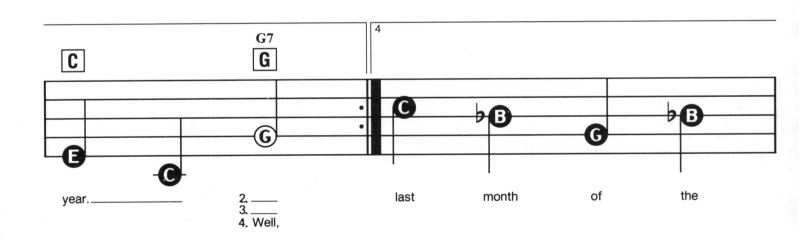

year.___ 2.___
3.___
4. Well,

last month of the

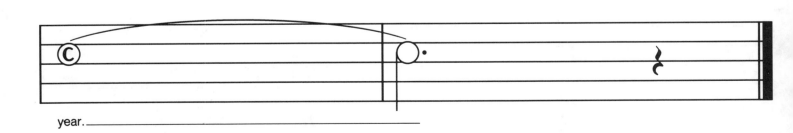

year.___

The Little Drummer Boy

Registration 2
Rhythm: March

Words and Music by Katherine Davis,
Henry Onorati and Harry Simeone

Come they told me pa - rum pum pum pum,_____
Lit - tle Ba - by pa - rum pum pum pum,_____
(Ba - by Ge - su)

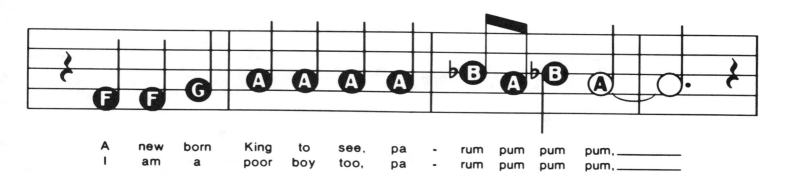

A new born King to see, pa - rum pum pum pum,_____
I am a poor boy too, pa - rum pum pum pum,_____

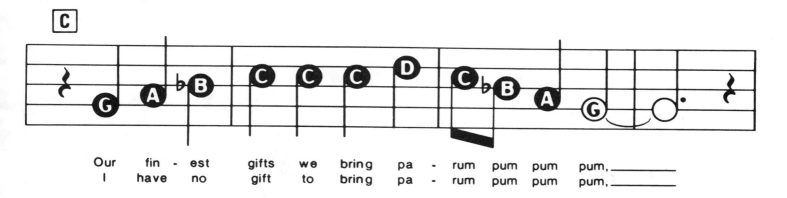

Our fin - est gifts we bring pa - rum pum pum pum,_____
I have no gift to bring pa - rum pum pum pum,_____

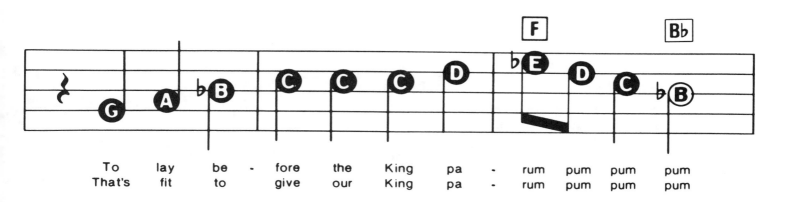

To lay be - fore the King pa - rum pum pum pum
That's fit to give our King pa - rum pum pum pum

118

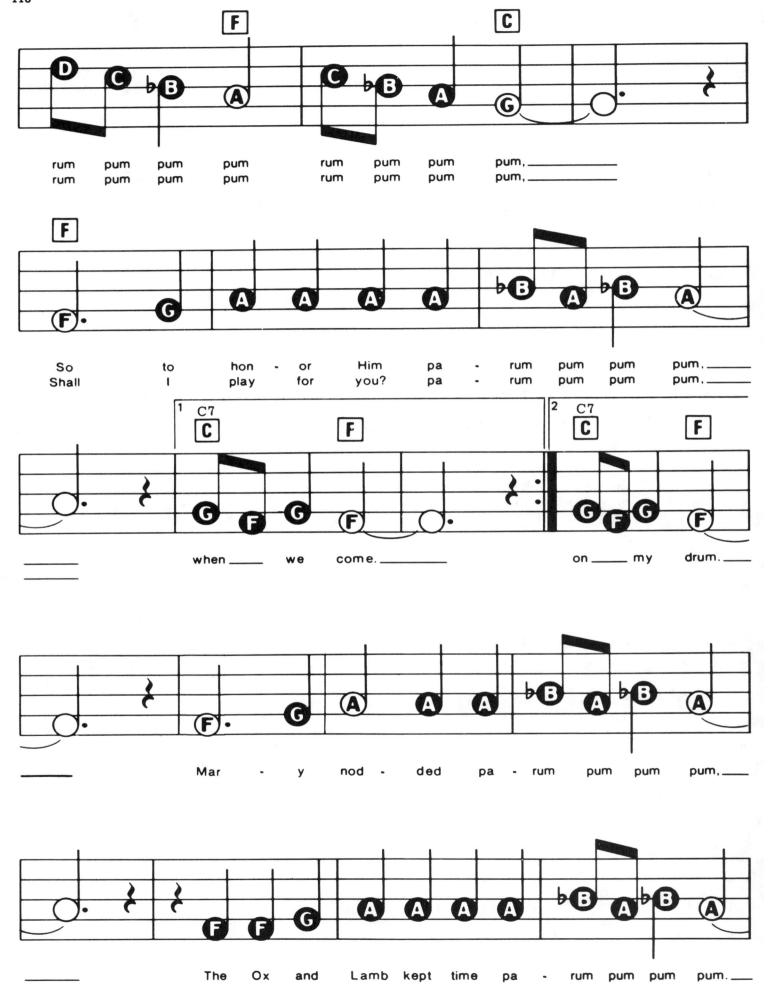

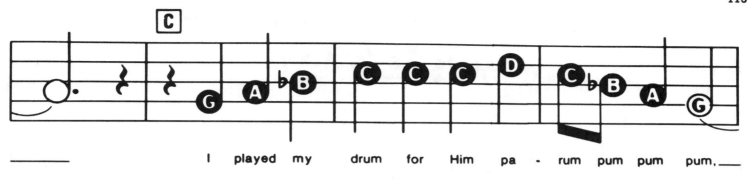

I played my drum for Him pa - rum pum pum pum,___

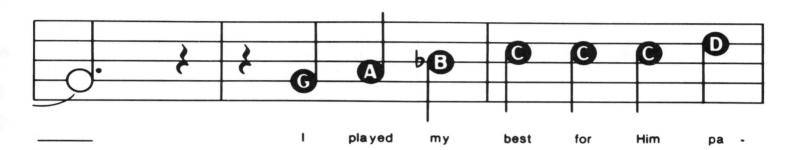

I played my best for Him pa -

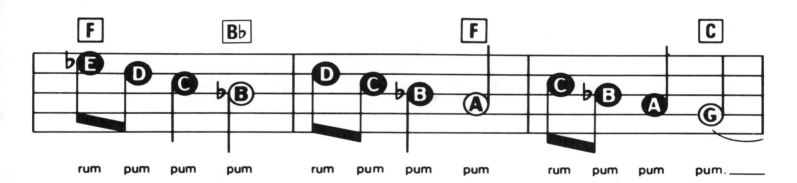

rum pum pum pum rum pum pum pum rum pum pum pum.___

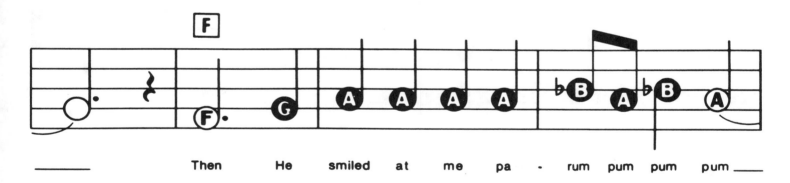

Then He smiled at me pa - rum pum pum pum___

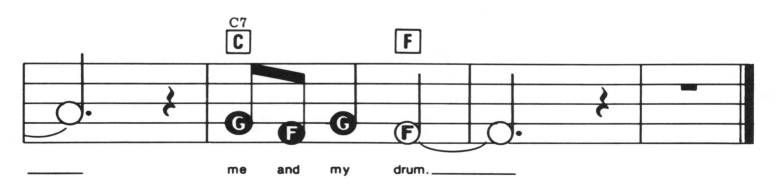

me and my drum.___

Let It Snow! Let It Snow! Let It Snow!

Registration 2
Rhythm: Fox Trot or Swing

Words by Sammy Cahn
Music by Jule Styne

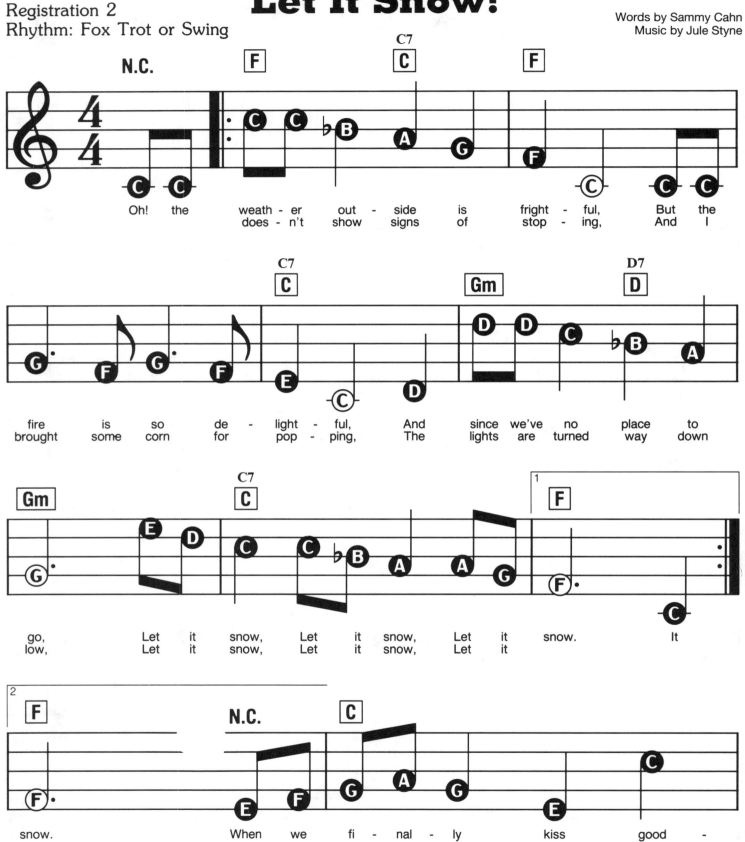

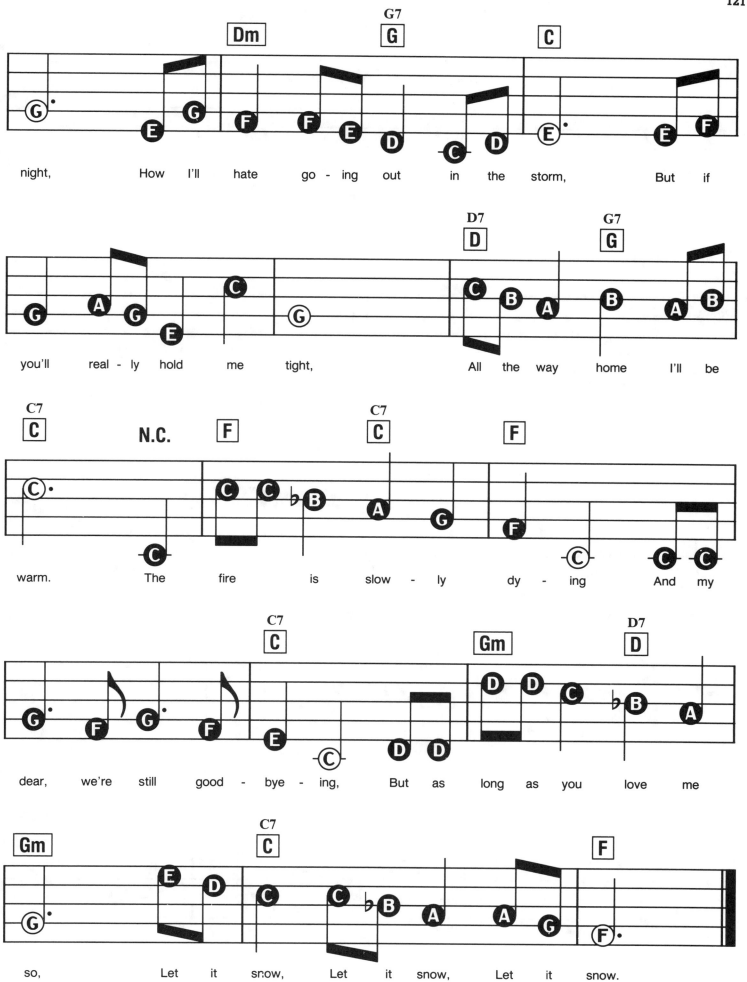

March Of The Toys

Registration 5
Rhythm: 6/8 March

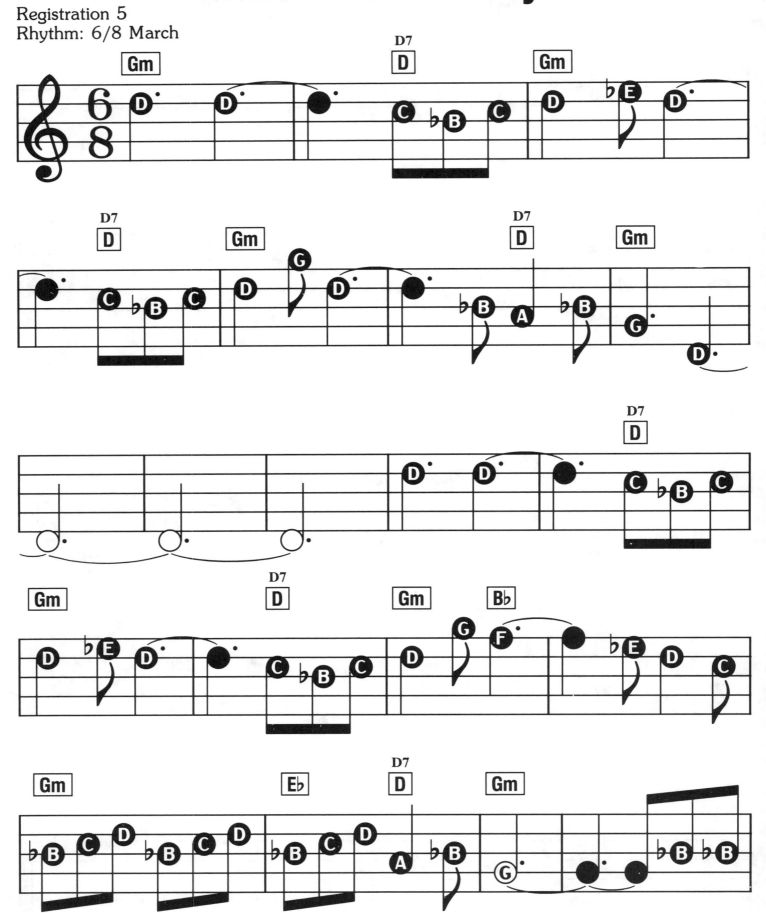

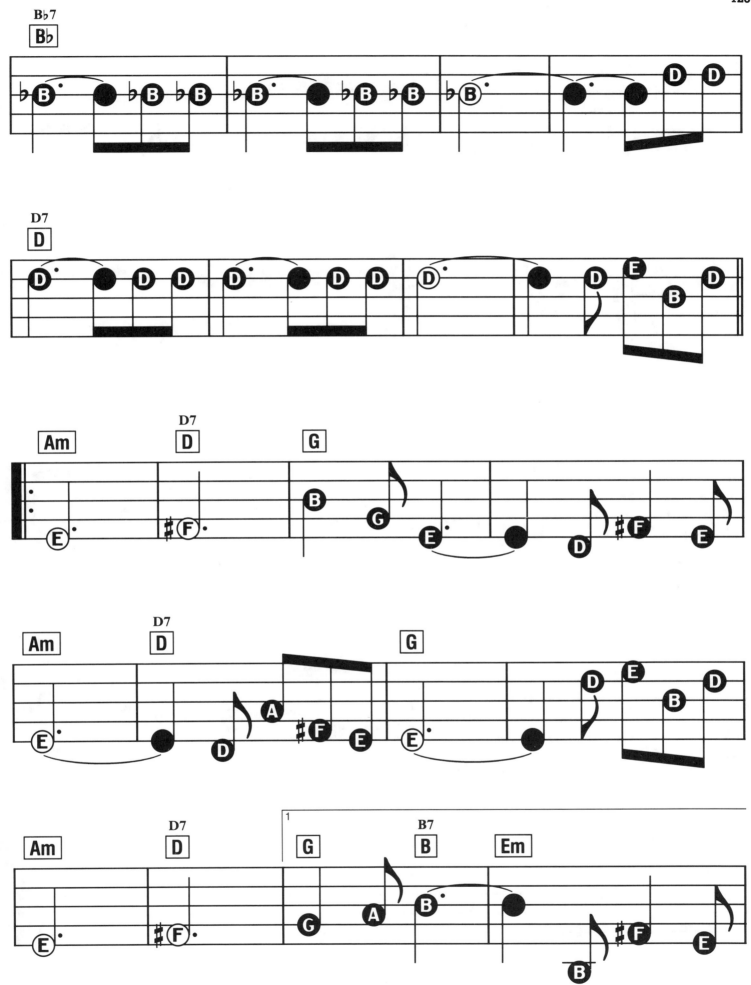

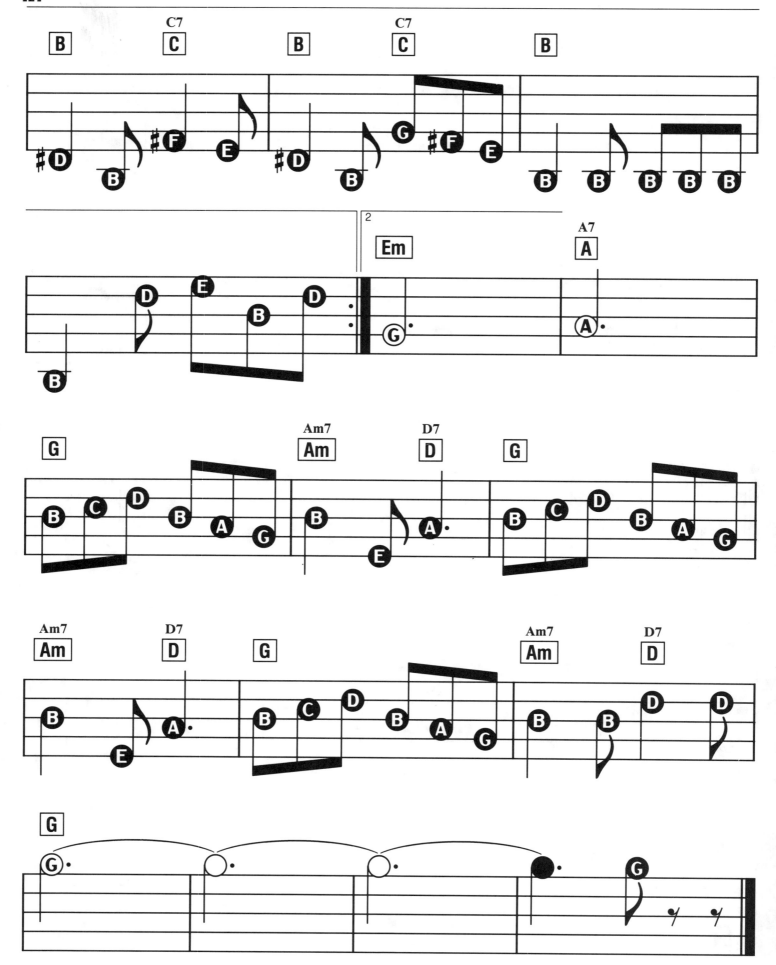

The Most Wonderful Day Of The Year

Registration 3
Rhythm: Waltz

Music and Lyrics by
Johnny Marks

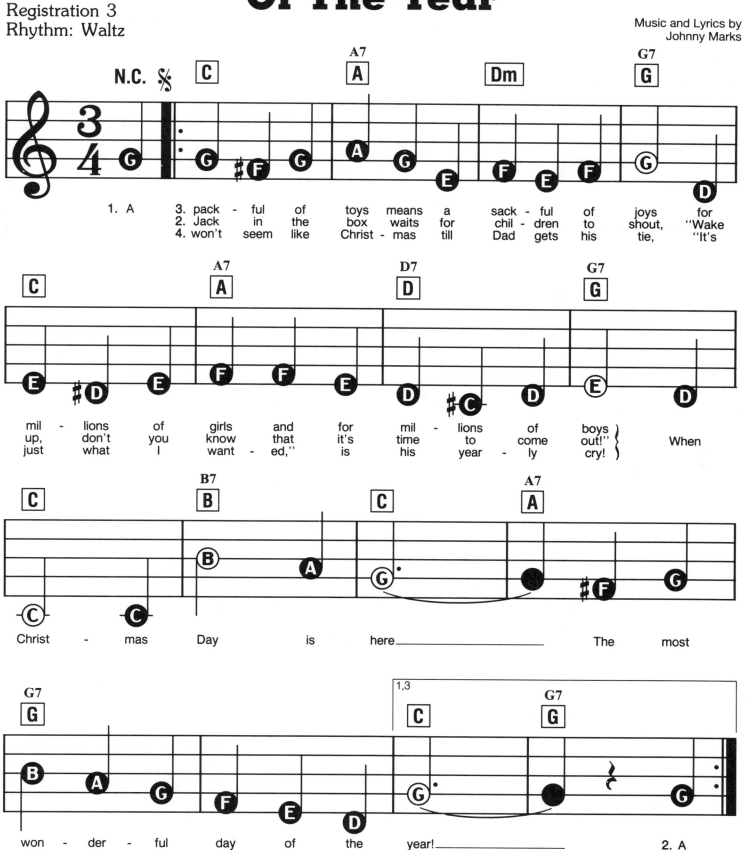

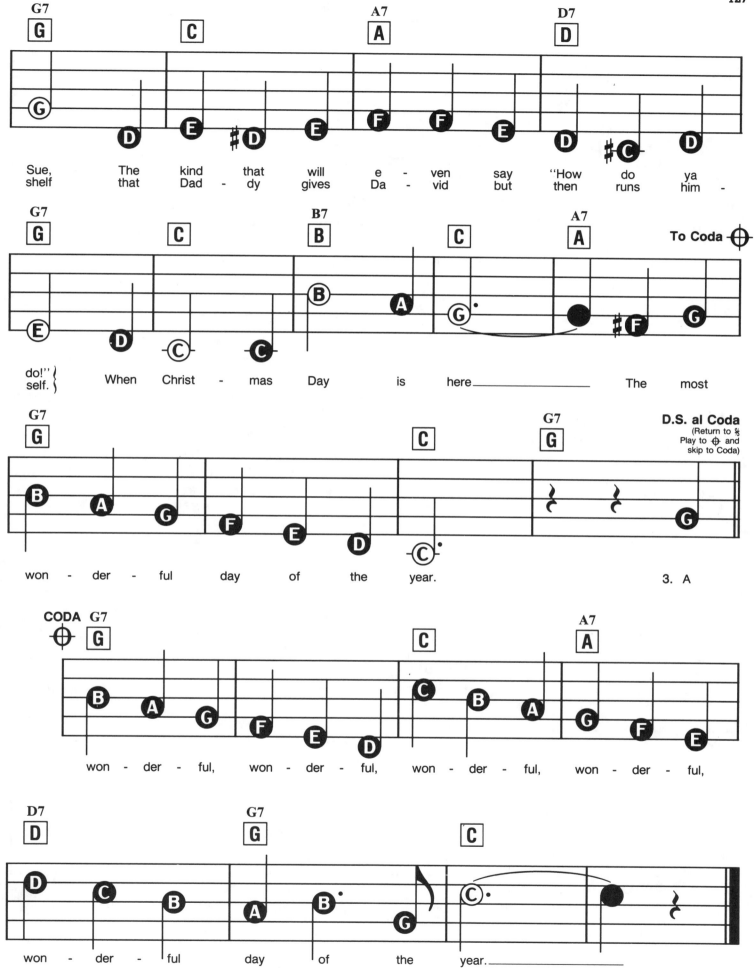

A Marshmallow World

Registration 2
Rhythm: Fox Trot or Polka

Words by Carl Sigman
Music by Peter De Rose

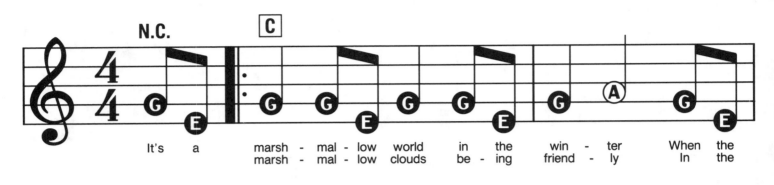

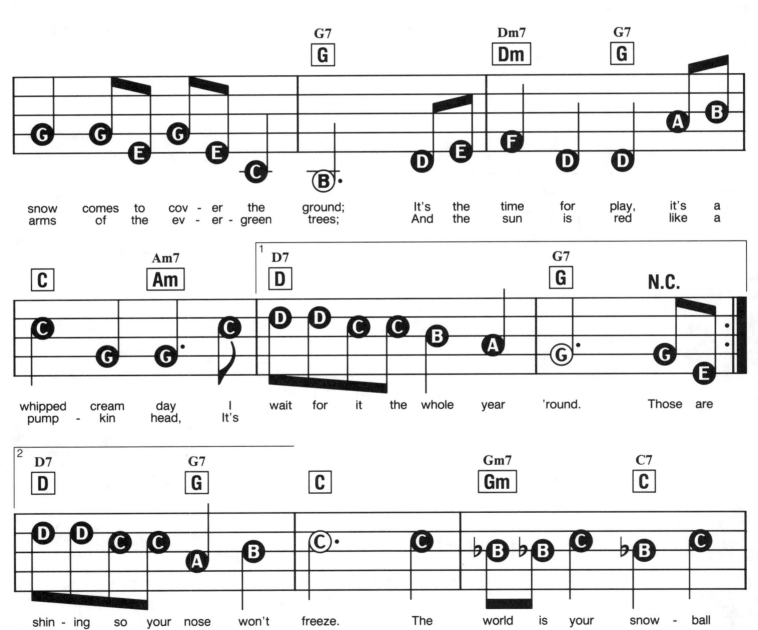

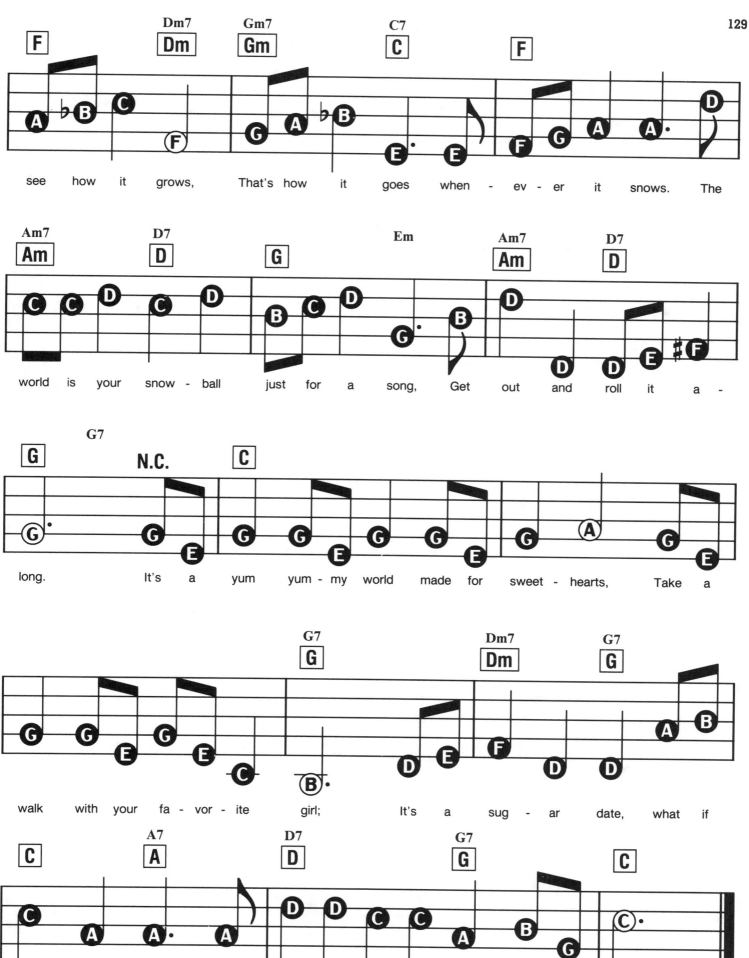

Mele Kalikimaka

Registration 5
Rhythm: Fox Trot or Swing

Words and Music by
Alex Anderson

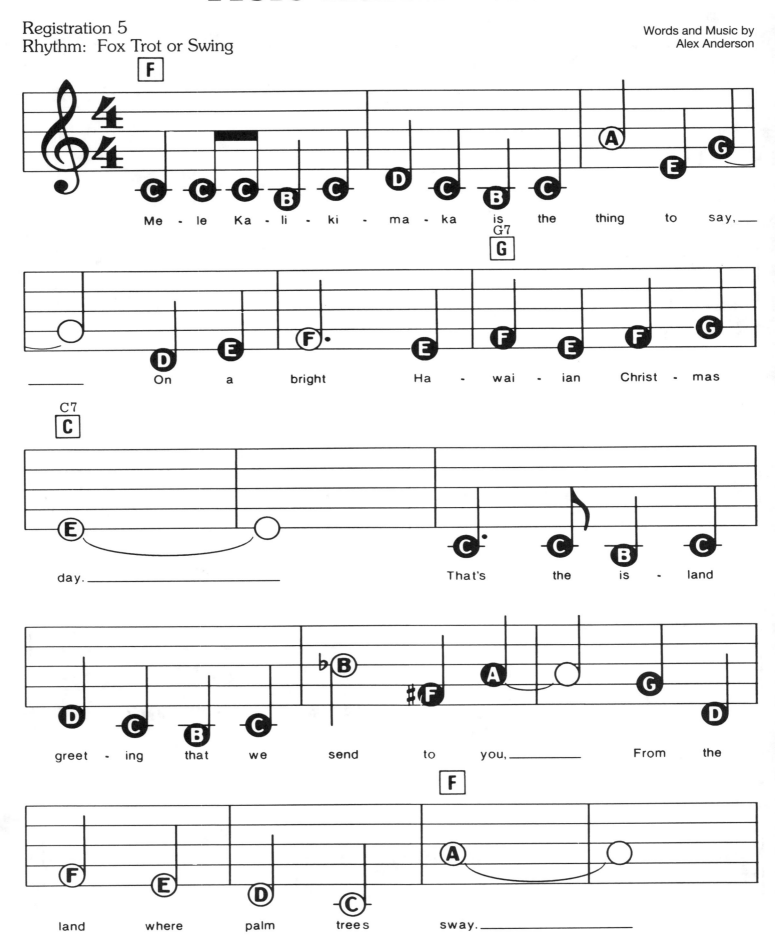

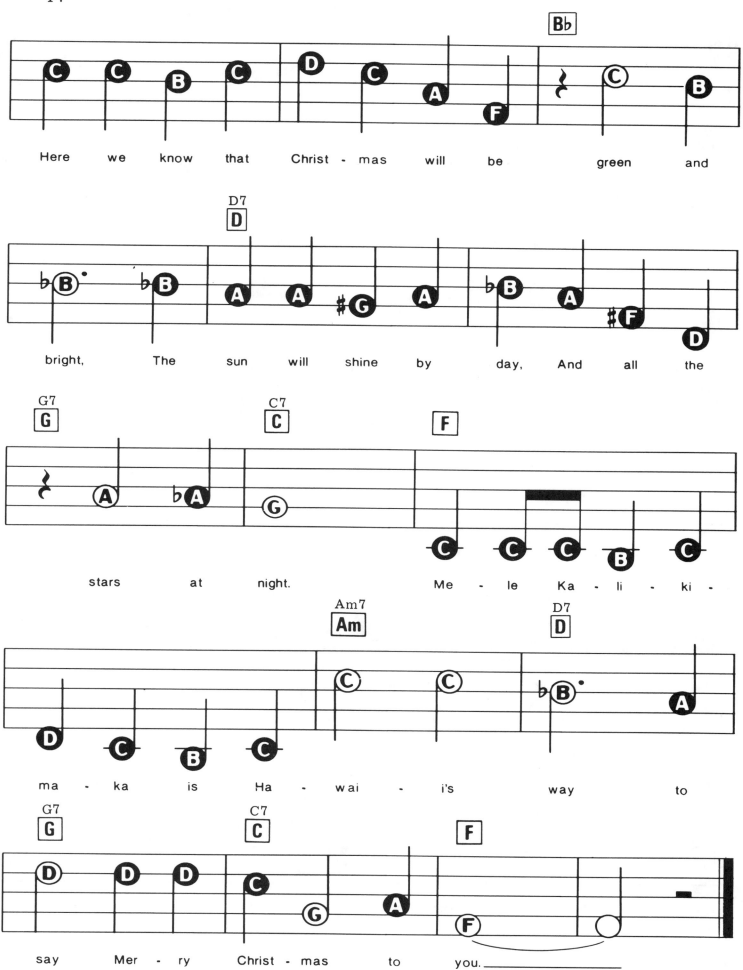

Mistletoe And Holly

Registration 2
Rhythm: Swing

Words and Music by
Frank Sinatra,
Dok Stanford and
Henry Sanicola

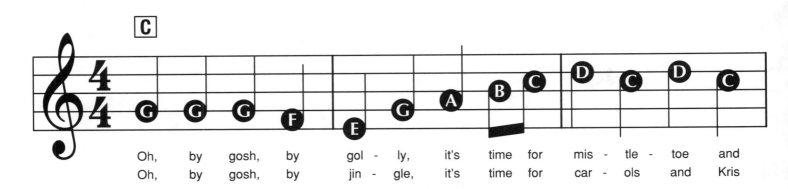

Oh, by gosh, by gol - ly, it's time for mis - tle - toe and
Oh, by gosh, by jin - gle, it's time for car - ols and Kris

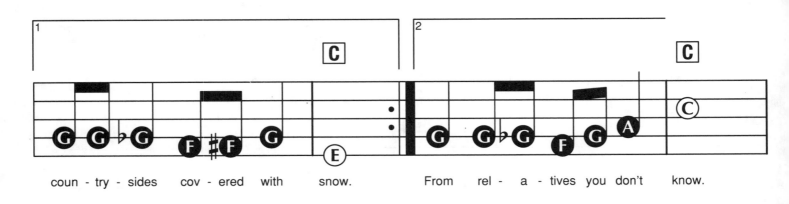

hol - ly,　　　tast - y pheas - ants,　christ - mas pre - sents,
Krin - gle;　　　o - ver - eat - ing,　mer - ry greet - ings,

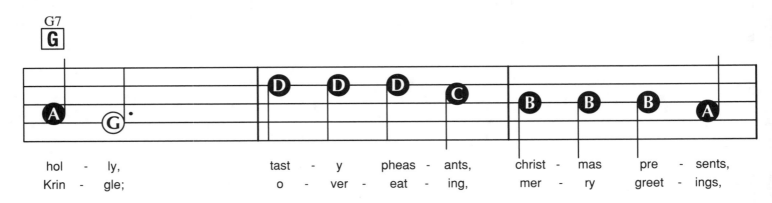

coun - try - sides cov - ered with snow.　　From rel - a - tives you don't know.

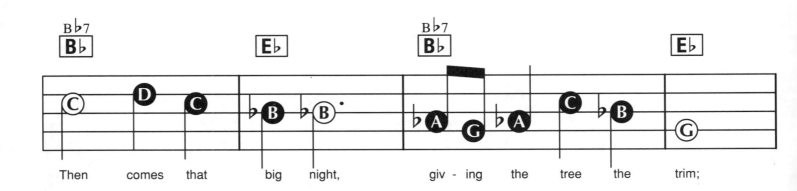

Then comes that big night,　giv - ing the tree the trim;

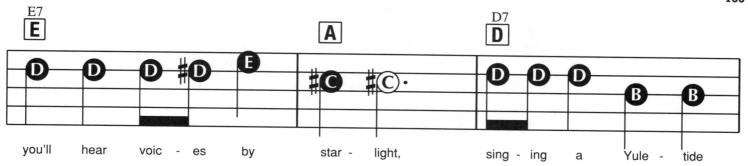

you'll hear voic - es by star - light, sing - ing a Yule - tide

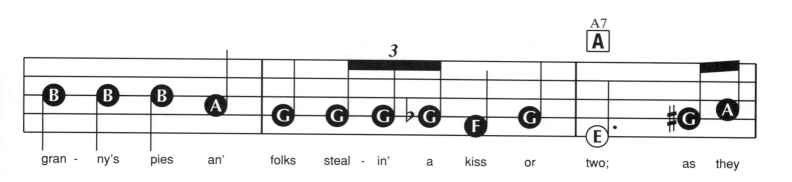

hymn. Oh, by gosh, by gol - ly, _____ it's time for

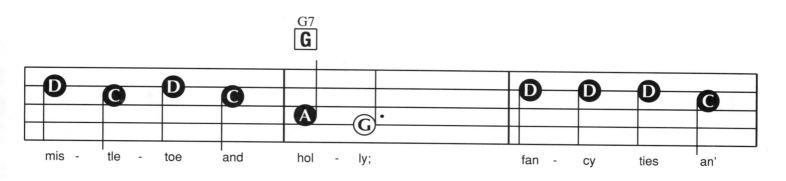

mis - tle - toe and hol - ly; fan - cy ties an'

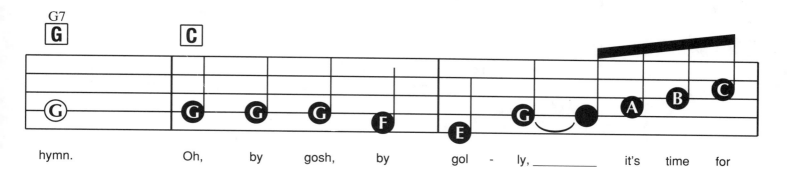

gran - ny's pies an' folks steal - in' a kiss or two; as they

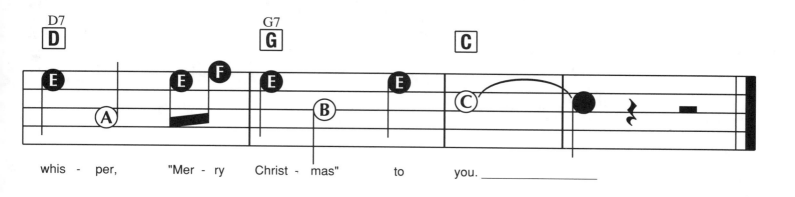

whis - per, "Mer - ry Christ - mas" to you. _____

My Favorite Things
(From "The Sound Of Music")

Registration 9
Rhythm: Waltz

Lyrics by Oscar Hammerstein II
Music by Richard Rodgers

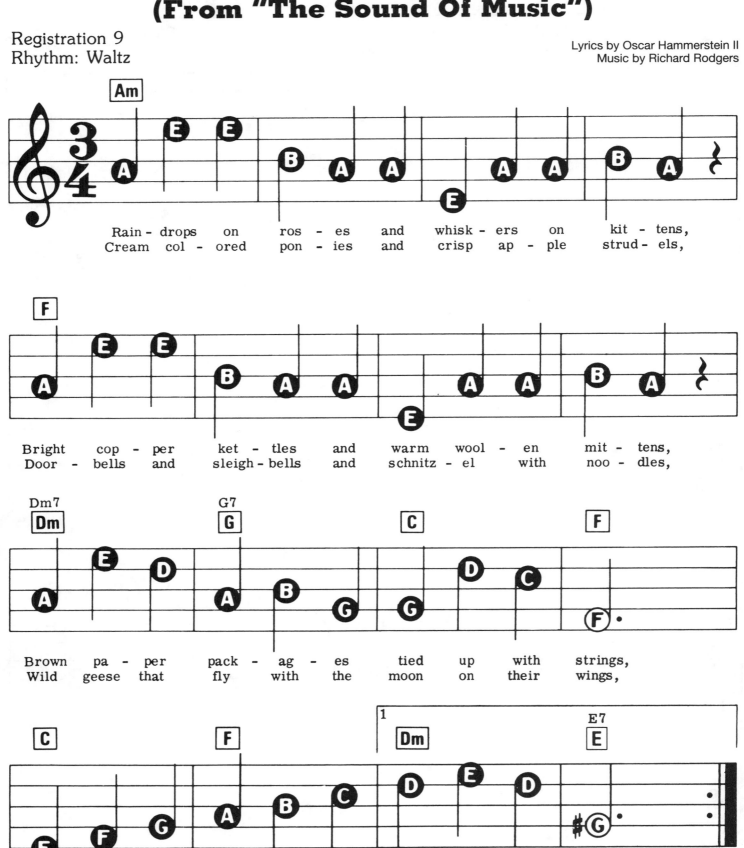

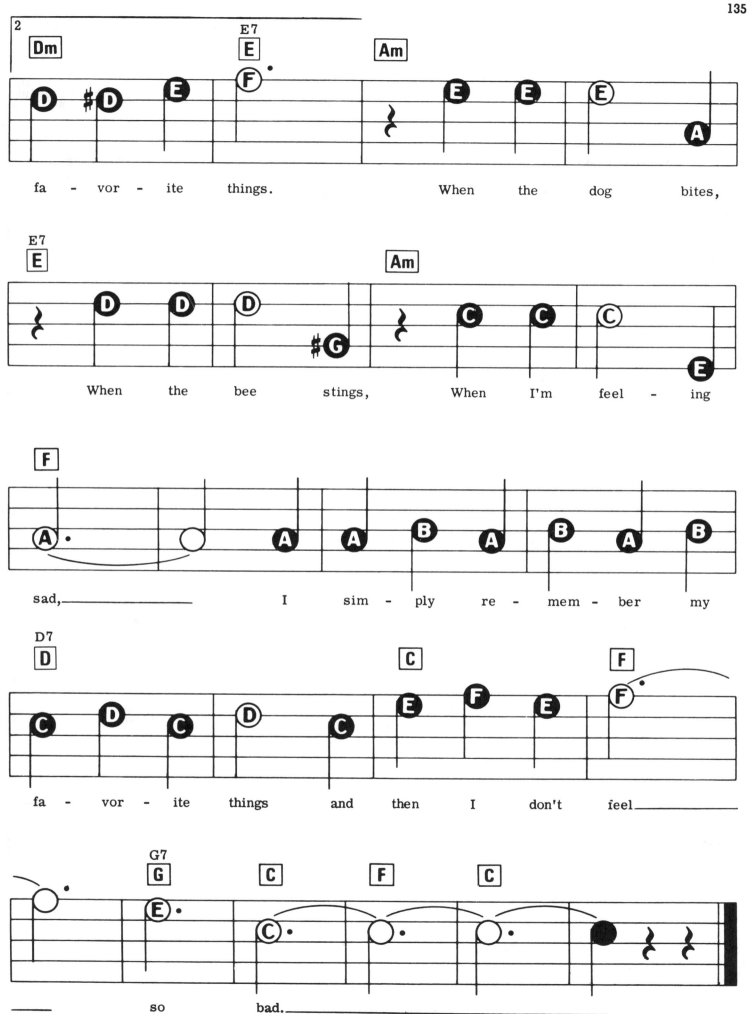

The Night Before Christmas Song

Registration 3
Rhythm: Waltz

Music by Johnny Marks
Lyrics adapted by Johnny Marks
from Clement Moore's poem

137

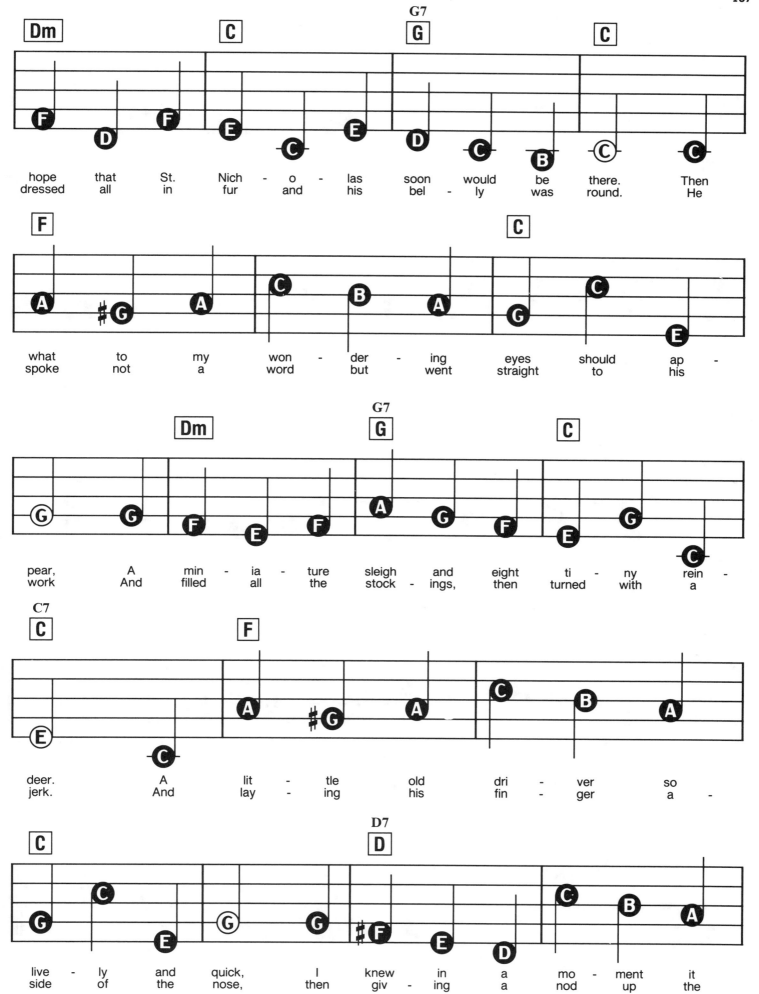

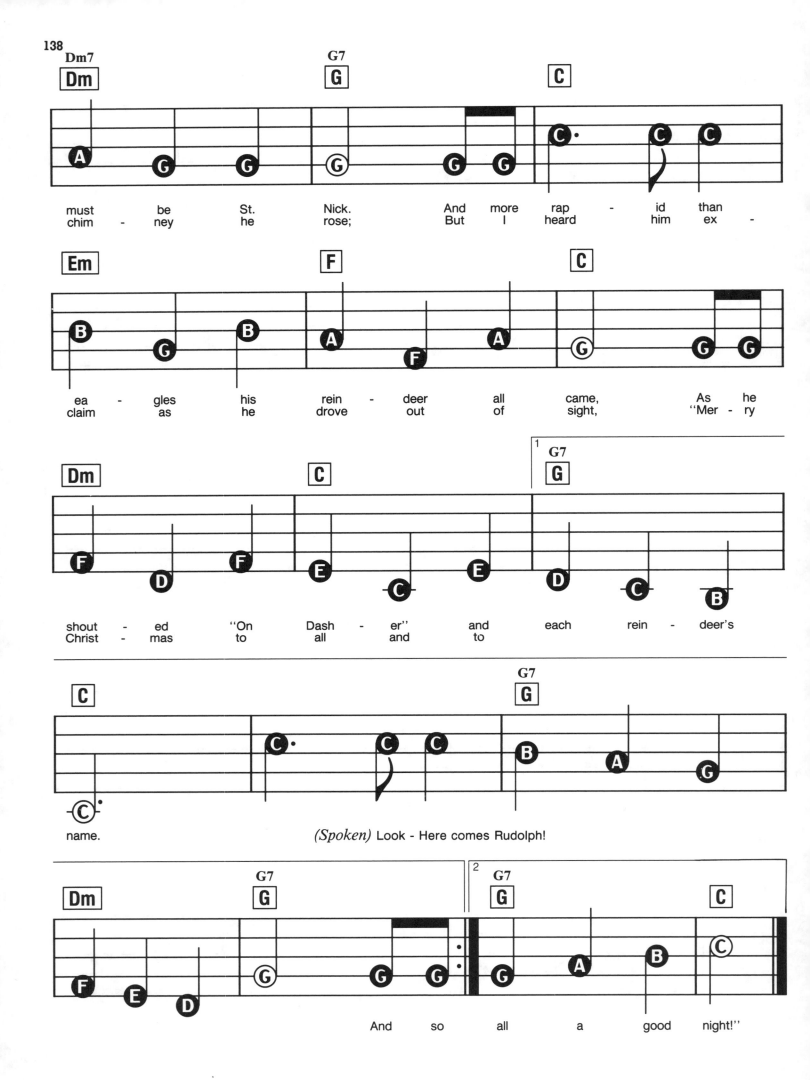

Parade Of The Wooden Soldiers

Registration 5
Rhythm: March or Polka

By Ballard MacDonald
and Leon Jessel

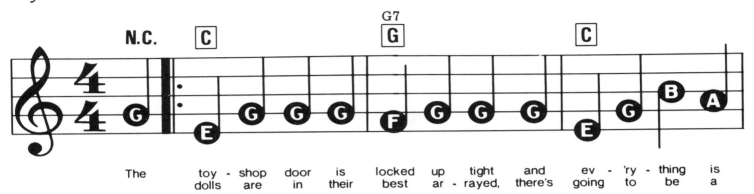

The toy - shop door is locked up tight and ev - 'ry - thing is
dolls are in their best ar - rayed, there's going to be a

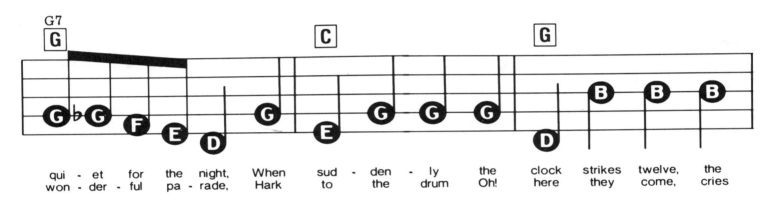

qui - et for the night, When sud - den - ly the clock strikes twelve, the
won - der - ful pa - rade, When Hark to the drum Oh! here they come, the cries

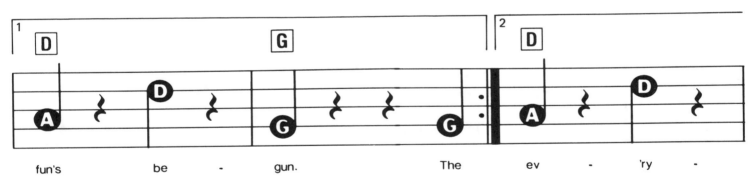

fun's be - gun. The ev - 'ry -

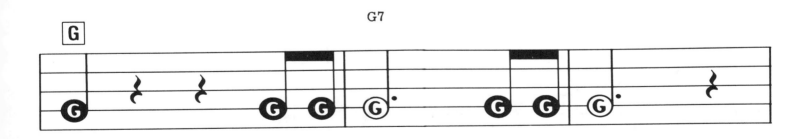

one

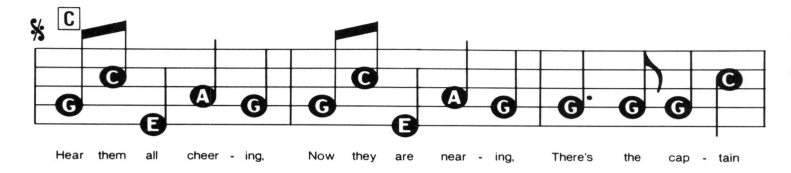

Hear them all cheer - ing, Now they are near - ing, There's the cap - tain

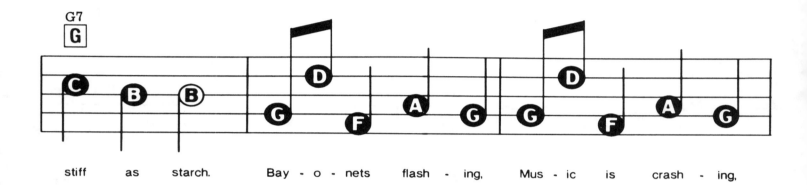

stiff as starch. Bay - o - nets flash - ing, Mus - ic is crash - ing,

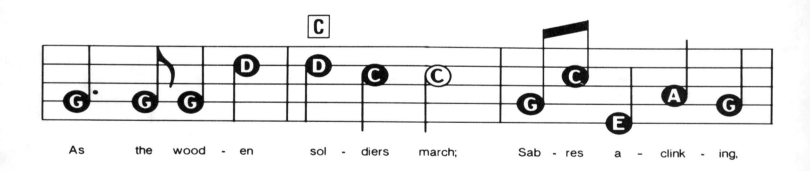

As the wood - en sol - diers march; Sab - res a - clink - ing,

To Coda

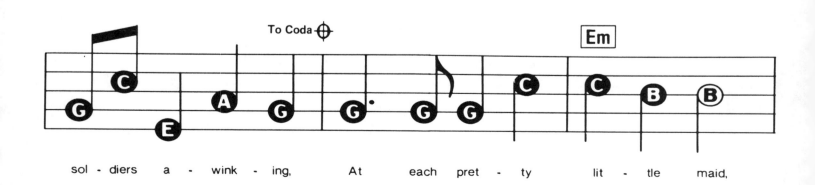

sol - diers a - wink - ing, At each pret - ty lit - tle maid,

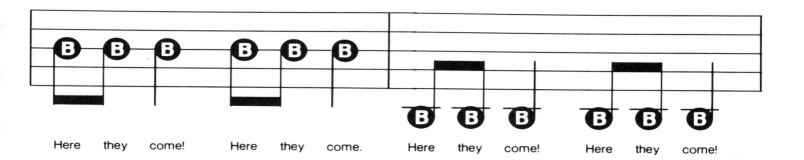

Here they come! Here they come. Here they come! Here they come!

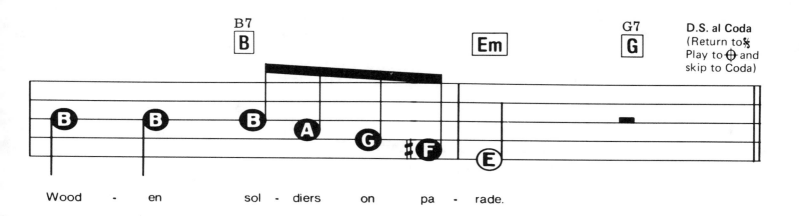

Wood - en sol - diers on pa - rade.

B7 · **Em** · **G7** · **D.S. al Coda** (Return to 𝄋 Play to ⊕ and skip to Coda)

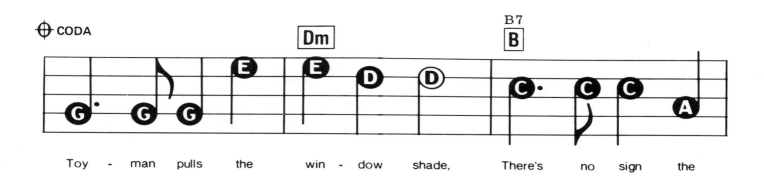

⊕ CODA

Dm · **B7**

Toy - man pulls the win - dow shade, There's no sign the

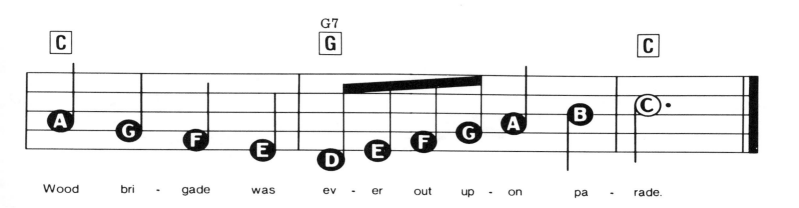

C · **G7** · **C**

Wood bri - gade was ev - er out up - on pa - rade.

Nuttin' For Christmas

Registration: 2
Rhythm: Fox Trot or Shuffle

Words and Music by Roy Bennett
and Sid Tepper

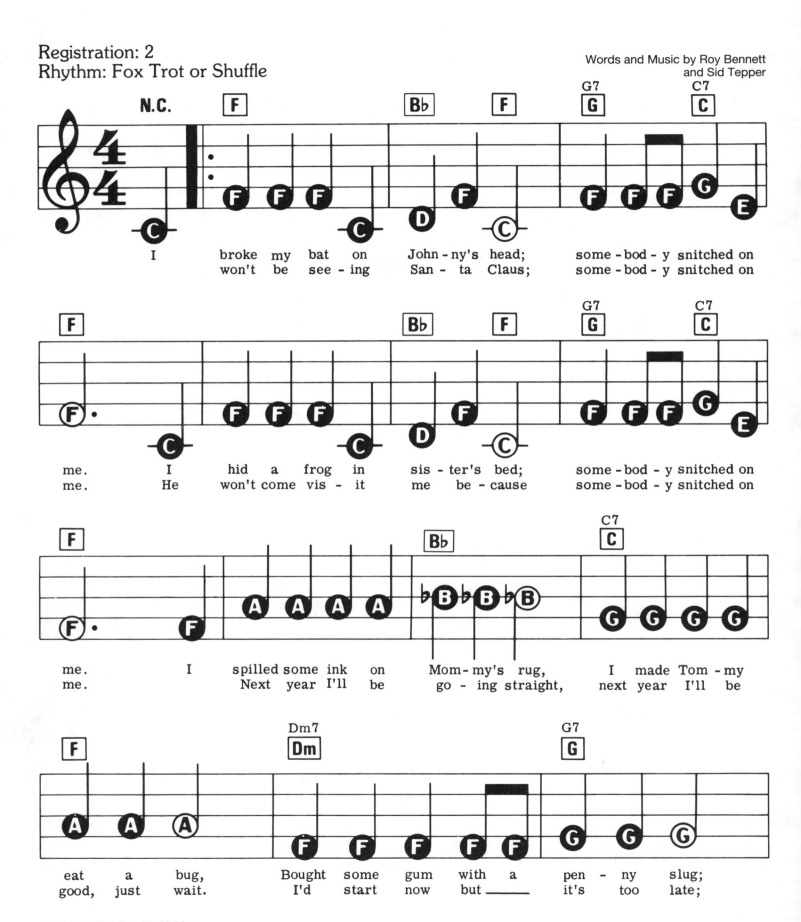

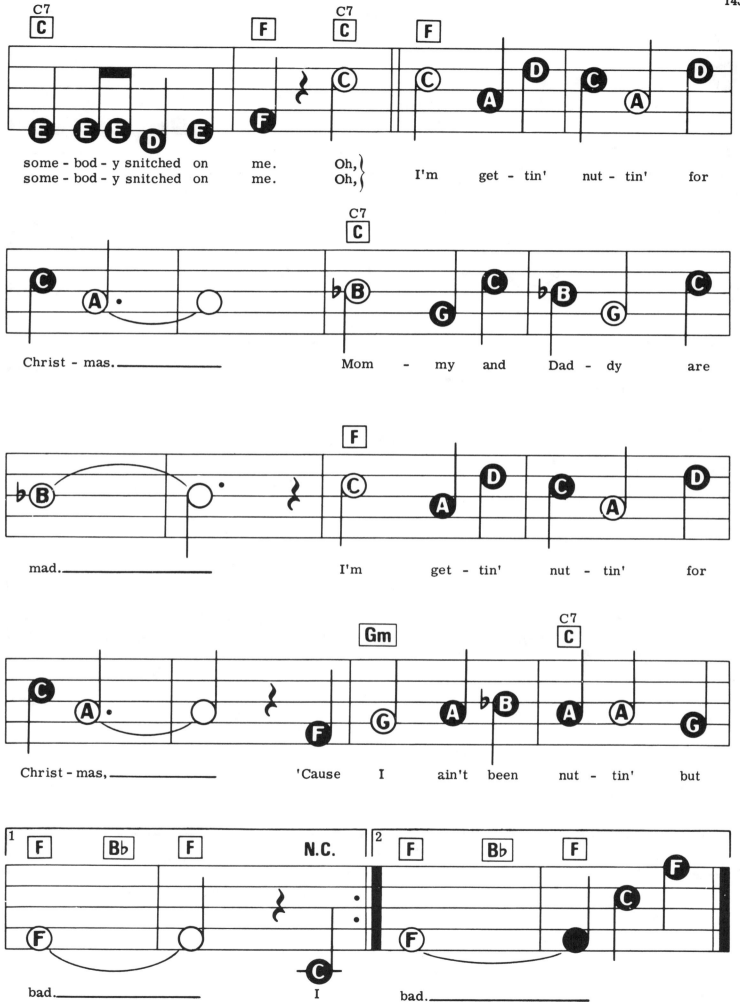

some - bod - y snitched on me. Oh,⎰
some - bod - y snitched on me. Oh,⎱ I'm get - tin' nut - tin' for

Christ - mas._____ Mom - my and Dad - dy are

mad._____ I'm get - tin' nut - tin' for

Christ - mas,_____ 'Cause I ain't been nut - tin' but

bad._____ I

bad._____

O Christmas Tree

Registration 3
Rhythm: None

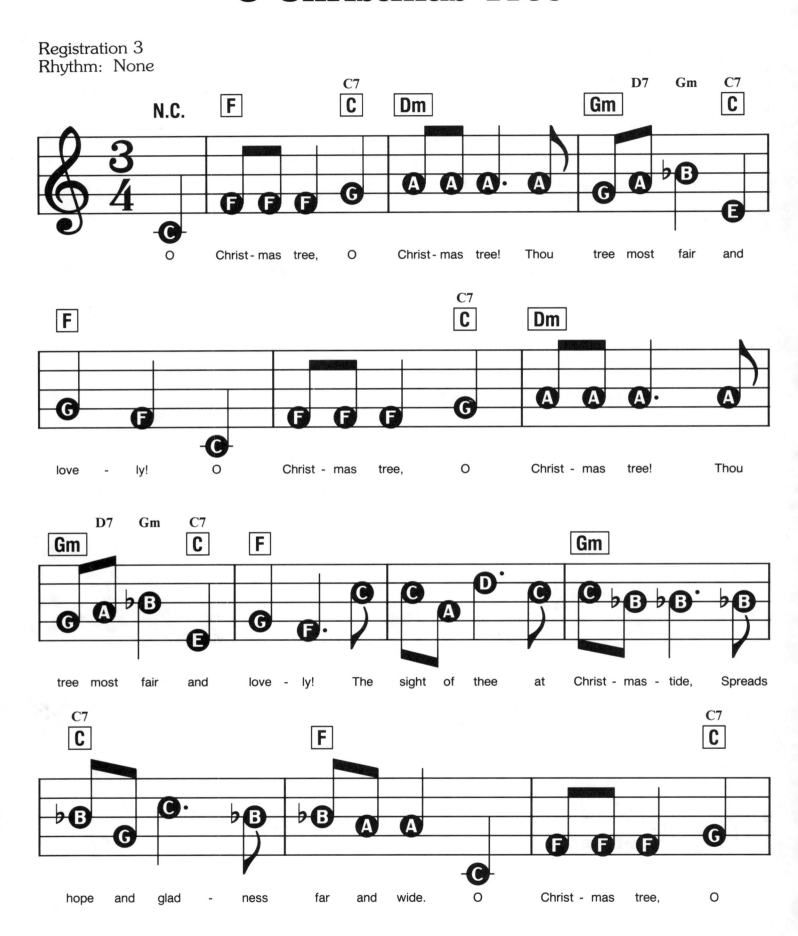

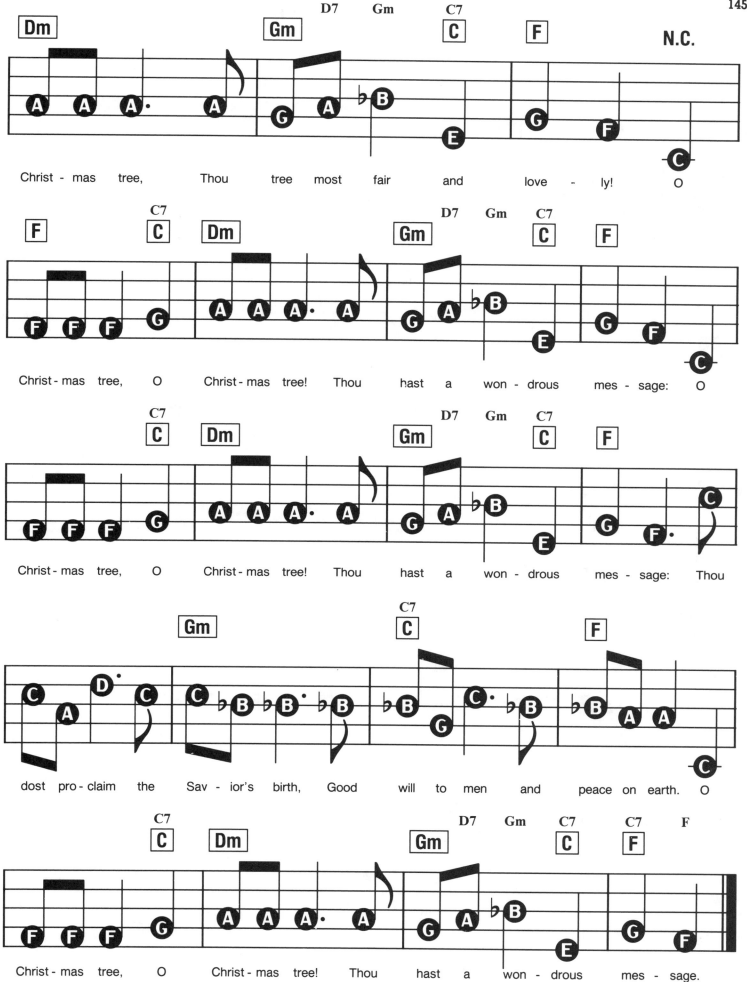

O Come All Ye Faithful

Registration 6
Rhythm: March or Pops

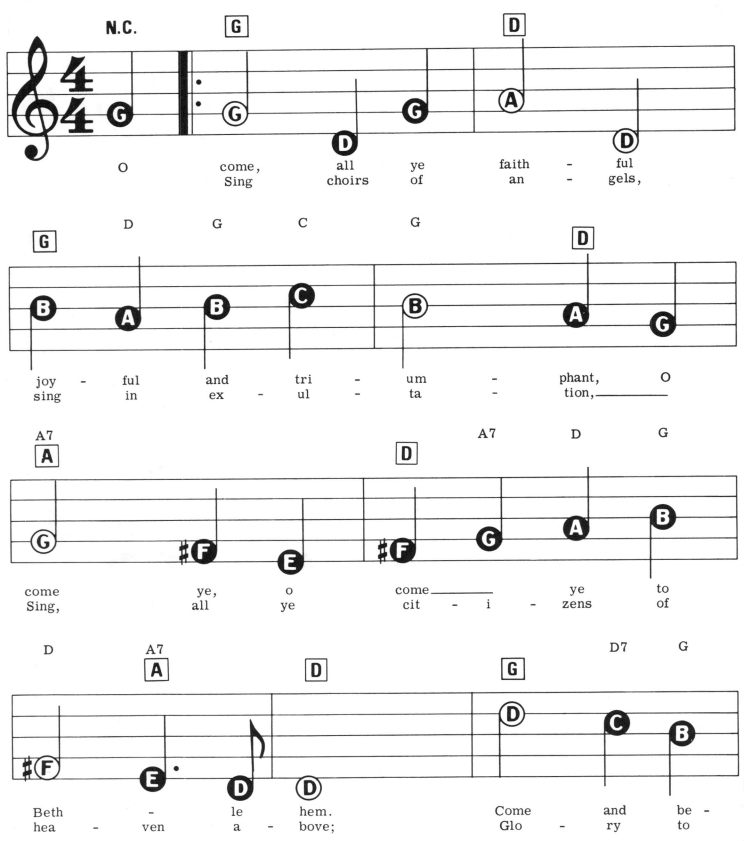

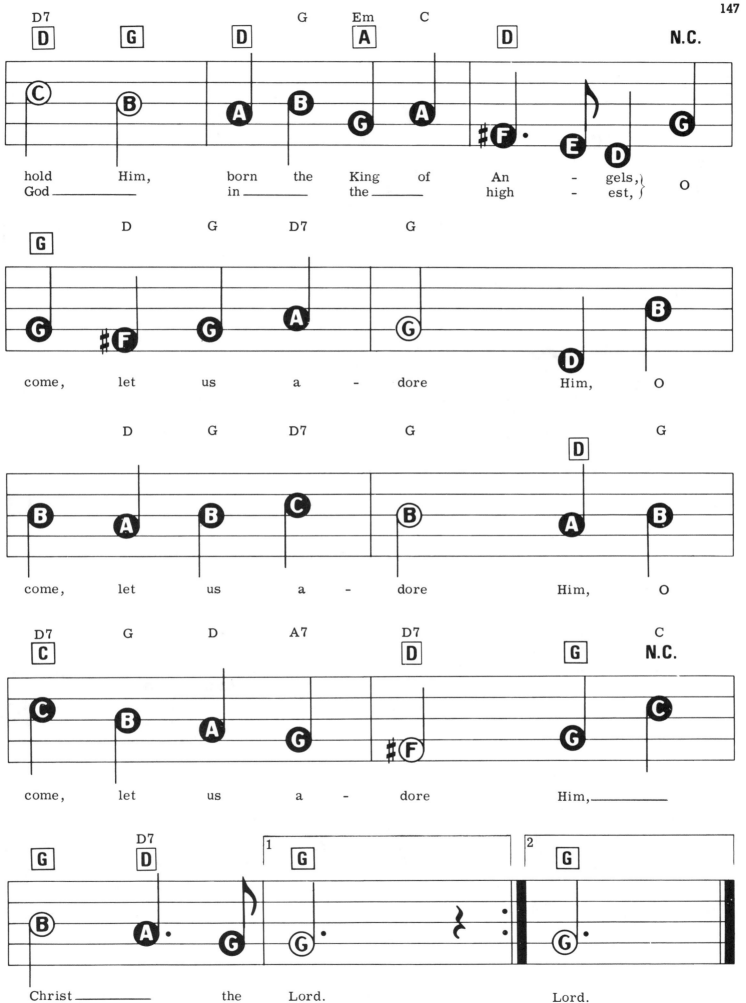

O Holy Night

Registration 6
Rhythm: None

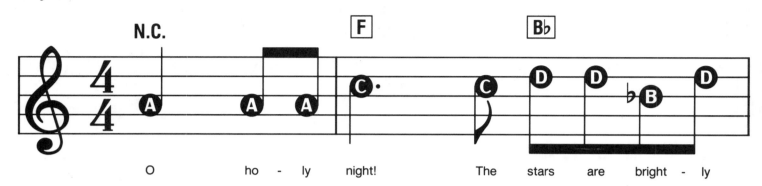

O ho-ly night! The stars are bright-ly

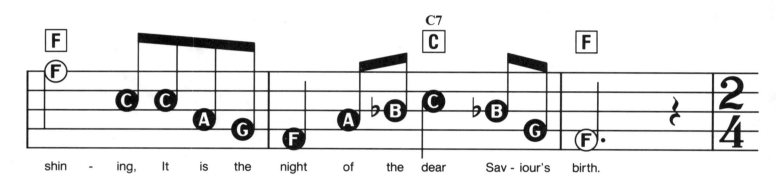

shin-ing, It is the night of the dear Sav-iour's birth.

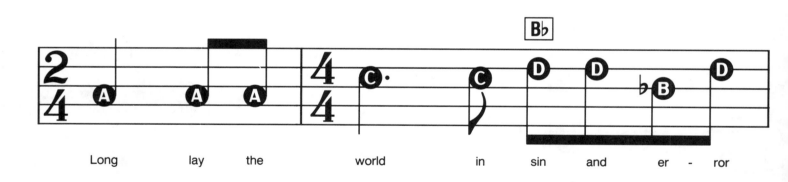

Long lay the world in sin and er-ror

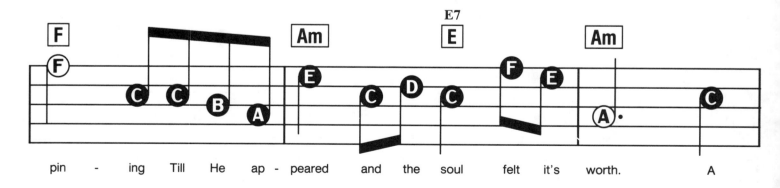

pin-ing Till He ap-peared and the soul felt it's worth. A

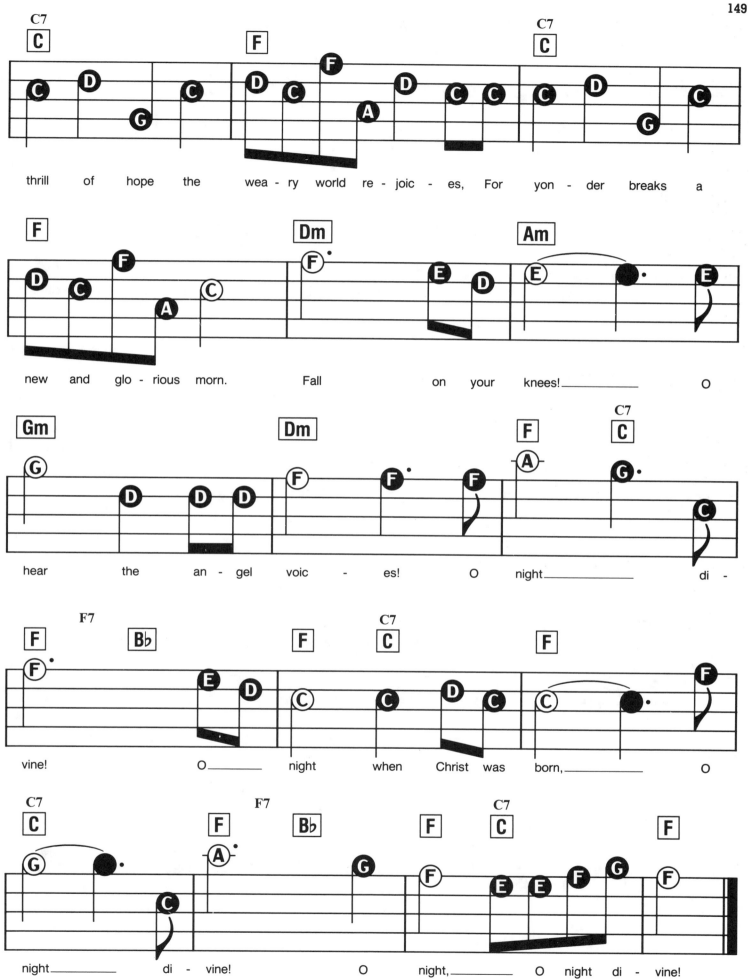

O Little Town Of Bethlehem

Registration 1
Rhythm: None

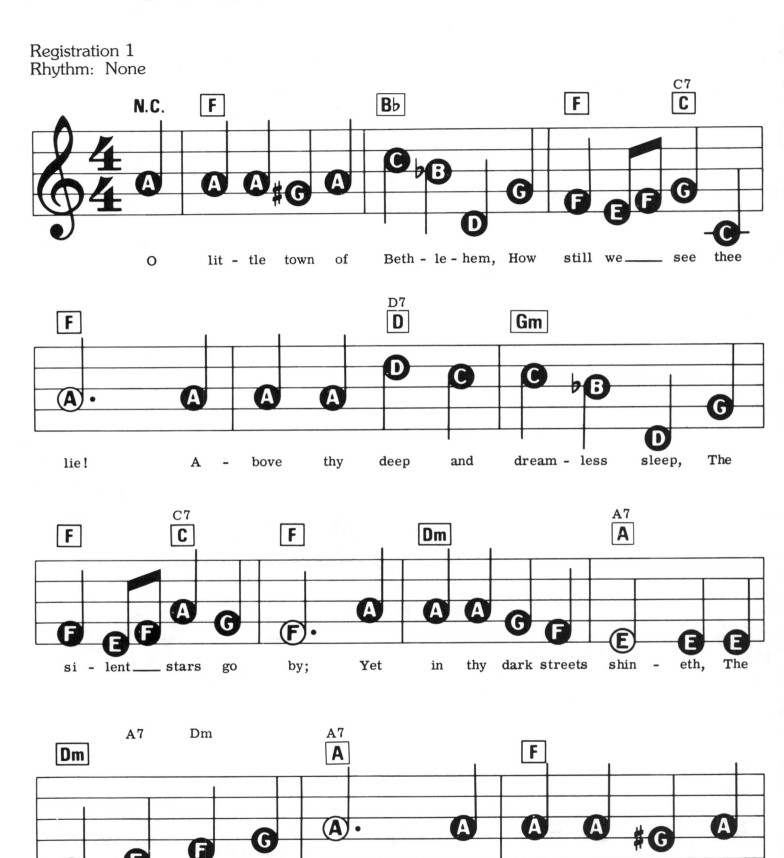

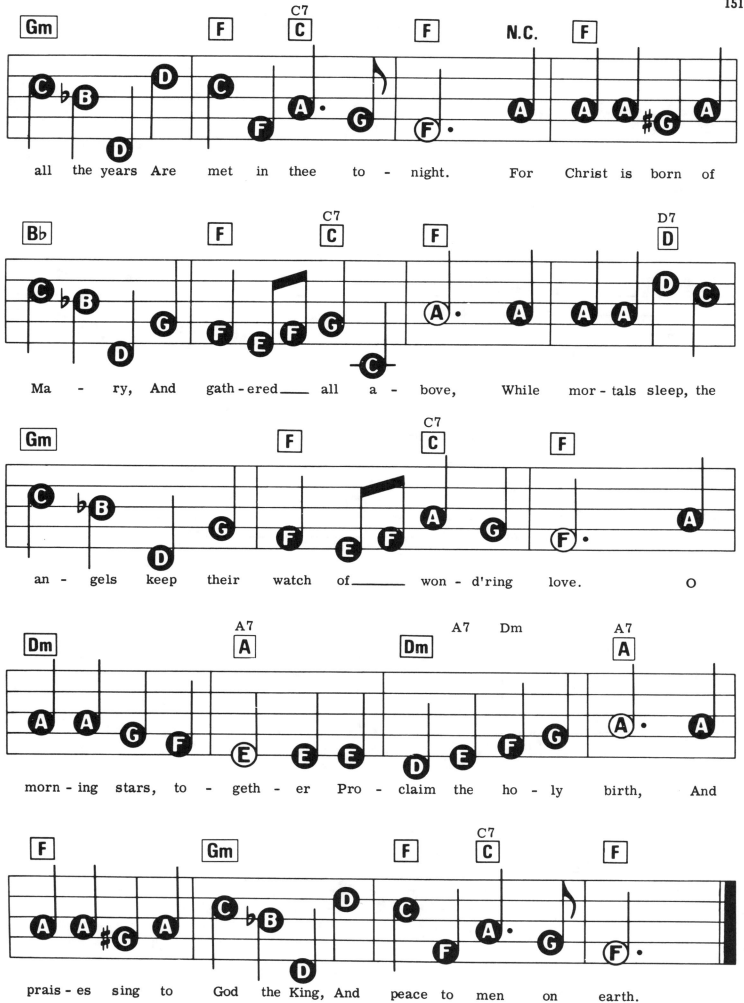

151

Old Toy Trains

Registration 3
Rhythm: Slow Rock

Words and Music by
Roger Miller

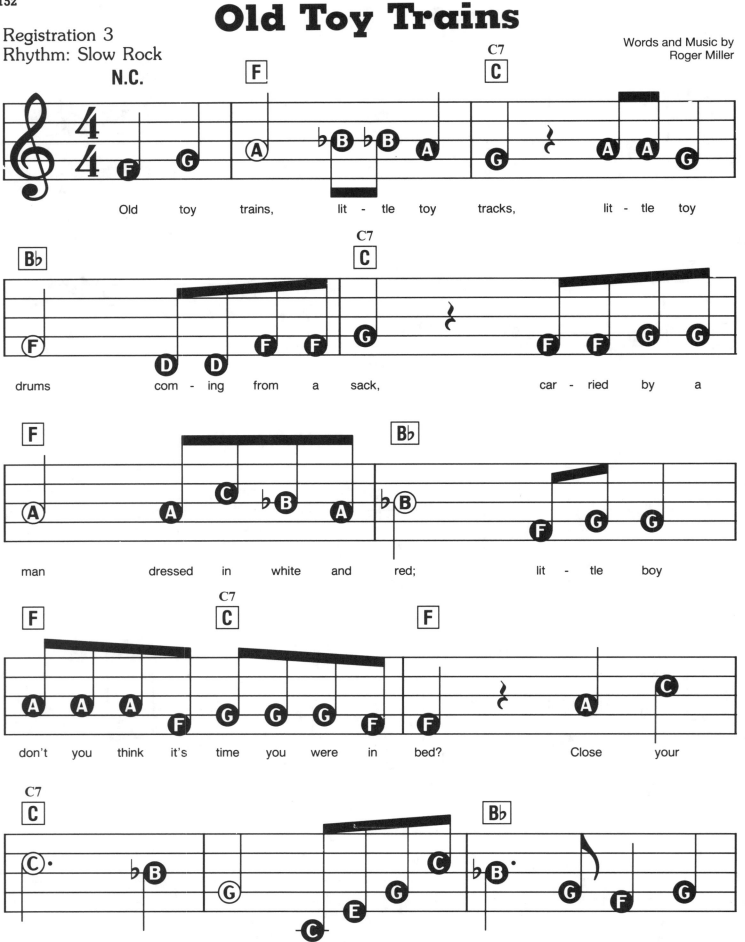

153

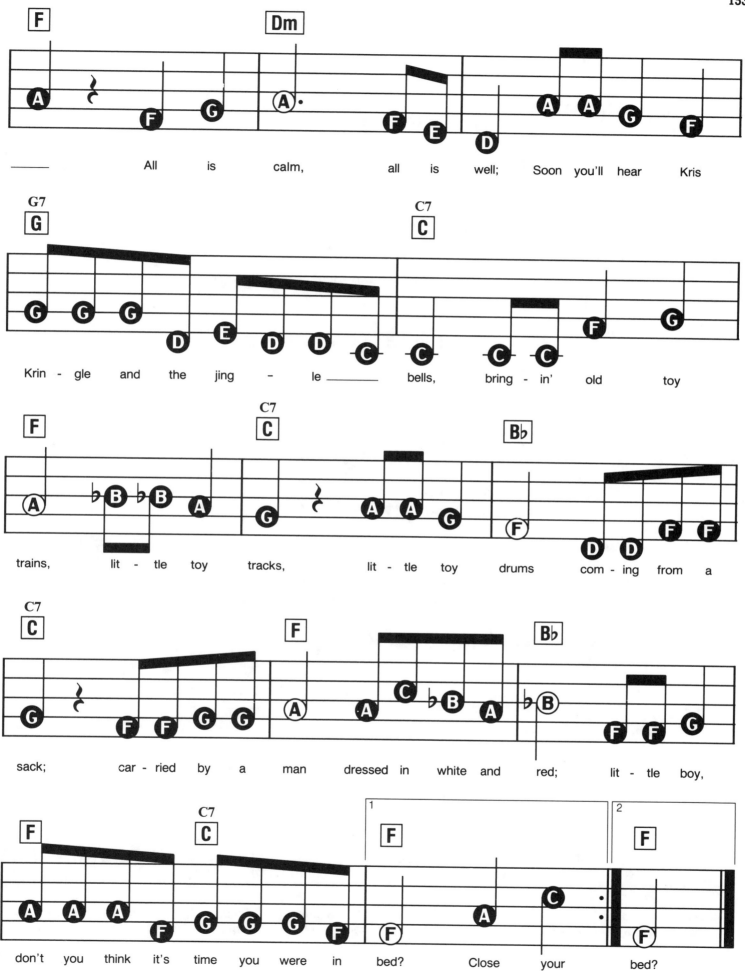

Once In Royal David's City

Registration 10
Rhythm: Pops

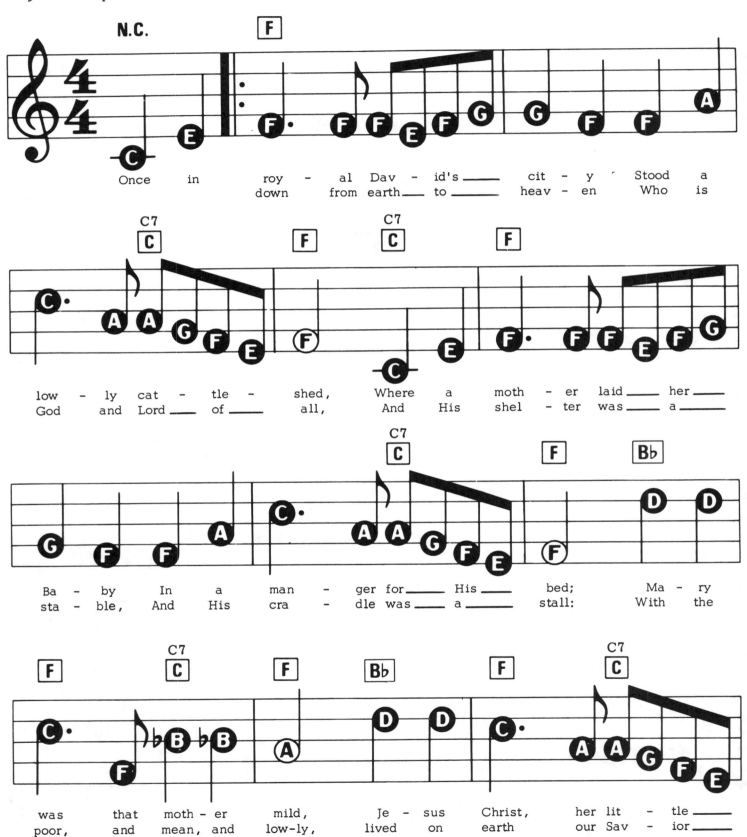

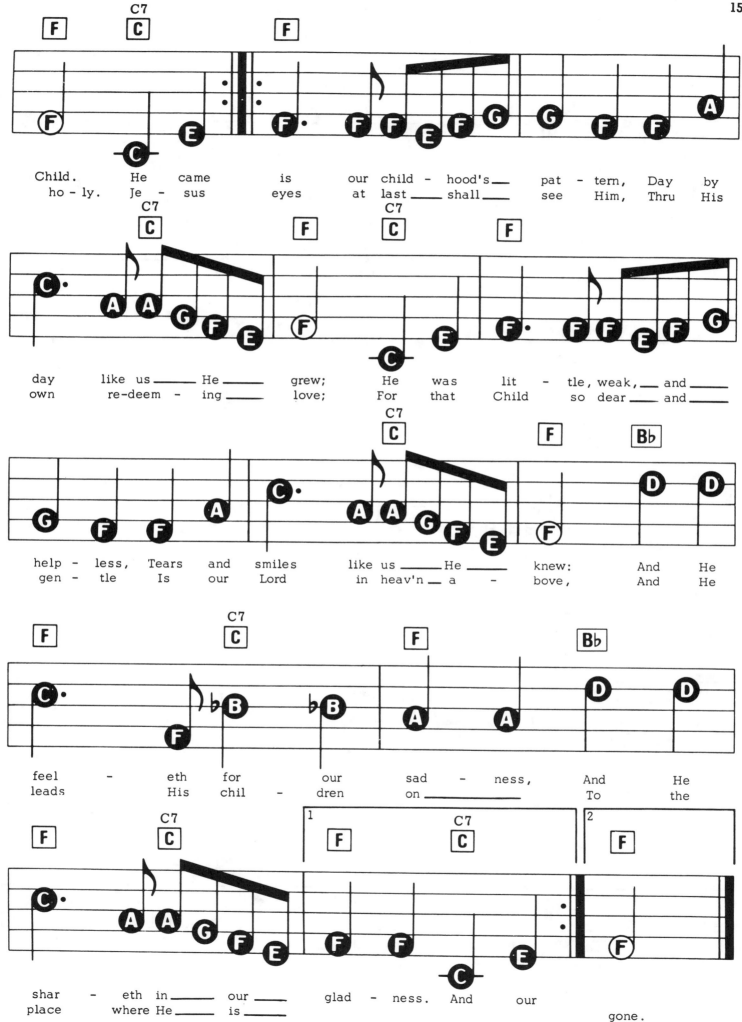

Pretty Paper

Registration 3
Rhythm: Waltz

Words and Music by
Willie Nelson

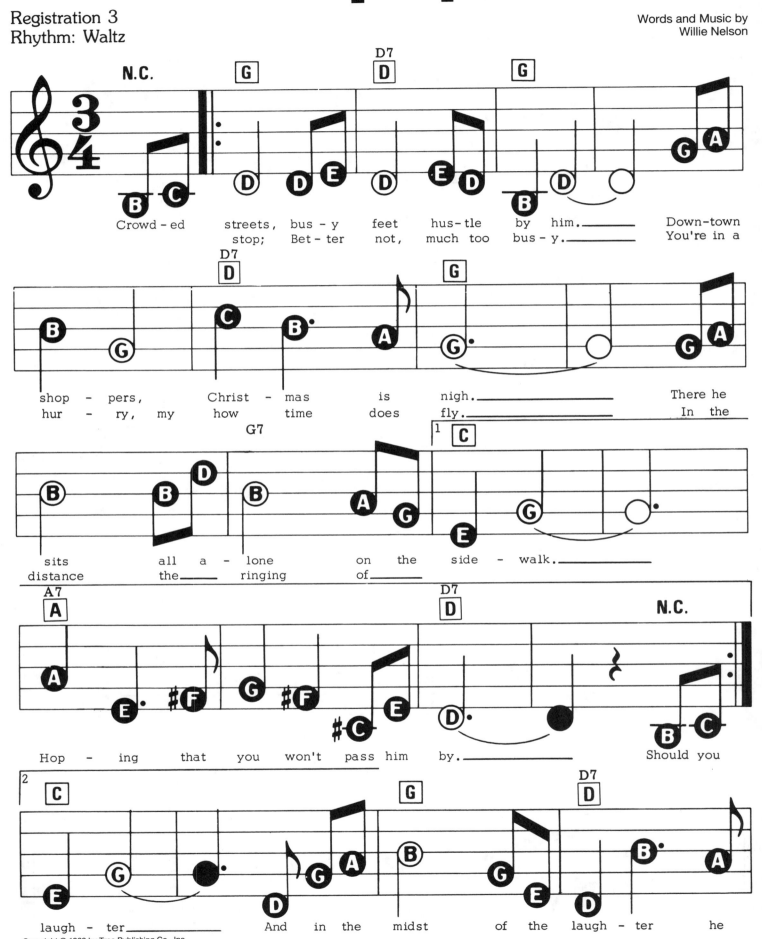

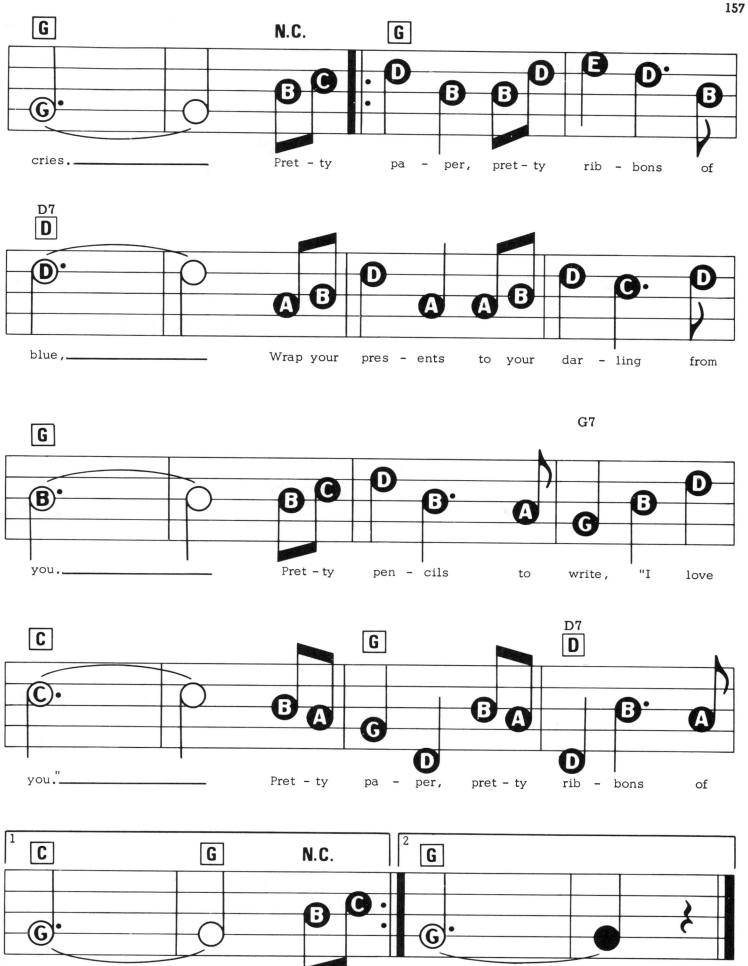

Rockin' Around The Christmas Tree

Registration 7
Rhythm: Fox Trot, Polka or Shuffle

Music and Lyrics by
Johnny Marks

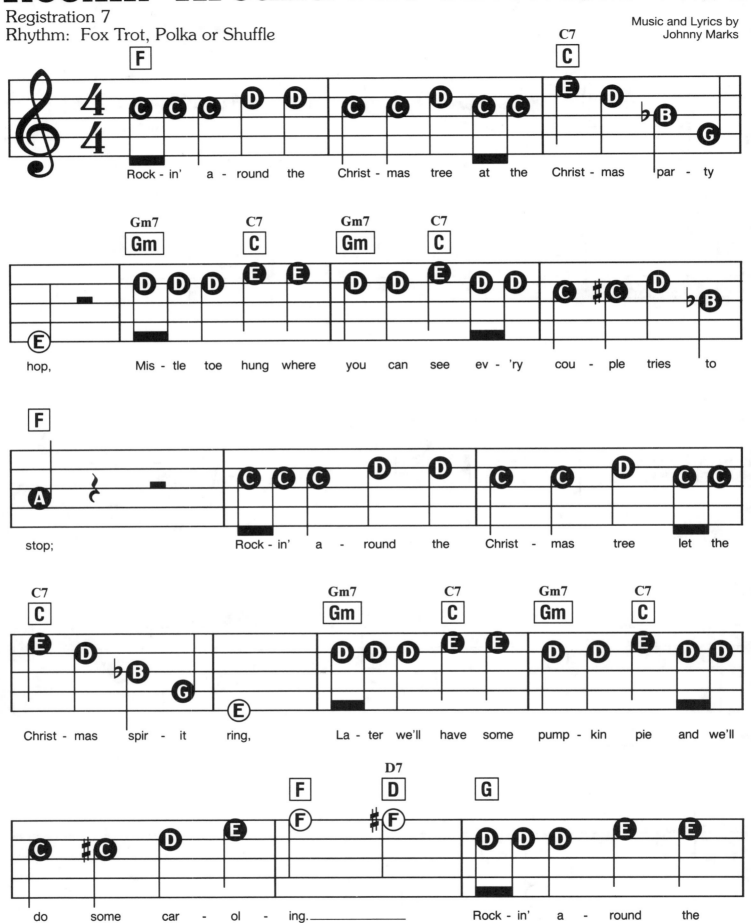

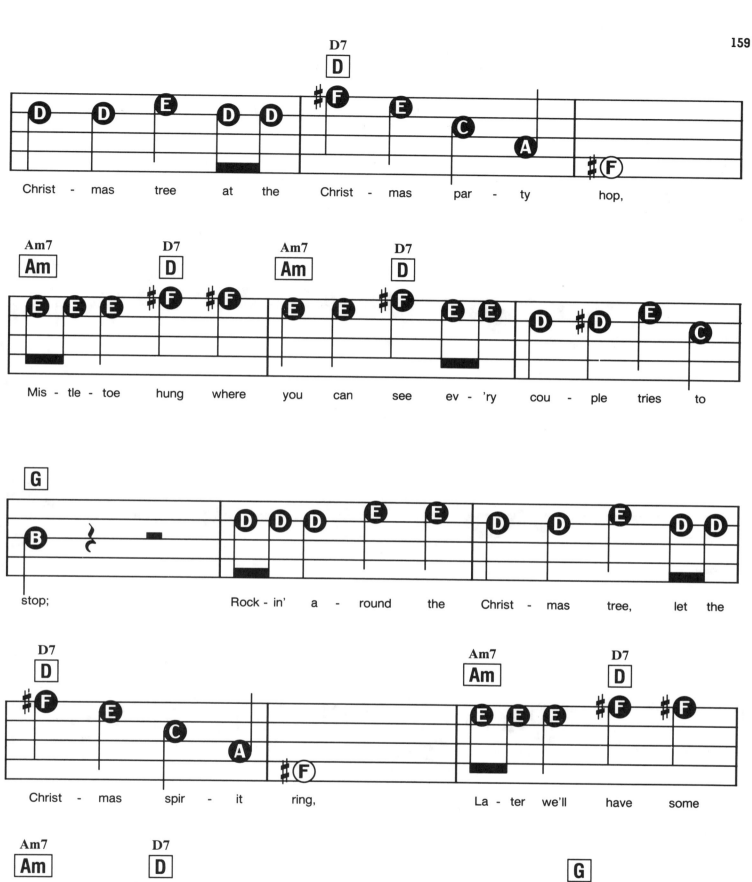

Christ - mas tree at the Christ - mas par - ty hop,

Mis - tle - toe hung where you can see ev - 'ry cou - ple tries to

stop; Rock - in' a - round the Christ - mas tree, let the

Christ - mas spir - it ring, La - ter we'll have some

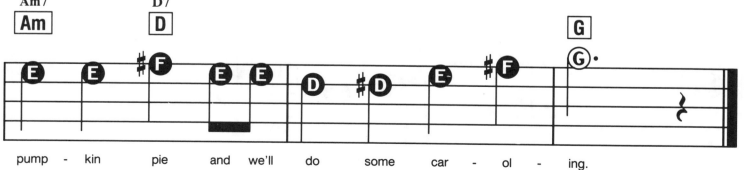

pump - kin pie and we'll do some car - ol - ing.

Rudolph The Red-Nosed Reindeer

Registration 4
Rhythm: Fox Trot or Swing

Music and Lyrics by
Johnny Marks

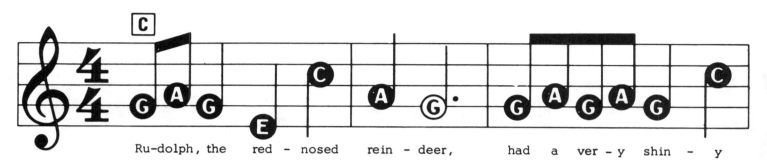

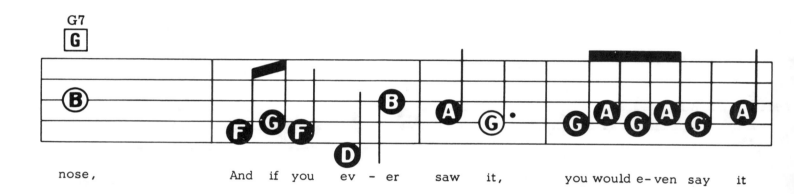

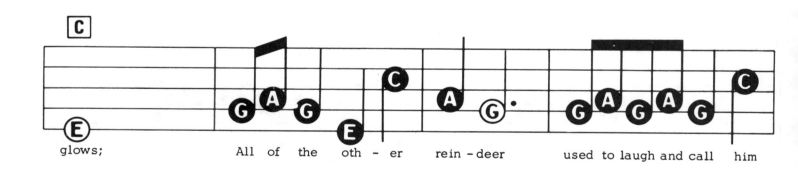

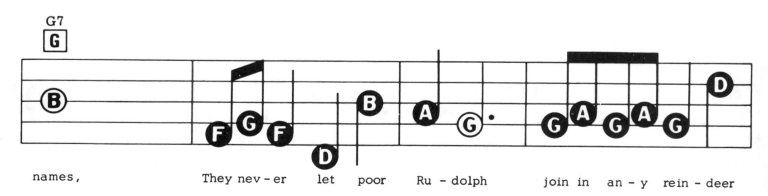

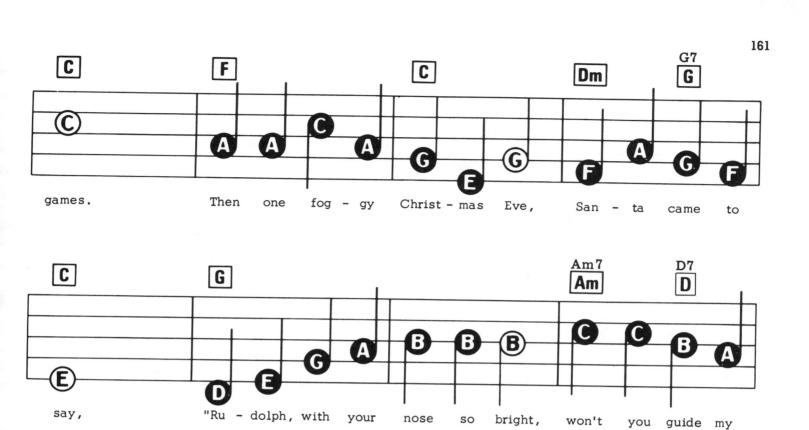

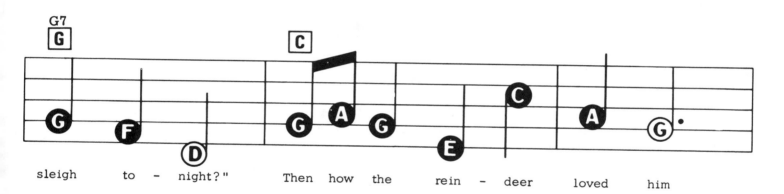

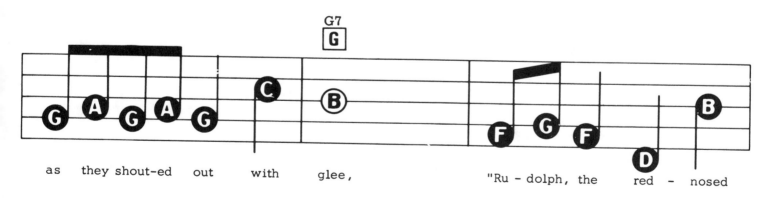

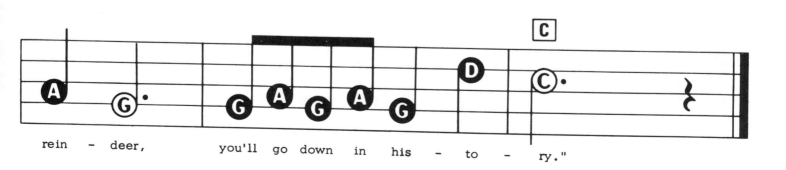

Santa Baby

Registration 3
Rhythm: Swing

Words and Music by
Joan Javits,
Phil Springer
and Tony Springer

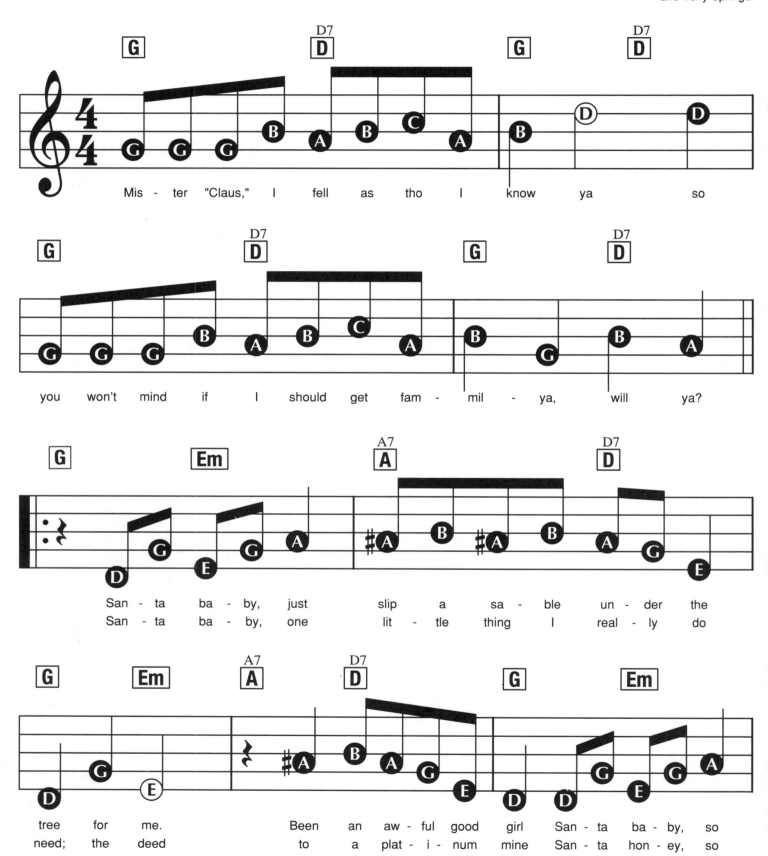

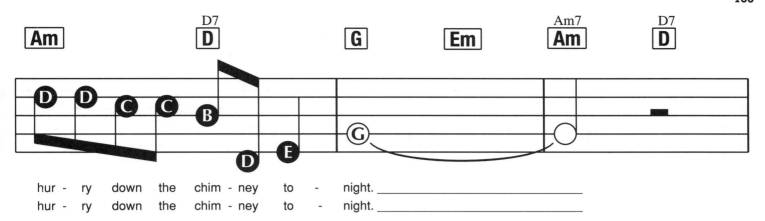

hur - ry down the chim - ney to - night. _____
hur - ry down the chim - ney to - night. _____

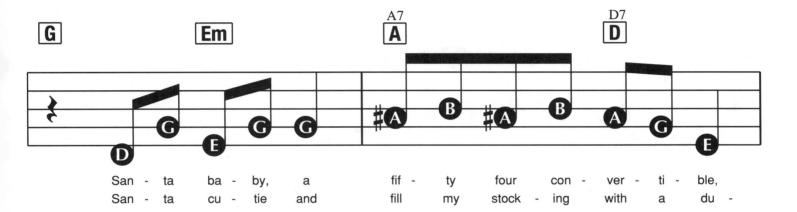

San - ta ba - by, a fif - ty four con - ver - ti - ble,
San - ta cu - tie and fill my stock - ing with a du -

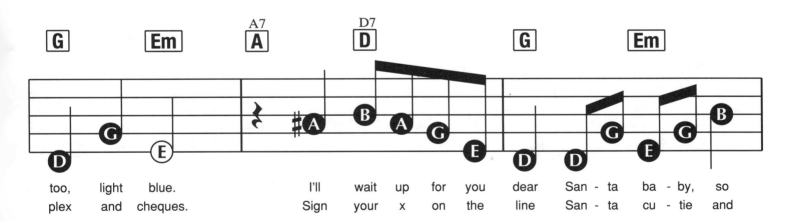

too, light blue. I'll wait up for you dear San - ta ba - by, so
plex and cheques. Sign your x on the line San - ta cu - tie and

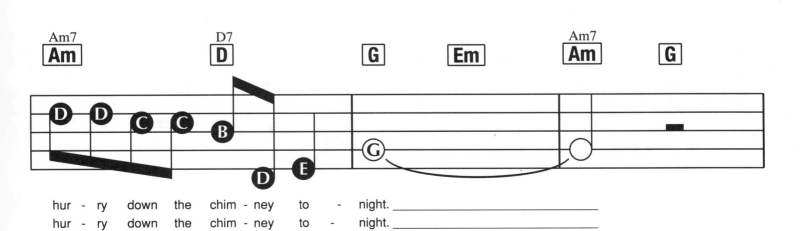

hur - ry down the chim - ney to - night. _____
hur - ry down the chim - ney to - night. _____

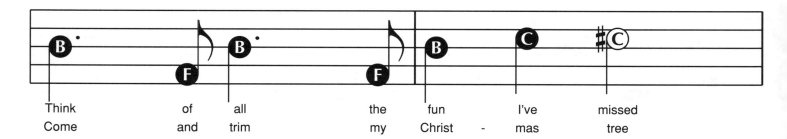

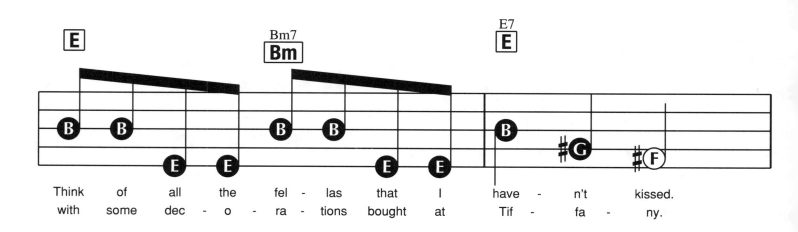

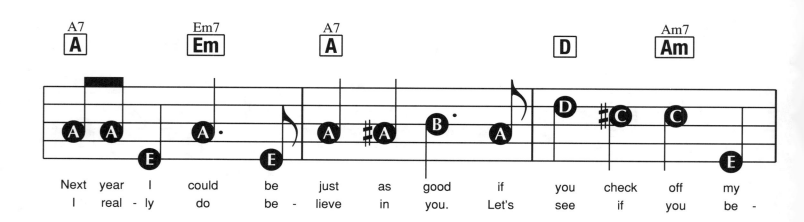

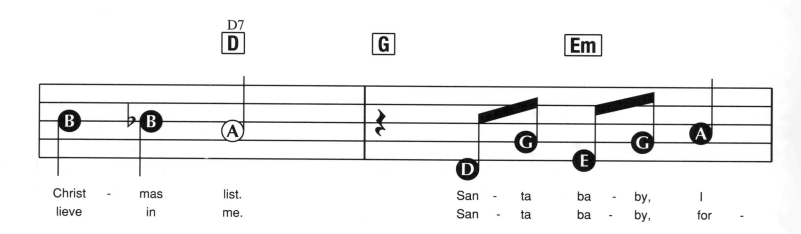

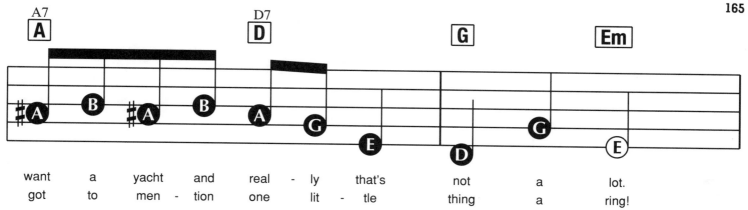

want a yacht and real - ly that's not a lot.
got to men - tion one lit - tle thing a ring!

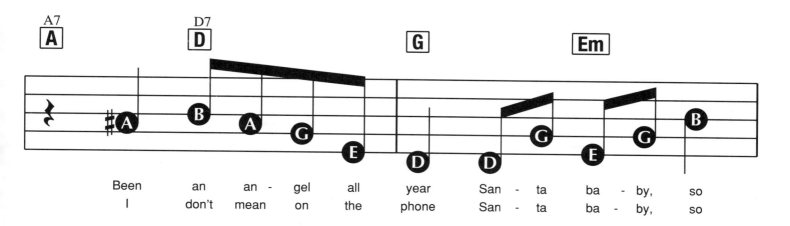

Been an an - gel all year San - ta ba - by, so
I don't mean on all the phone San - ta ba - by, so

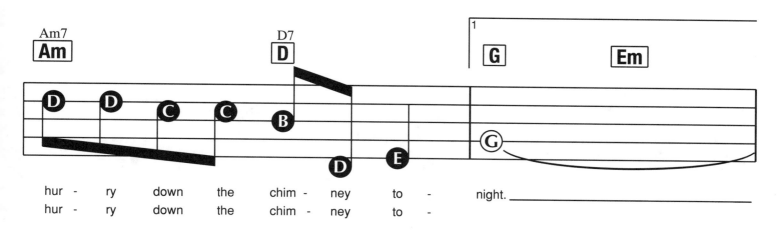

hur - ry down the chim - ney to - night. _____
hur - ry down the chim - ney to -

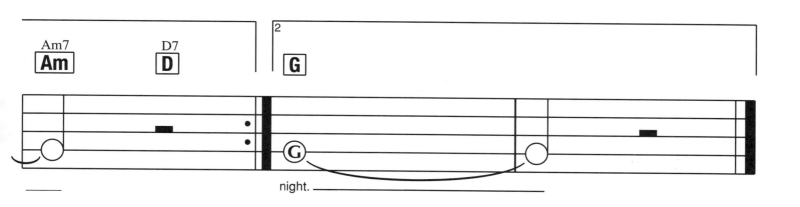

night. _____

Santa, Bring My Baby Back (To Me)

Registration 5
Rhythm: March

Words and Music by Claude DeMetrius
and Aaron Schroeder

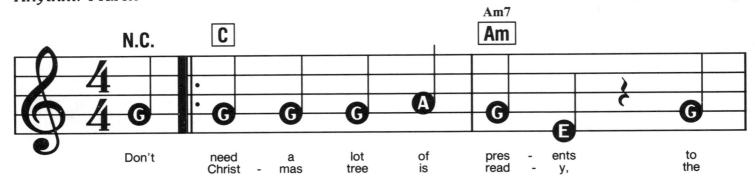

Don't need a lot of pres - ents to
Christ - mas tree is read - y, the

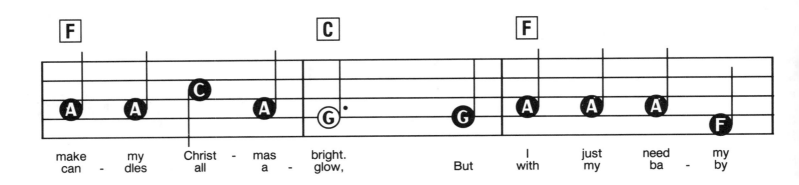

make my Christ - mas bright.
can - dles all a - glow, But I with just need my
my ba - by

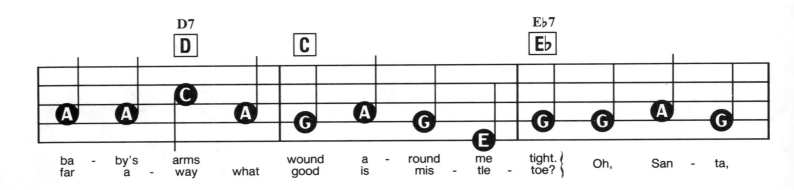

ba - by's arms wound a - round me tight. Oh, San - ta,
far a - way what good is mis - tle - toe?

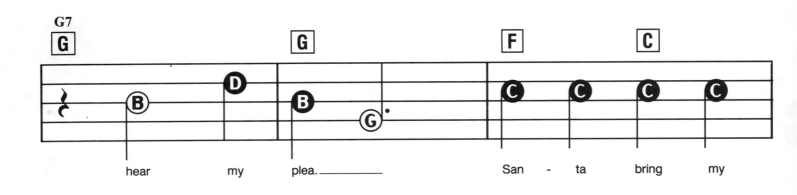

hear my plea. San - ta bring my

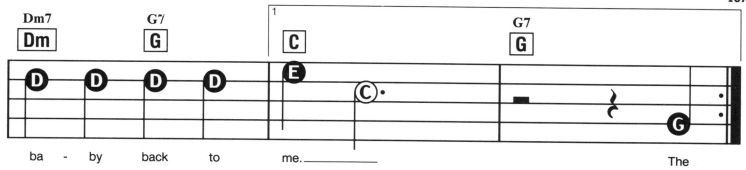

ba - by back to me._____ The

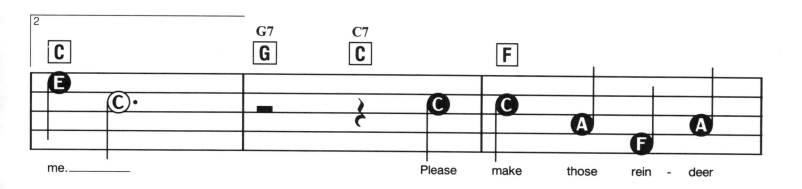

me._____ Please make those rein - deer

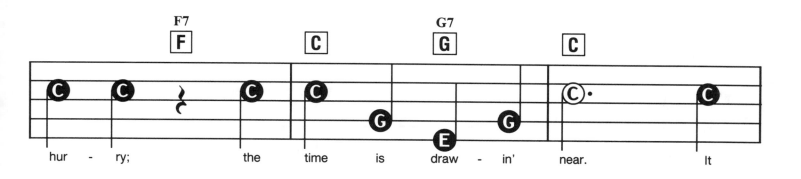

hur - ry; the time is draw - in' near. It

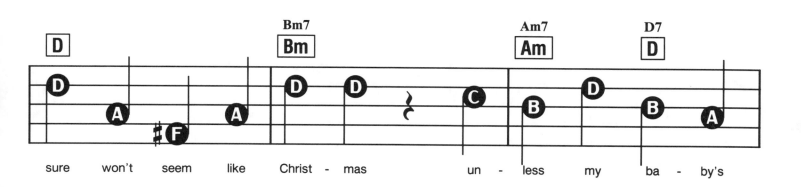

sure won't seem like Christ - mas un - less my ba - by's

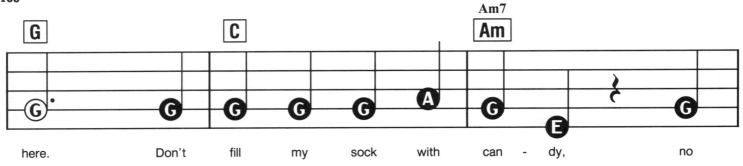

here. Don't fill my sock with can - dy, no

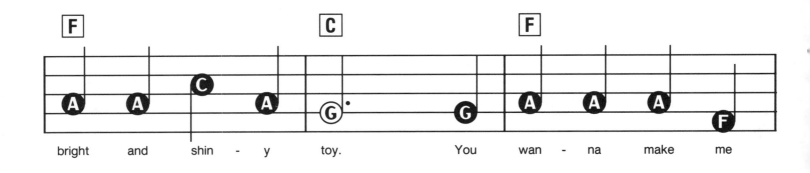

bright and shin - y toy. You wan - na make me

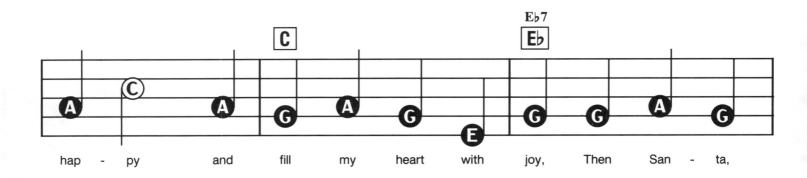

hap - py and fill my heart with joy, Then San - ta,

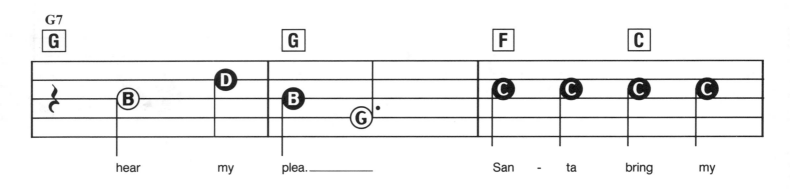

hear my plea._____ San - ta bring my

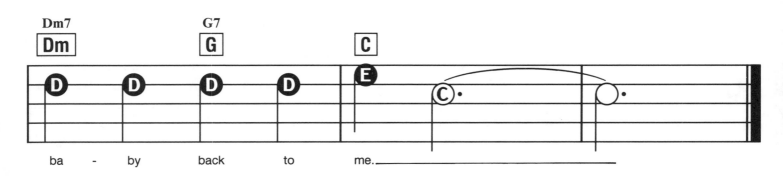

ba - by back to me._____

Shake Me I Rattle
(Squeeze Me I Cry)

Registration 3
Rhythm: Waltz

Words and Music by Hal Hackady
and Charles Naylor

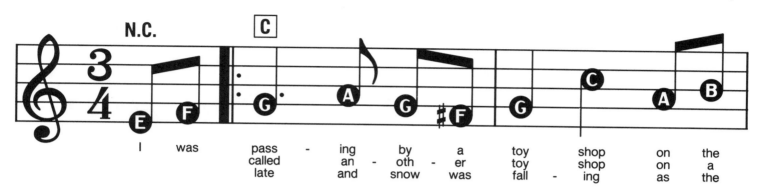

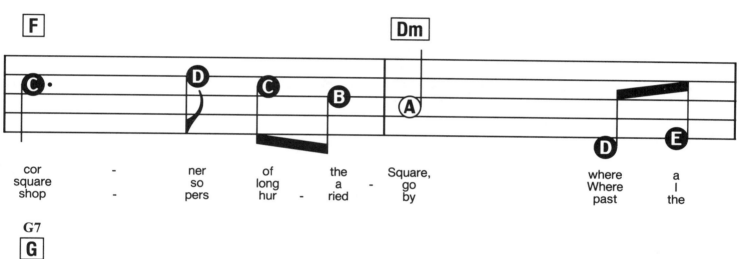

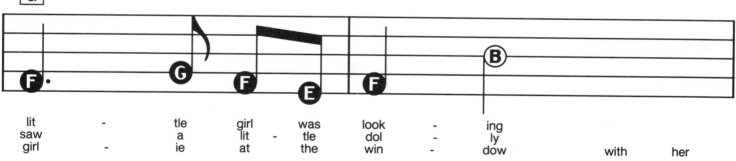

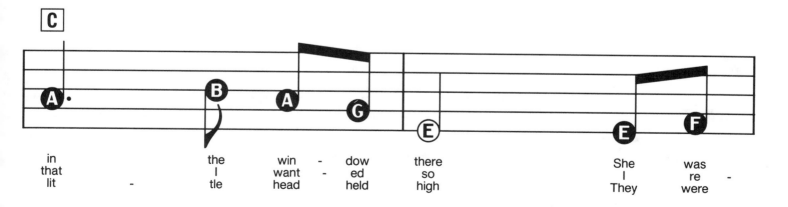

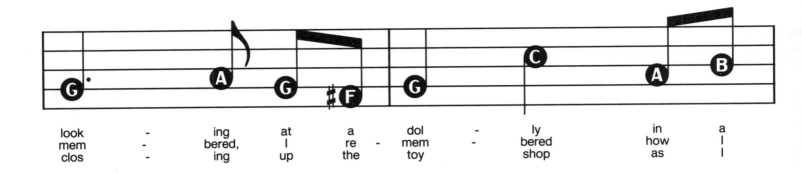

look	-		ing	at	a	dol	-	ly		in	a
mem	-		bered,	I	re -	mem	-	bered		how	all
clos	-		ing	up	the	toy		shop		as	I

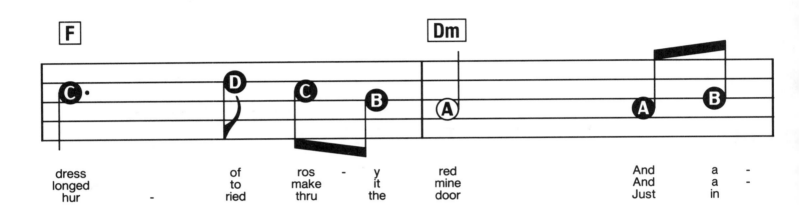

dress			of	ros	-	y	red		And	a -
longed			to	make		it	mine		And	a -
hur	-		ried	thru	the		door		Just	in

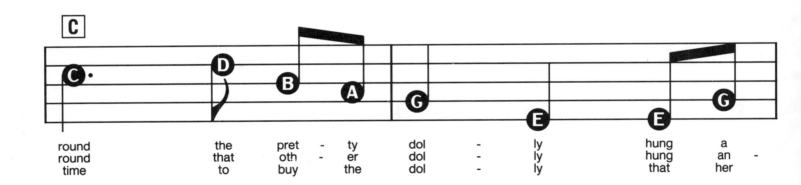

round			the	pret	-	ty	dol	-	ly		hung	a
round			that	oth	-	er	dol	-	ly		hung	an -
time			to	buy	the	dol	-	ly		that	her

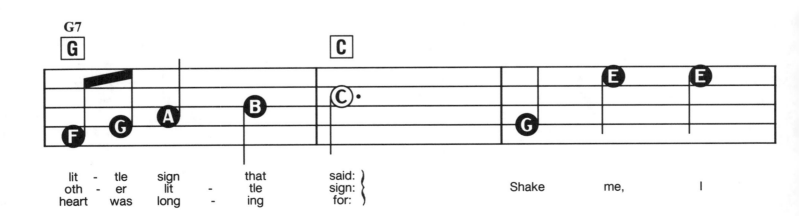

lit	-	tle	sign		that	said:	Shake	me,	I
oth	-	er	sign	lit -	tle	sign:			
heart	was	long	-	ing	for:				

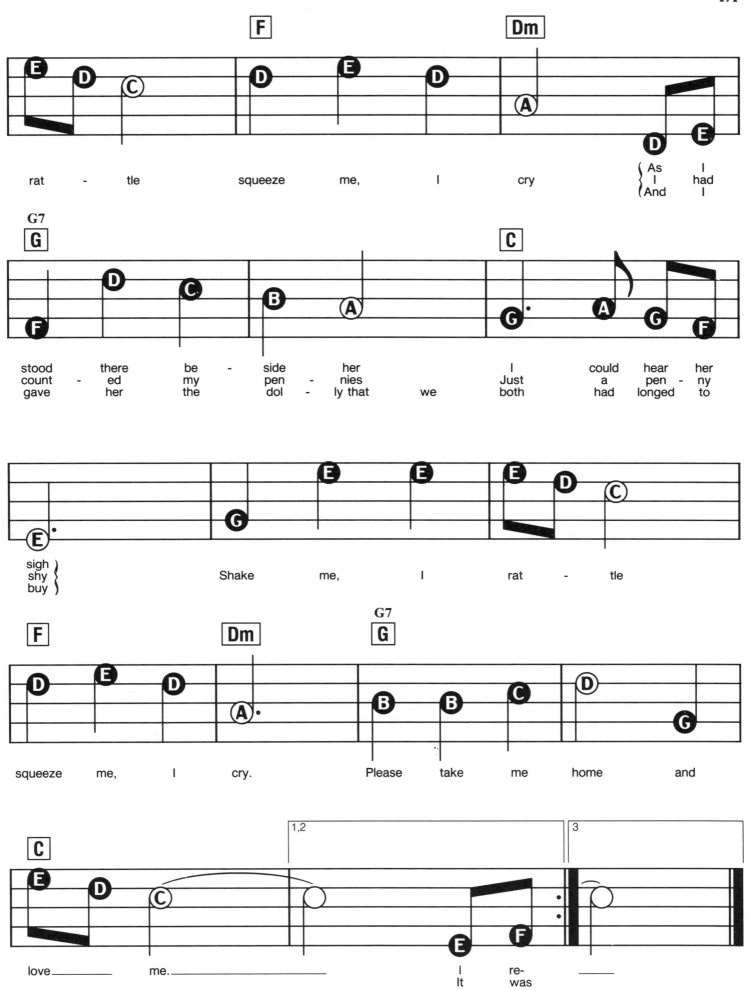

Santa Claus Is Coming To Town

Registration 3
Rhythm: Swing or Big Band

Words by Haven Gillespie
Music by J. Fred Coots

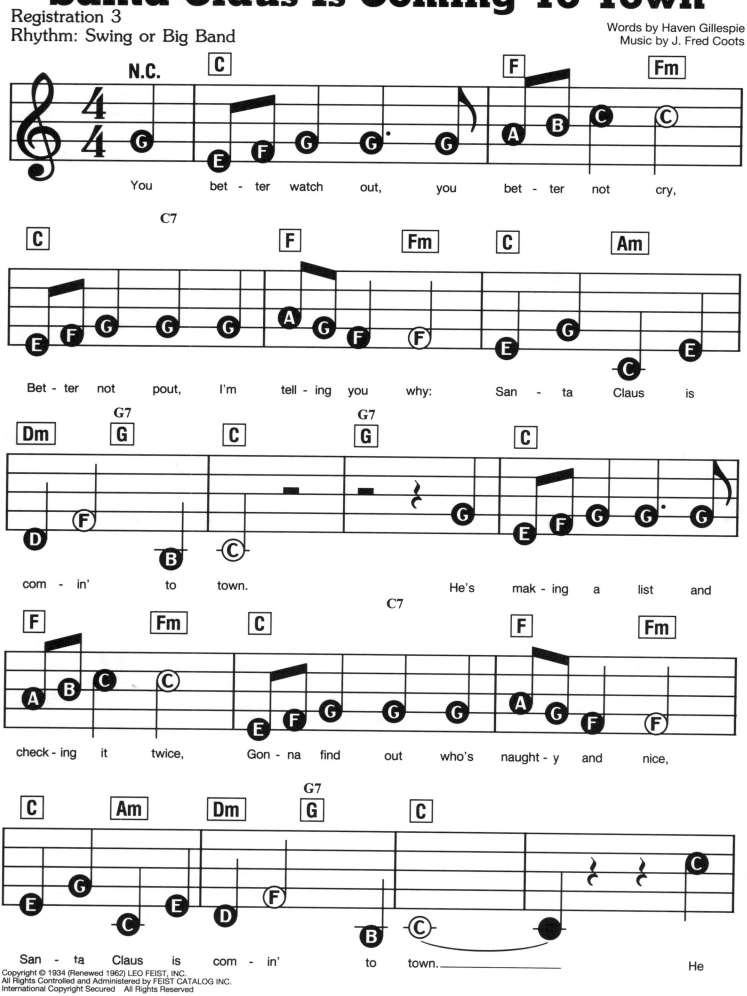

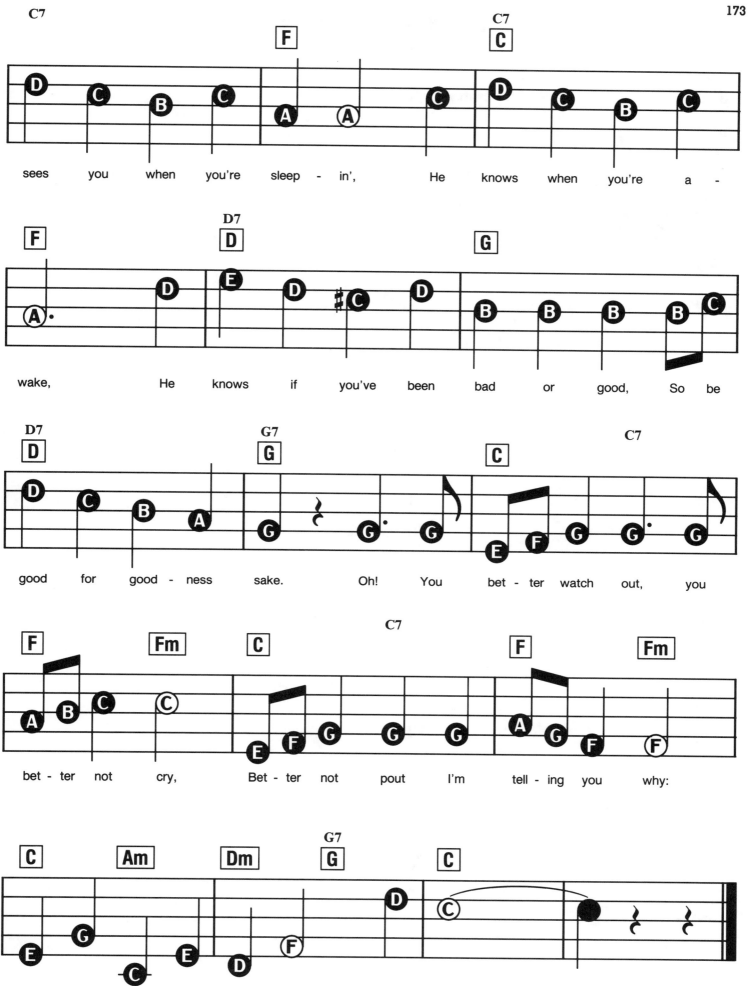

Silent Night

Registration 1
Rhythm: Waltz

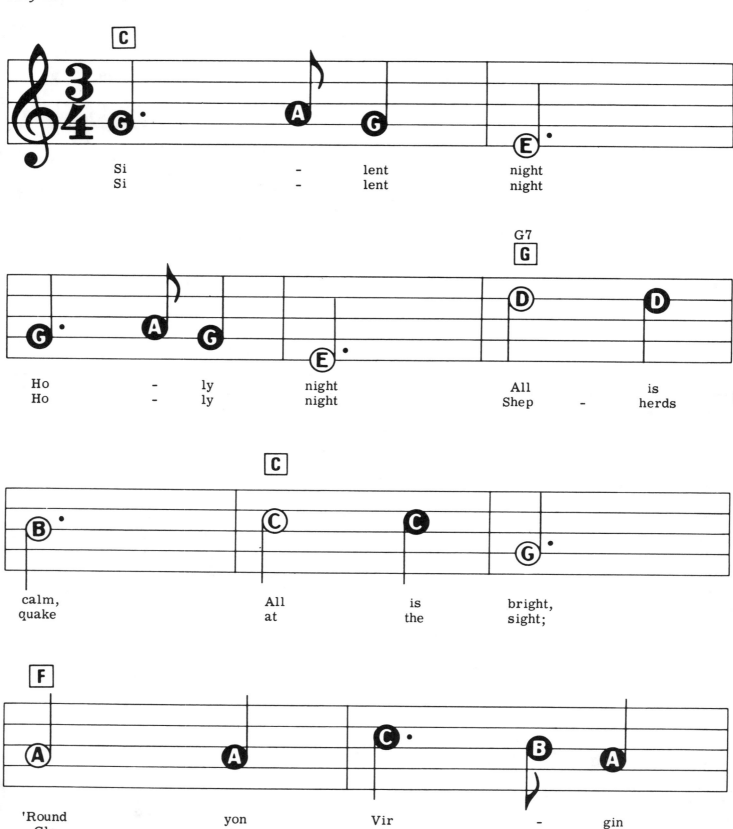

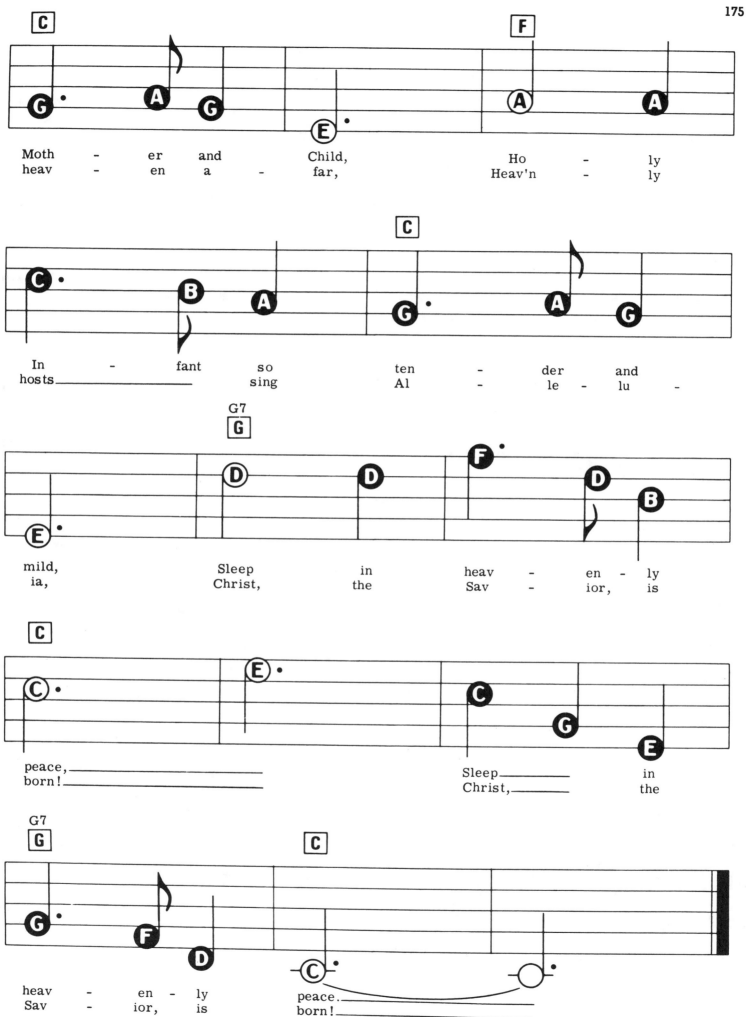

Silver And Gold

Registration 2
Rhythm: Waltz

Music and Lyrics by
Johnny Marks

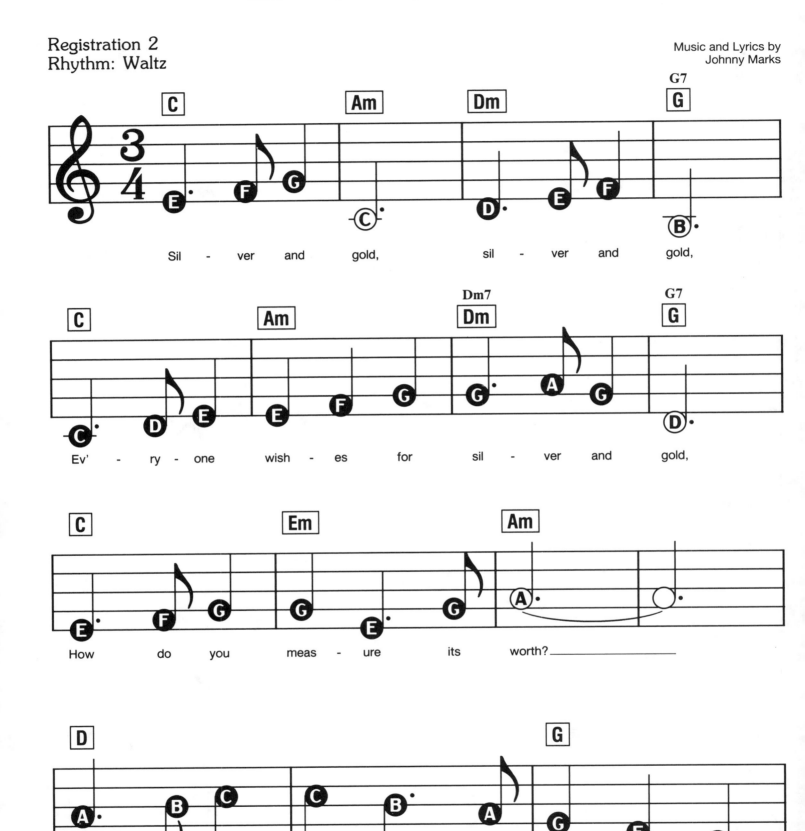

Silver Bells

Registration 7
Rhythm: Waltz

Words and Music by Jay Livingston
and Ray Evans

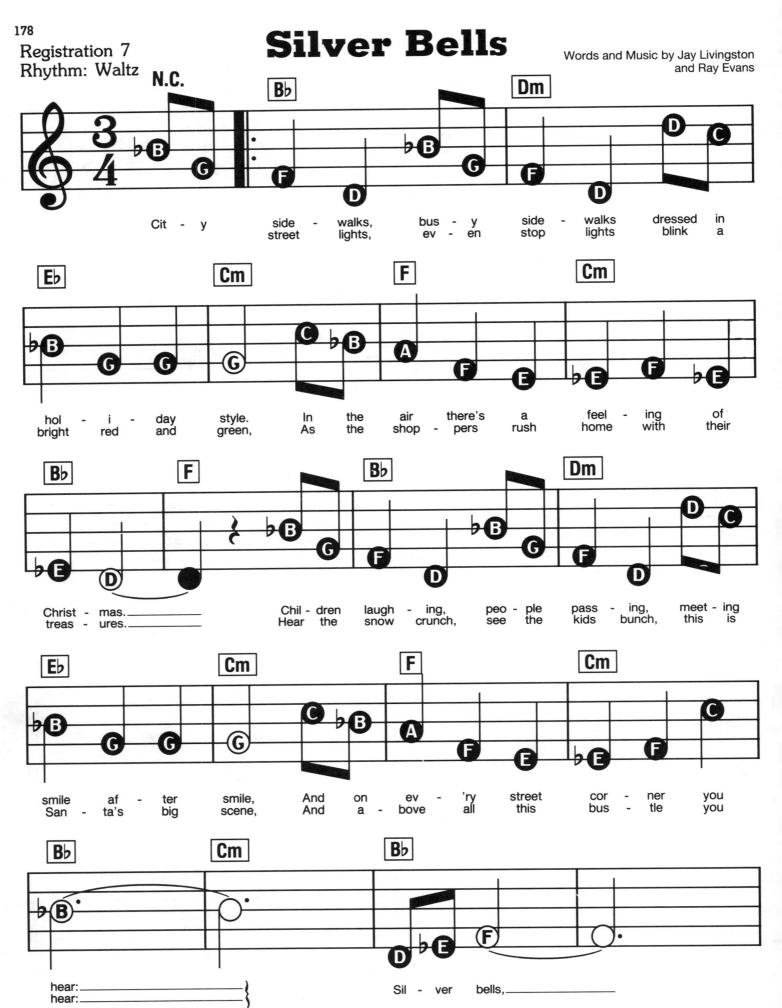

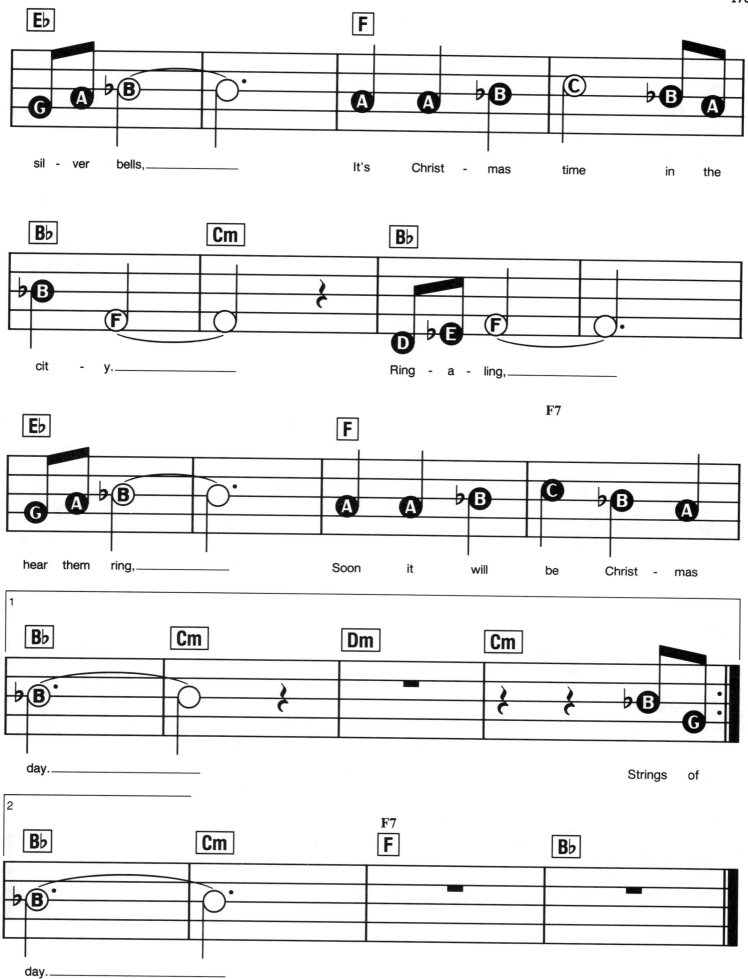

Sleigh Ride

Words by Mitchell Parish
Music by LeRoy Anderson

Registration 8
Rhythm: Fox Trot or Swing

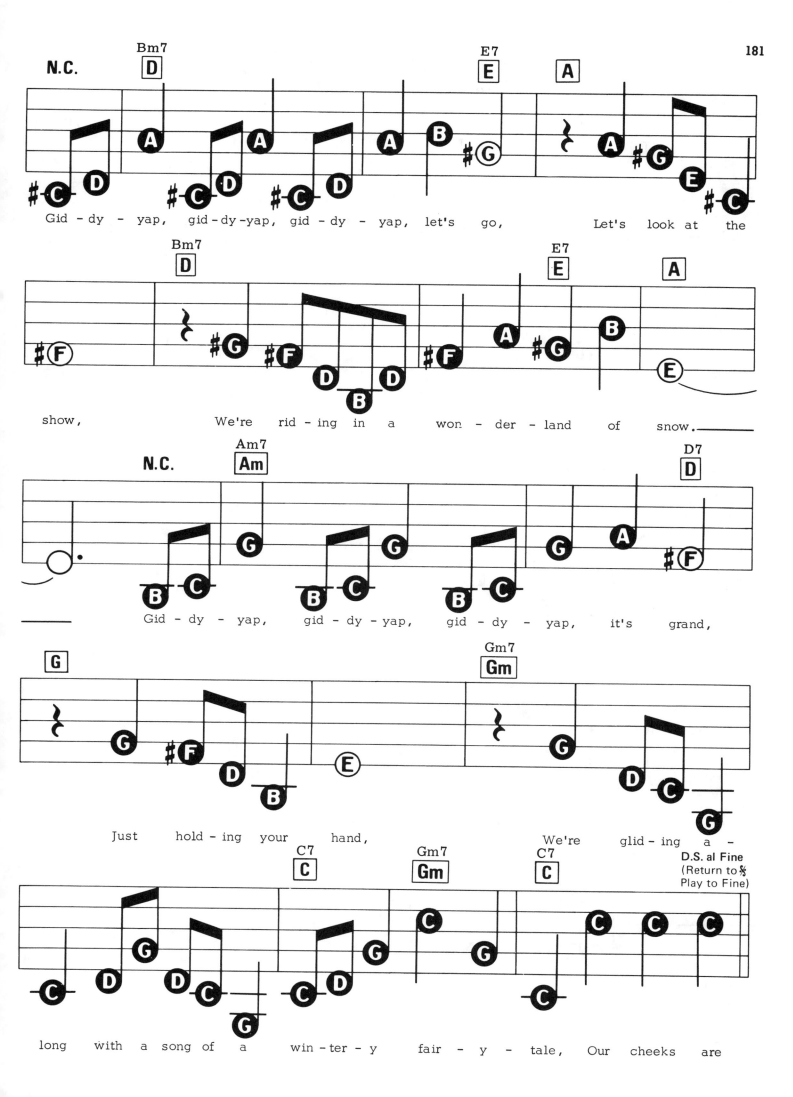

Suzy Snowflake

Registration 2
Rhythm: Fox Trot or Swing

Words and Music by Sid Tepper
and Roy Bennett

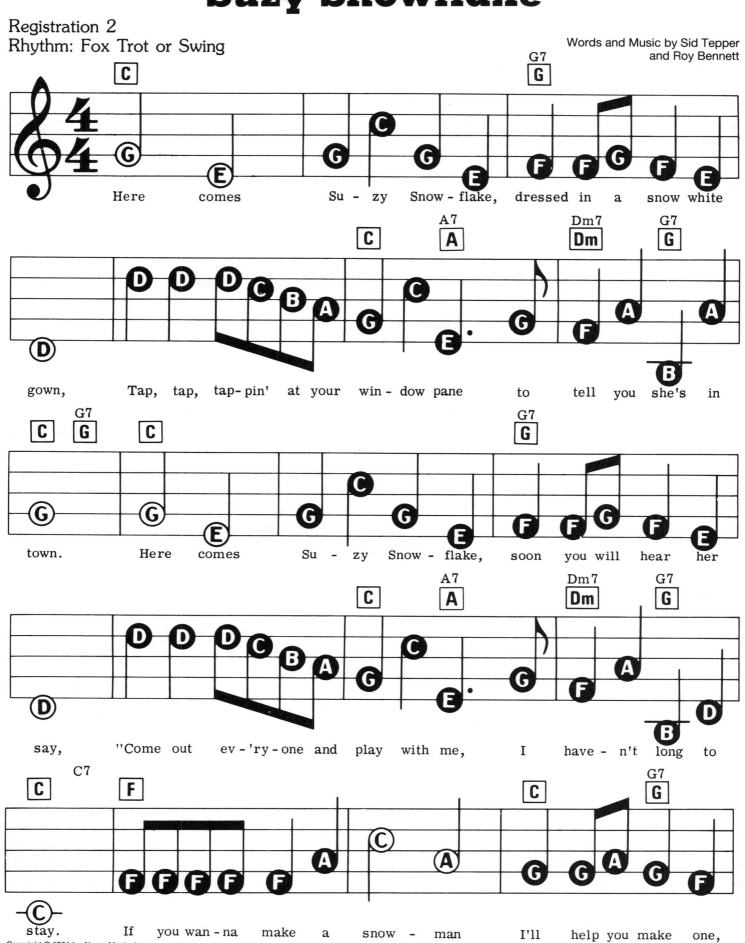

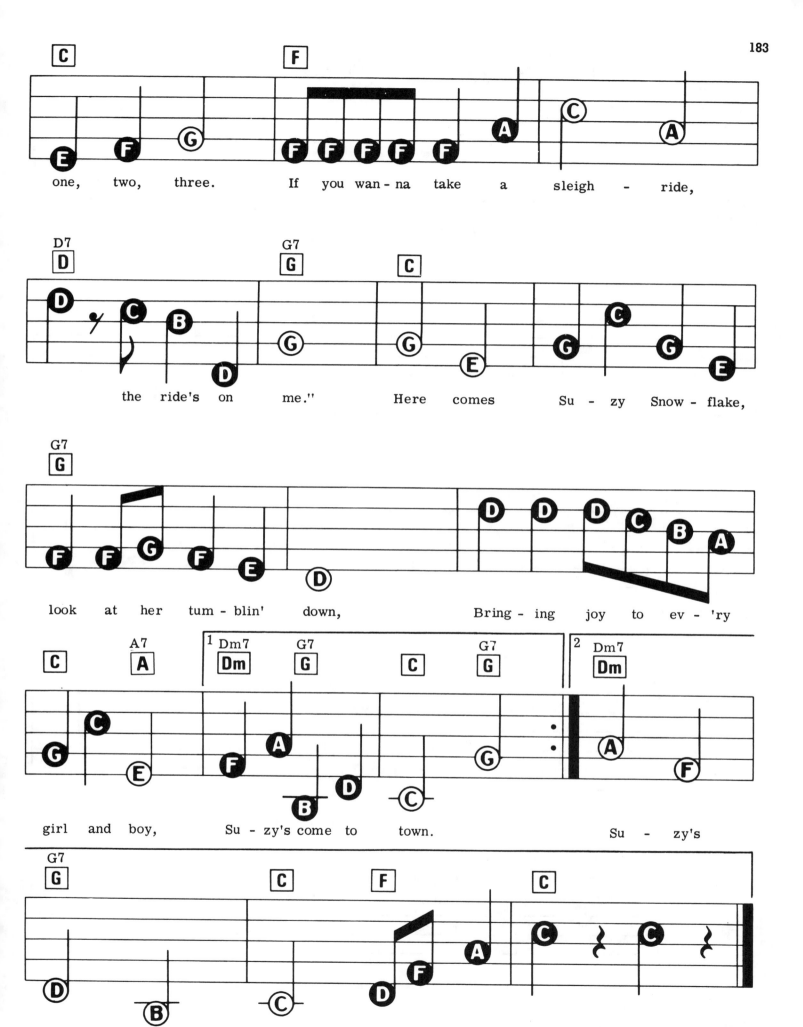

That Christmas Feeling

Registration 1
Rhythm: Fox Trot or Swing

Words and Music by Bennie Benjamin
and George Weiss

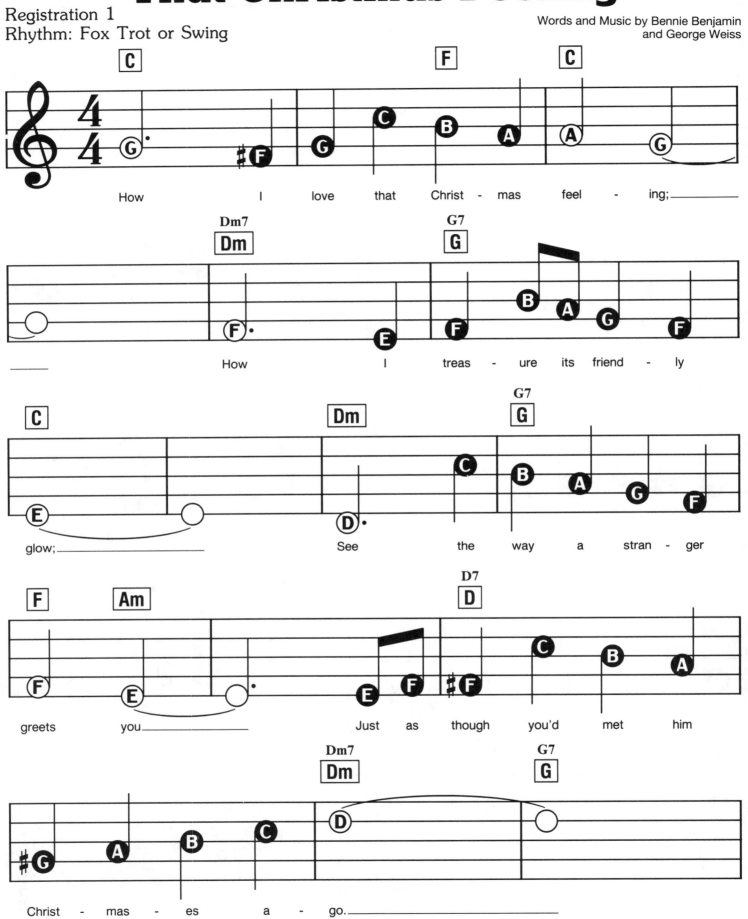

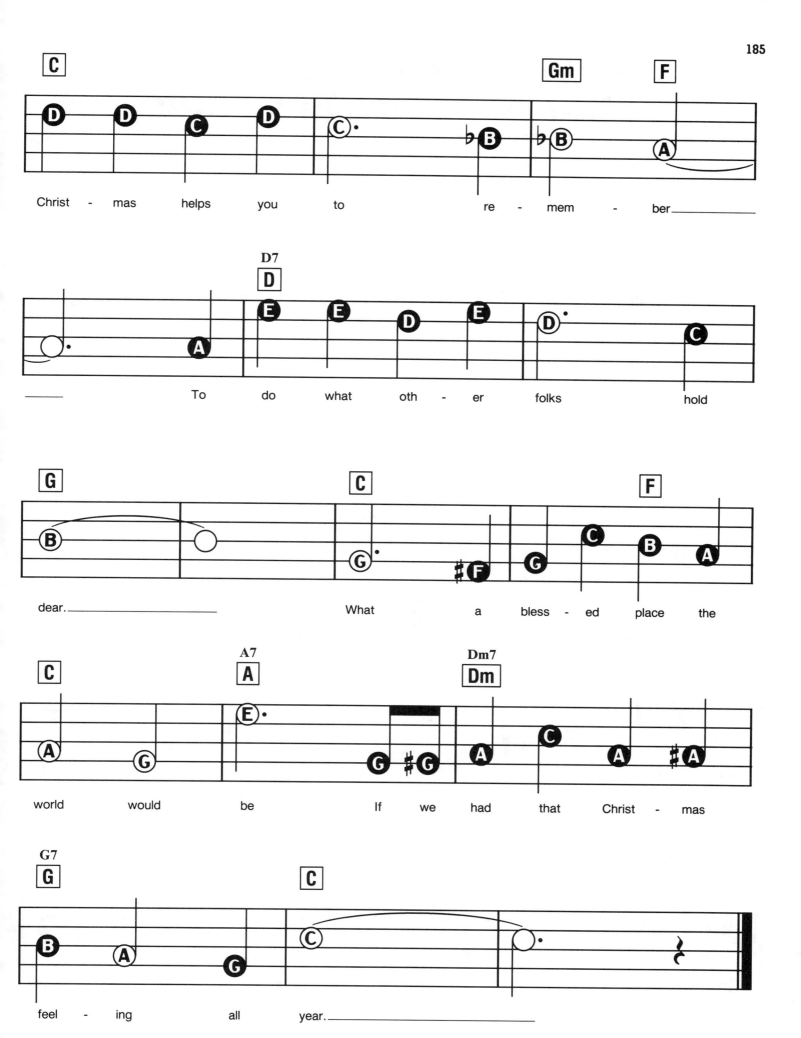

There Is No Christmas Like A Home Christmas

Registration 4
Rhythm: Fox Trot or Swing

Words by Carl Sigman
Music by Mickey J. Addy

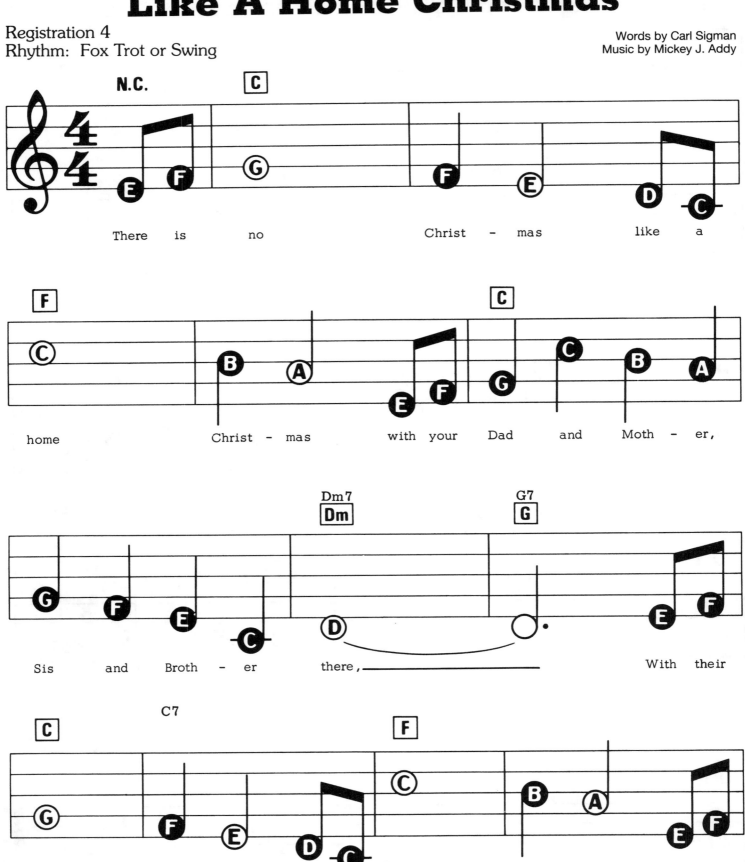

Toyland

Registration 4
Rhythm: Waltz

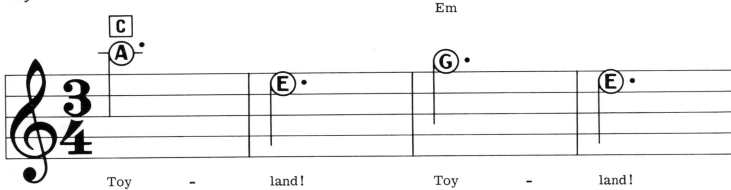

Toy - land! Toy - land!

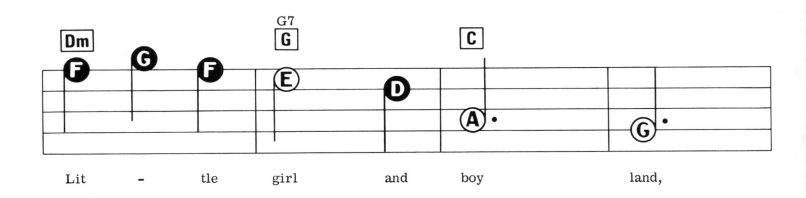

Lit - tle girl and boy land,

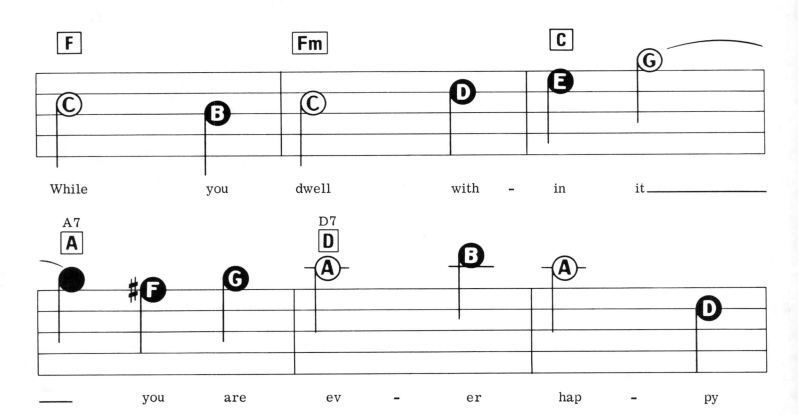

While you dwell with - in it _____

_____ you are ev - er hap - py

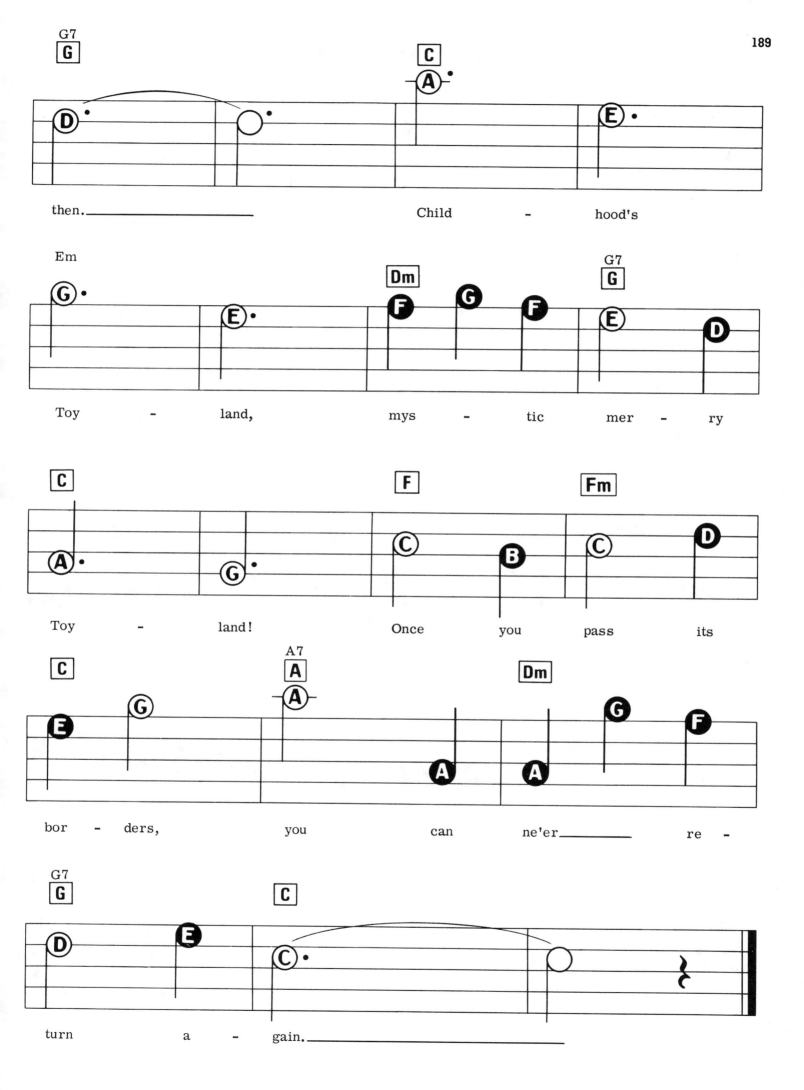

then._____ Child - hood's

Toy - land, mys - tic mer - ry

Toy - land! Once you pass its

bor - ders, you can ne'er_____ re -

turn a - gain._____

The Twelve Days Of Christmas

Registration 5
Rhythm: None

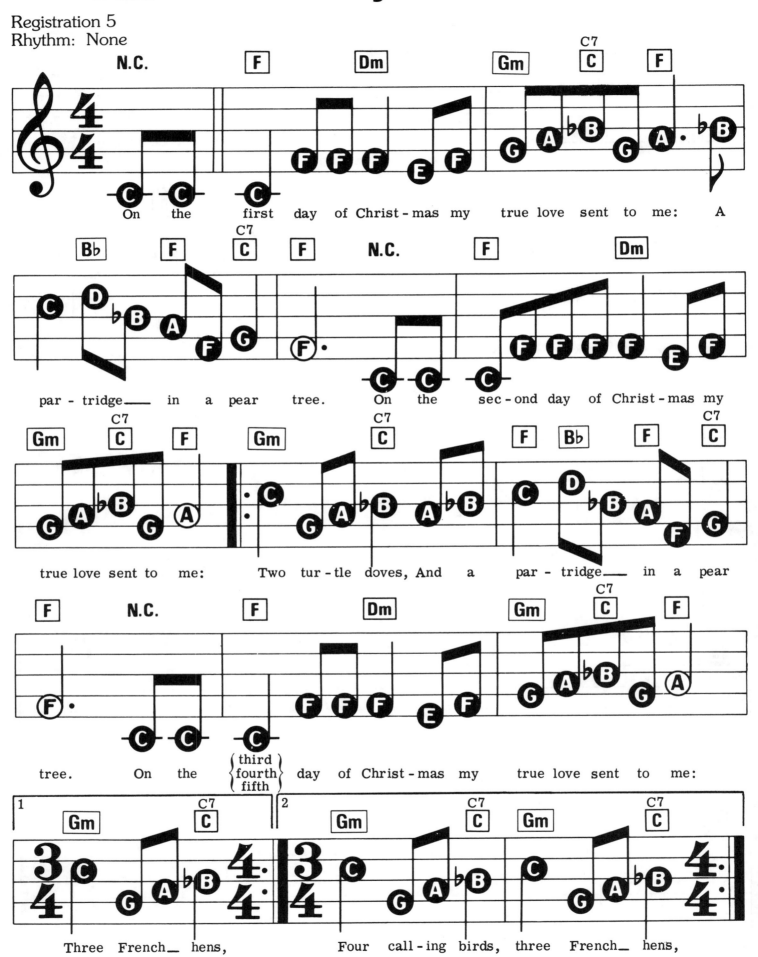

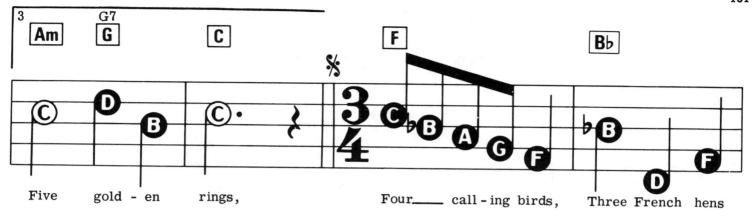

Five gold - en rings, Four___ call - ing birds, Three French hens

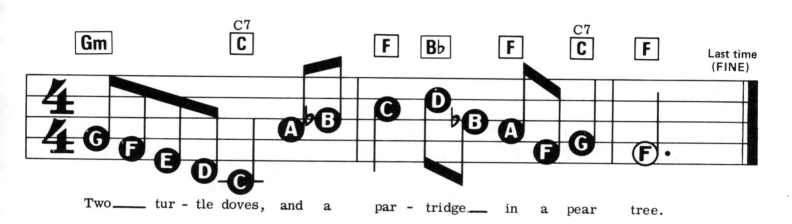

Two___ tur - tle doves, and a par - tridge___ in a pear tree.

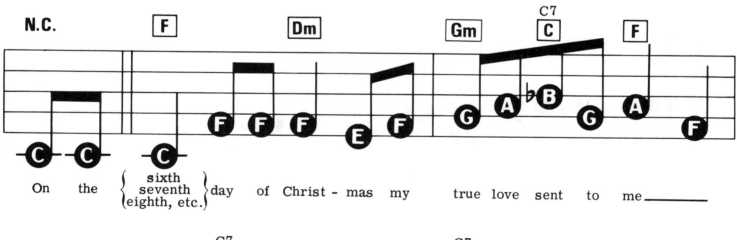

On the { sixth / seventh / eighth, etc. } day of Christ - mas my true love sent to me____

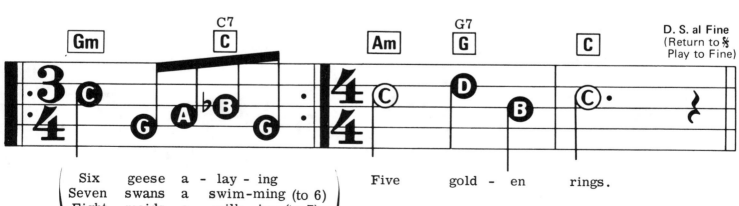

Six geese a - lay - ing
Seven swans a swim-ming (to 6)
Eight maids a milk - ing (to 7)
Nine la - dies danc - ing (to 8)
Ten lords a leap - ing (to 9)
Eleven pi - pers pip - ing (to10)
Twelve drum-mers drum-ming (to 11)

Five gold - en rings.

Up On The Housetop

Registration 5
Rhythm: Fox Trot or Ballad

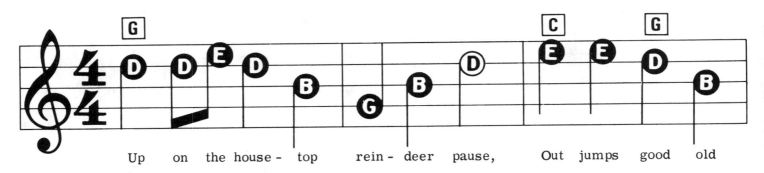

Up on the house - top rein - deer pause, Out jumps good old

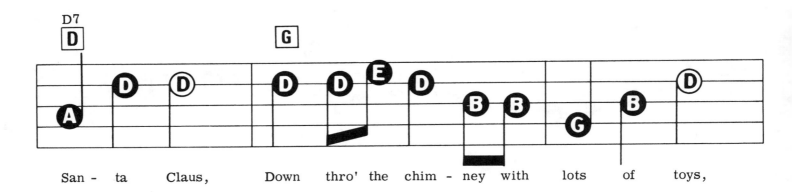

San - ta Claus, Down thro' the chim - ney with lots of toys,

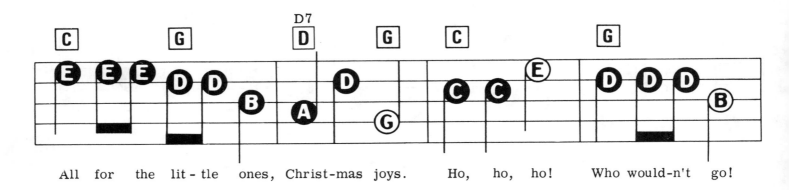

All for the lit - tle ones, Christ-mas joys. Ho, ho, ho! Who would-n't go!

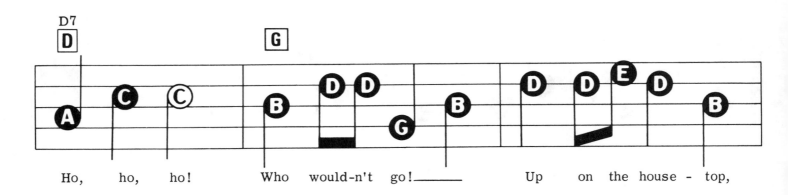

Ho, ho, ho! Who would-n't go!_____ Up on the house - top,

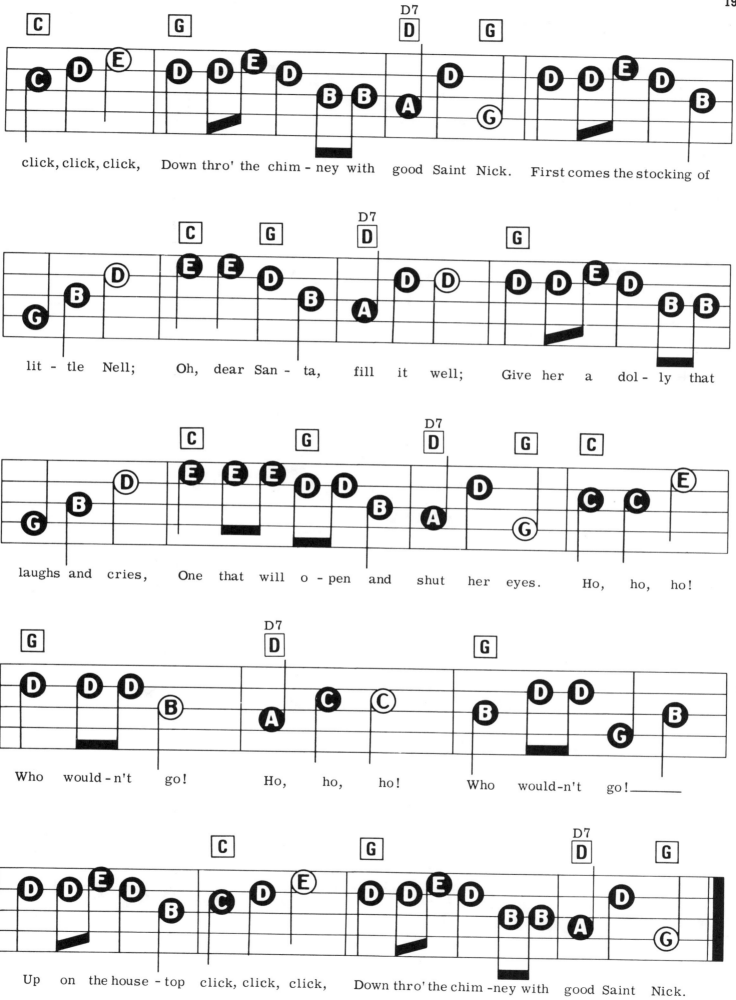

We Three Kings Of Orient Are

Registration 9
Rhythm: None

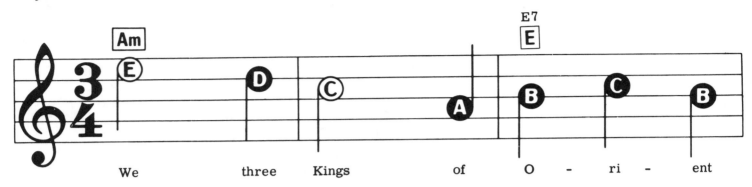

We   three   Kings   of   O - ri - ent

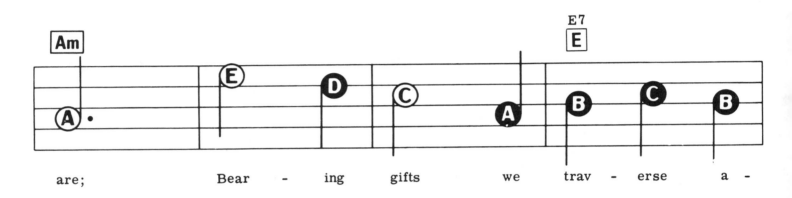

are;   Bear - ing   gifts   we   trav - erse   a -

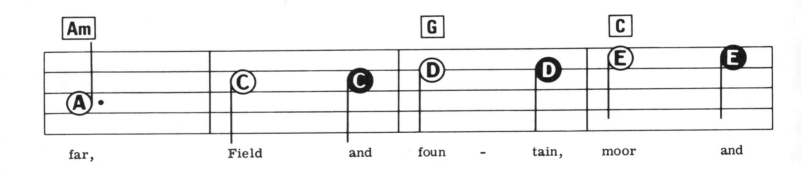

far,   Field   and   foun - tain,   moor   and

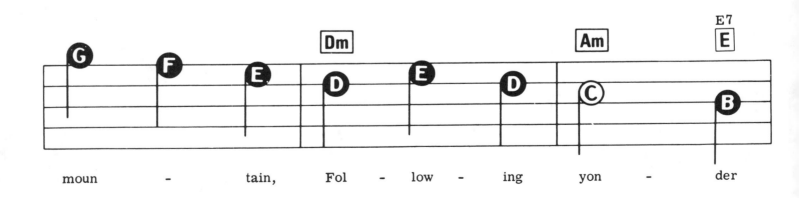

moun - tain,   Fol - low - ing   yon - der

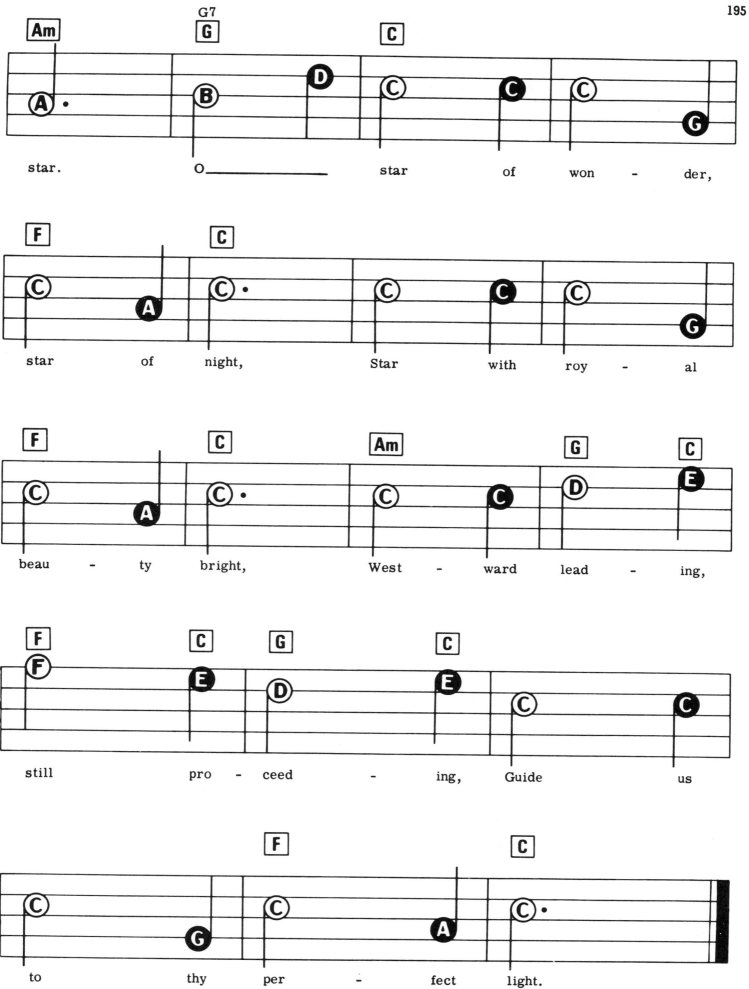

We Wish You A Merry Christmas

Registration 4
Rhythm: None

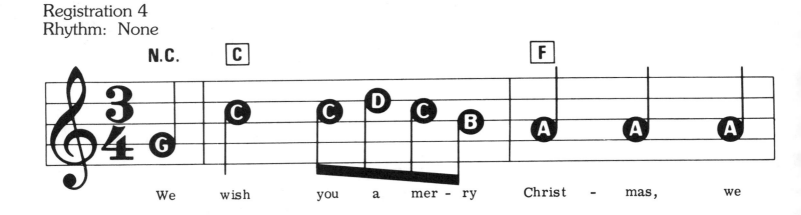

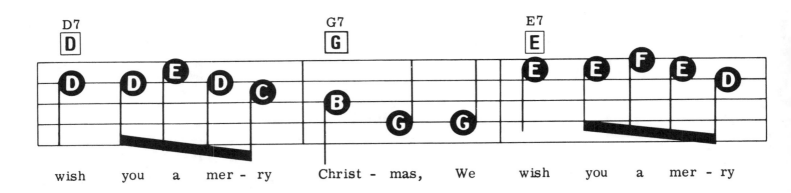

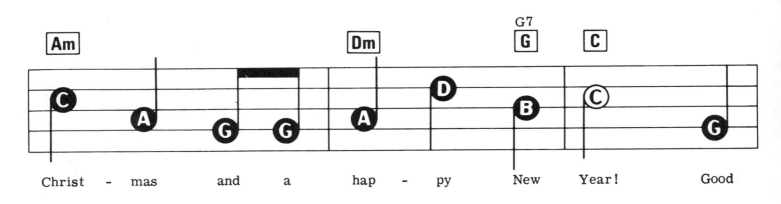

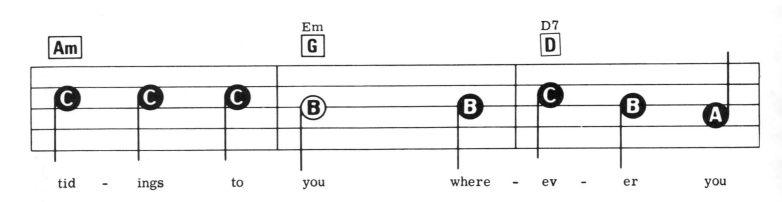

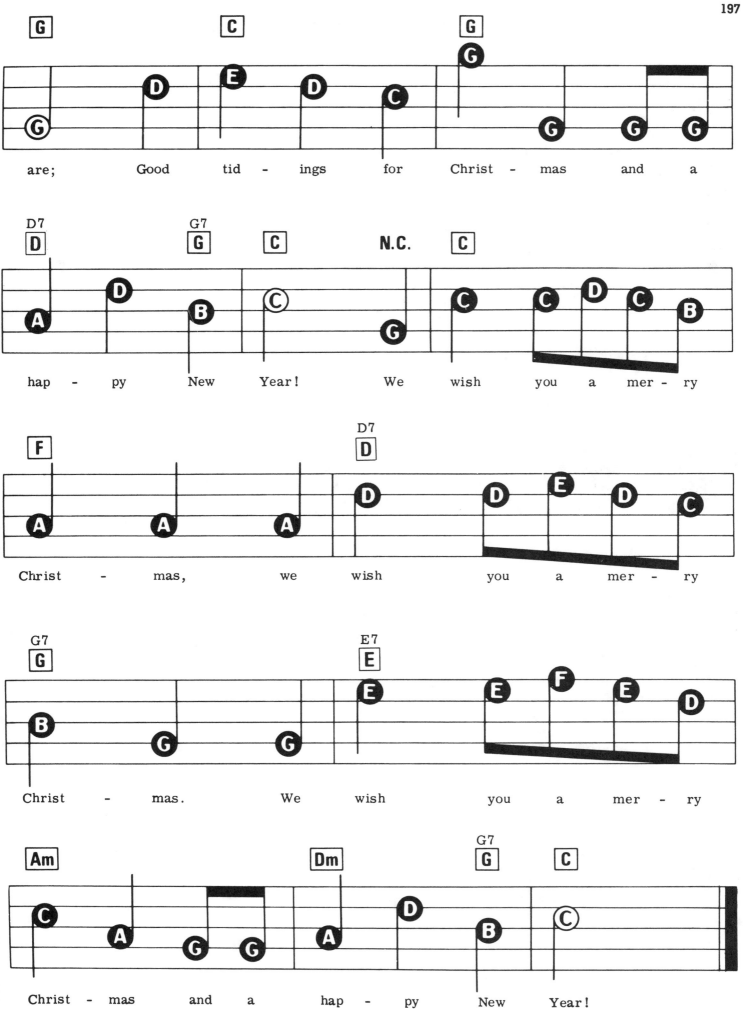

What Child Is This?

Registration 10
Rhythm: Waltz

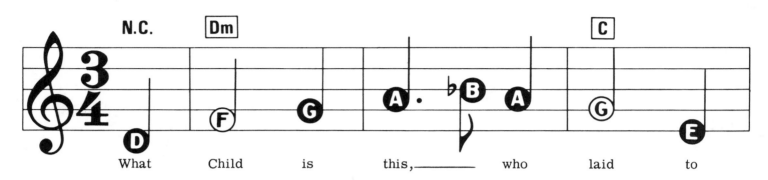

What Child is this, _____ who laid to

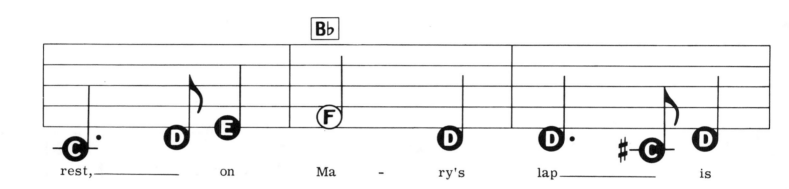

rest, _____ on Ma - ry's lap _____ is

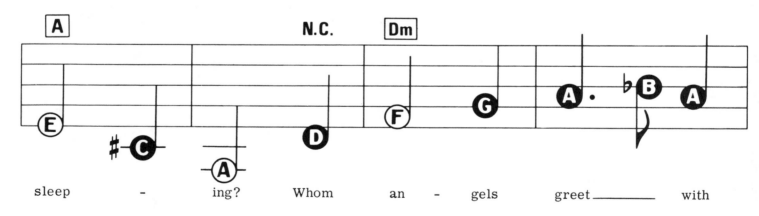

sleep - ing? Whom an - gels greet _____ with

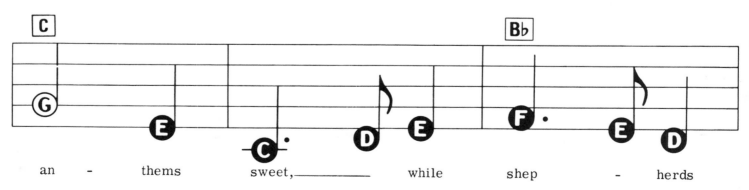

an - thems sweet, _____ while shep - herds

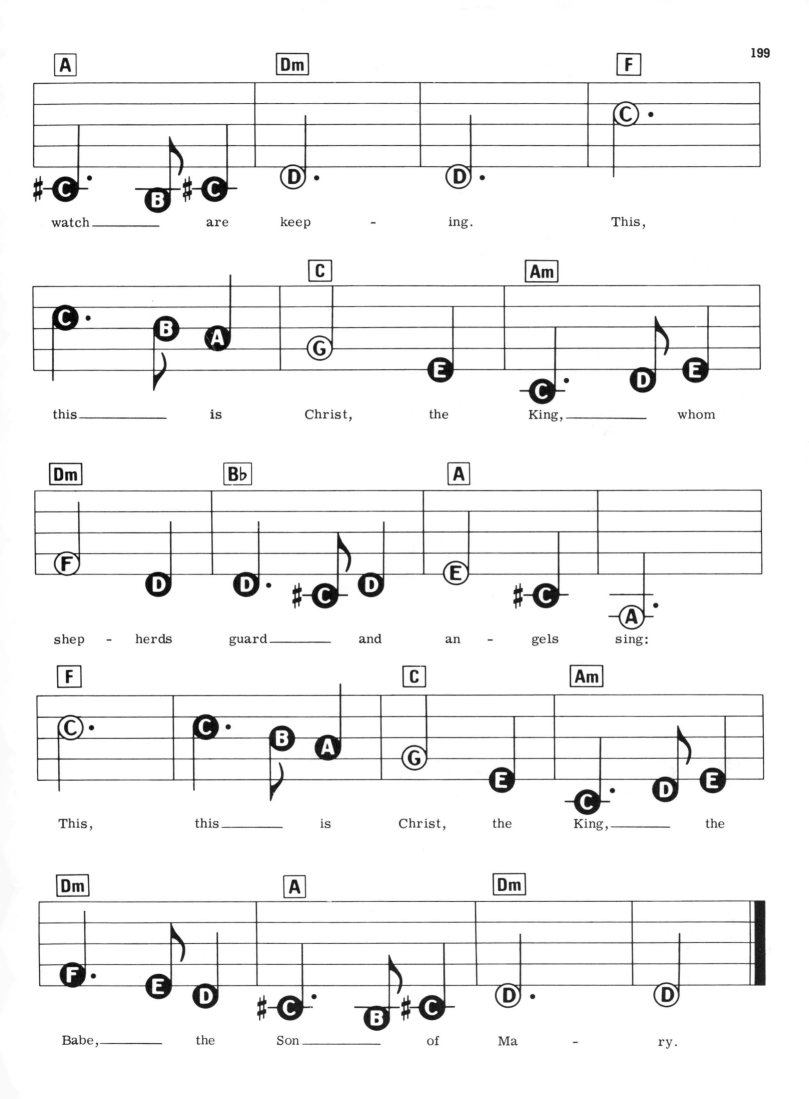

While Shepherds Watched Their Flocks By Night

Registration 1
Rhythm: 8 Beat or Pops

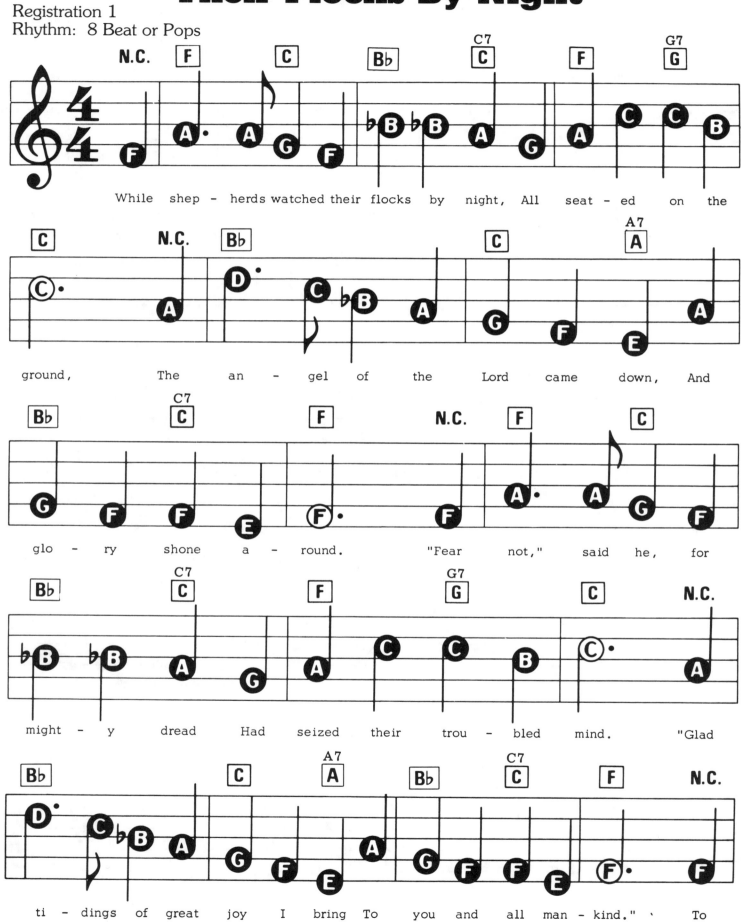

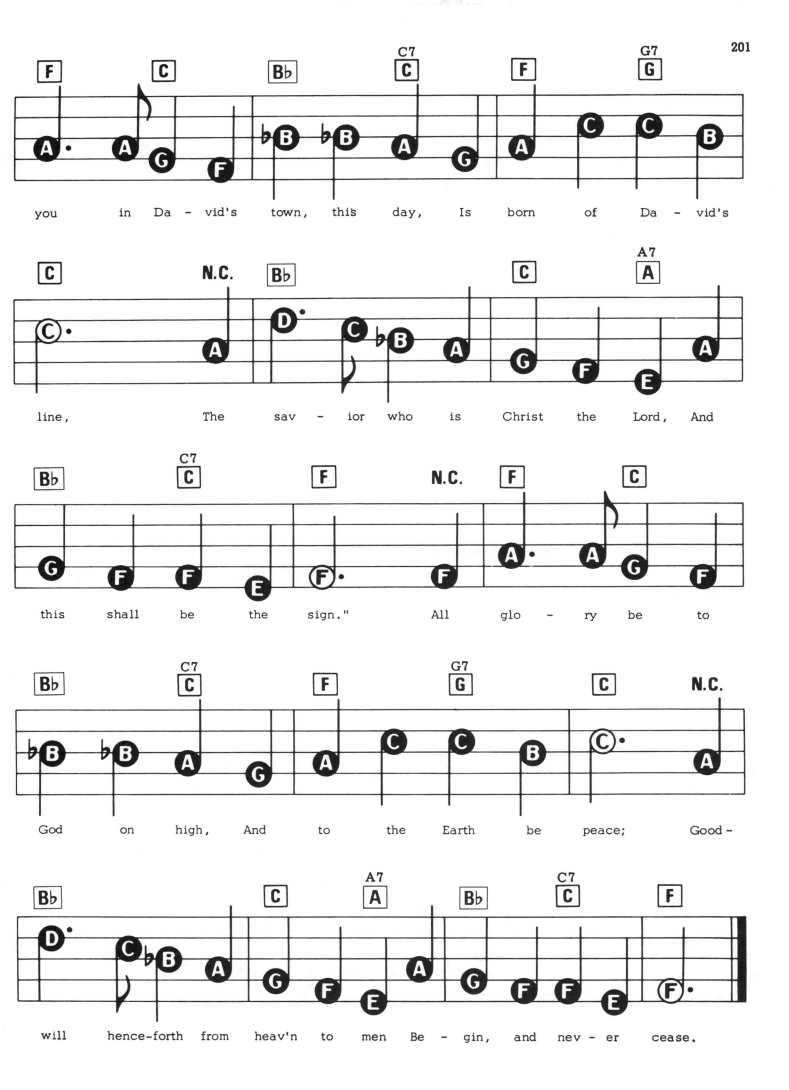

Winter Wonderland

Registration 4
Rhythm: Swing

Words by Dick Smith
Music by Felix Bernard

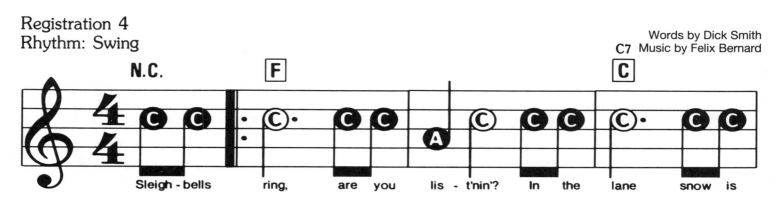

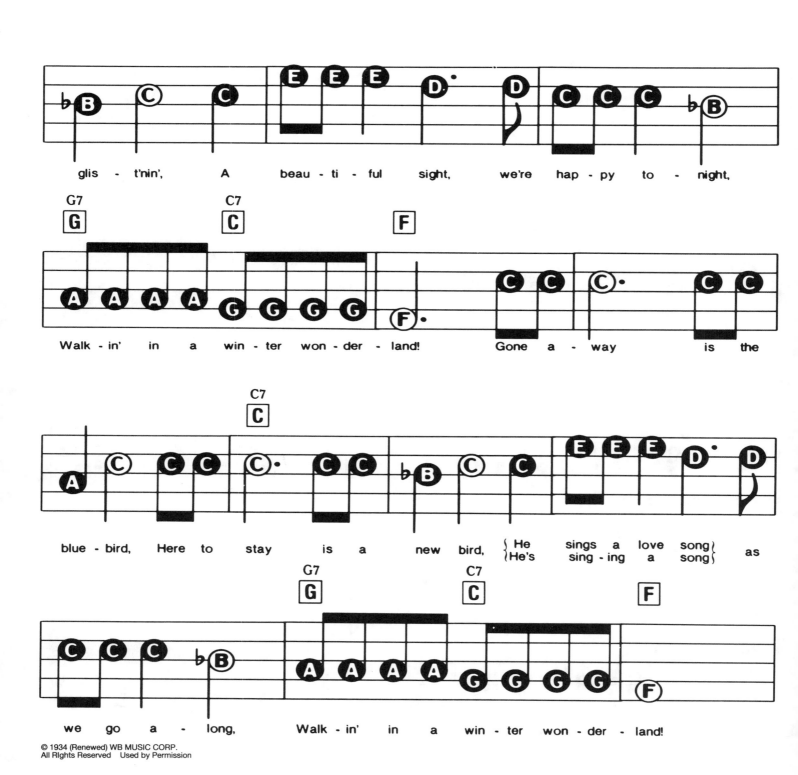

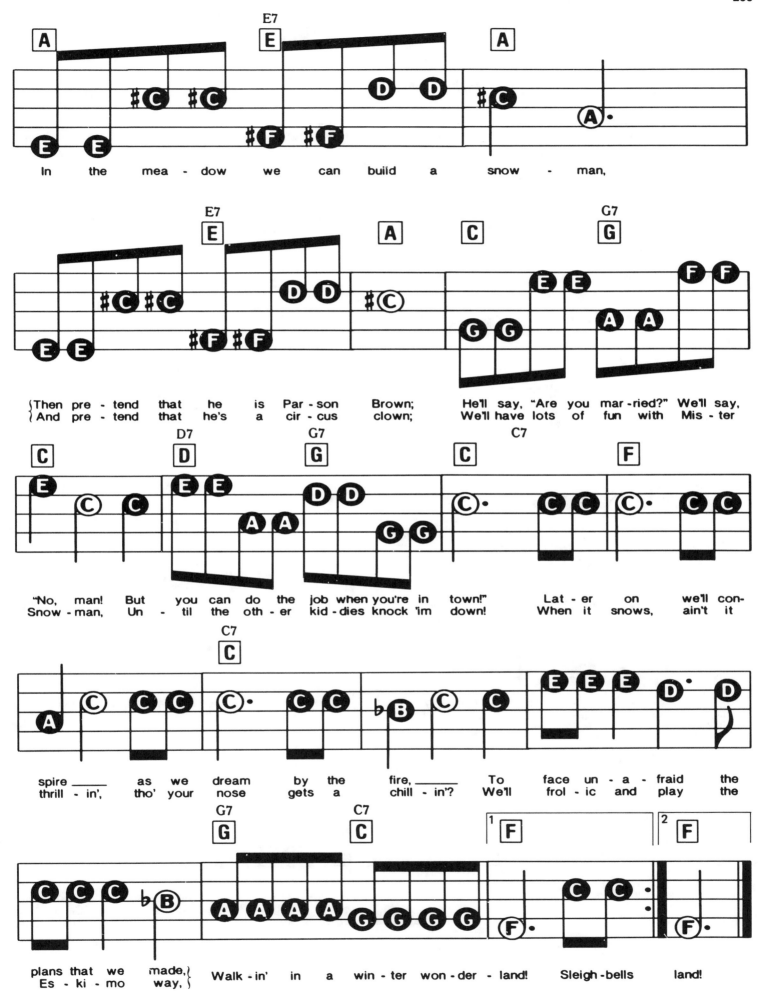

You Make It Feel Like Christmas

Registration 3
Rhythm: Ballad or Slow Rock

Words and Music by
Neil Diamond

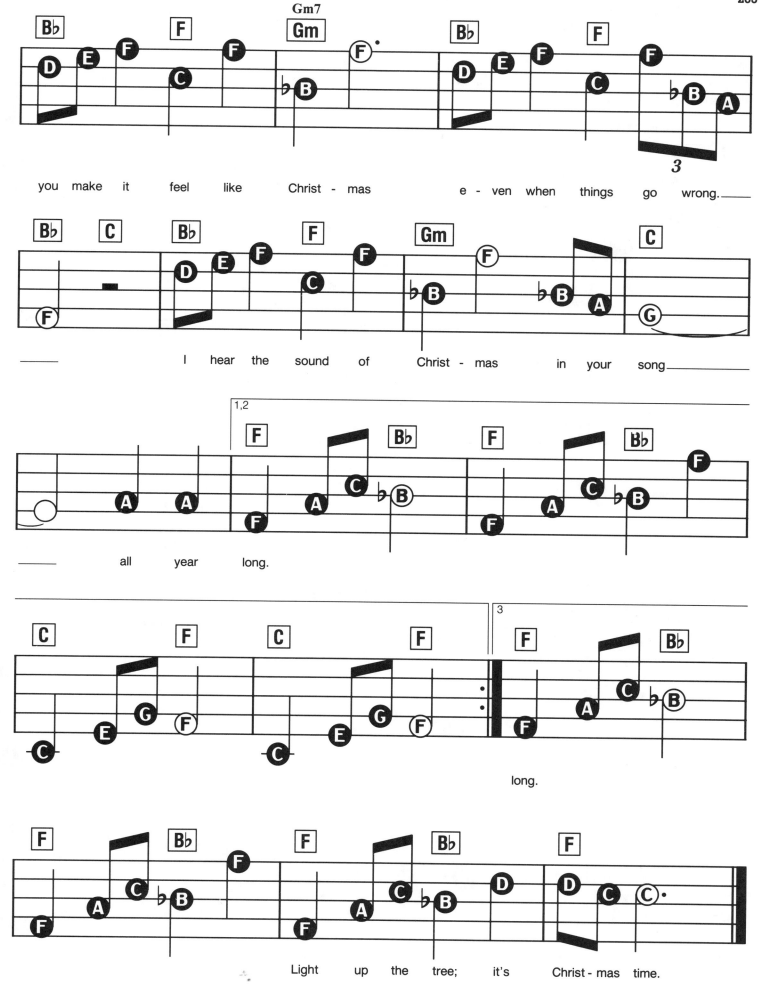

You're All I Want For Christmas

Registration 3
Rhythm: Pops or Ballad

Words and Music by Glen Moore
and Seger Ellis

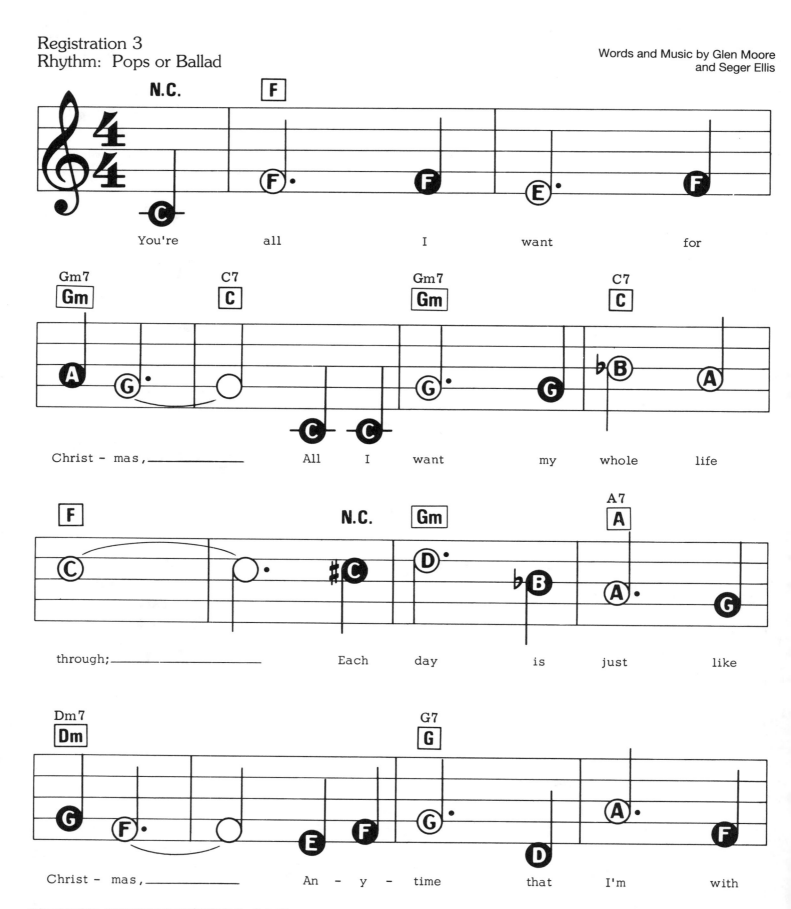

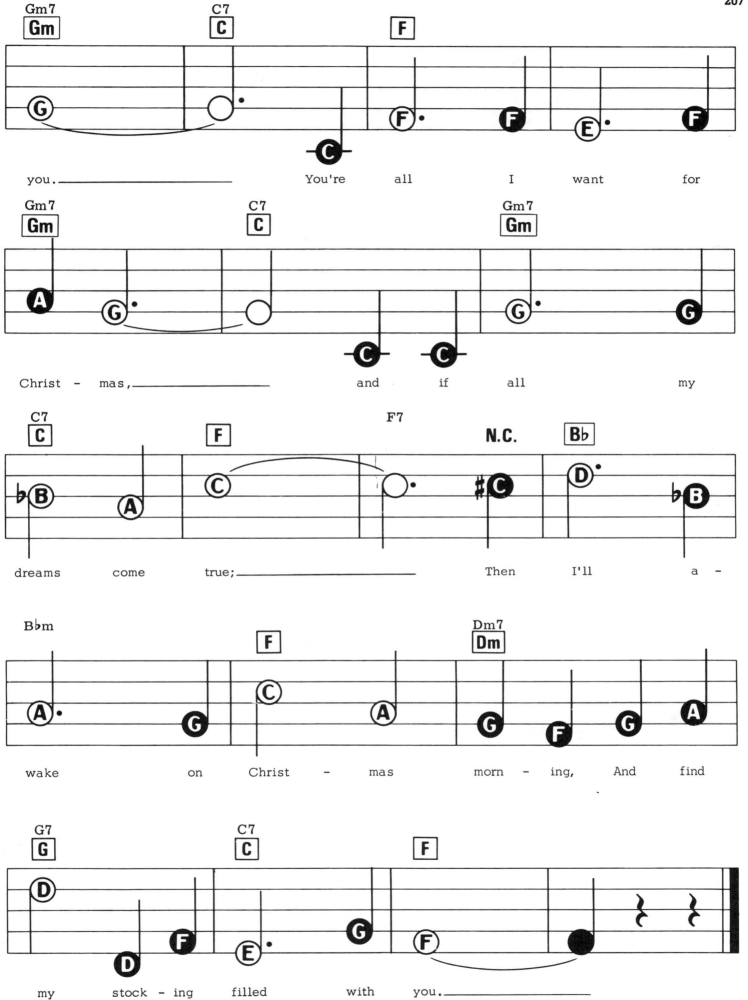

Registration Guide

- Match the Registration number on the song to the corresponding numbered category below. Select and activate an instrumental sound available on your instrument.
- Choose an automatic rhythm appropriate to the mood and style of the song. (Consult your Owner's Guide for proper operation of automatic rhythm features.)
- Adjust the tempo and volume controls to comfortable settings.

Registration

1	Flute, Pan Flute, Jazz Flute
2	Clarinet, Organ
3	Violin, Strings
4	Brass, Trumpet, Bass
5	Synth Ensemble, Accordion, Brass
6	Pipe Organ, Harpsichord
7	Jazz Organ, Vibraphone, Vibes, Electric Piano, Jazz Guitar
8	Piano, Electric Piano
9	Trumpet, Trombone, Clarinet, Saxophone, Oboe
10	Violin, Cello, Strings